Advance Praise for

Planet U

Timely and inspiring, *Planet U* is above all a call for action at a time when much is spoken and disappointingly little is done in respect of the practical implementation of sustainable principles into university life. Thanks to its scope and enriching sets of information and experiences, the book should motivate universities across the globe to take their rightful, but long neglected, place at the forefront of innovation for sustainability and thus honor the commitment to future generations.

— Professor Walter Leal Filho (BSc, PhD, DSc, DL), Distinguished Professor of Environmental Management and Editor of the *International Journal of Sustainability in Higher Education*. TuTech Innovation, Hamburg, Germany

The modern university is at a tipping point. It can either continue its contemporary flirtation with the corporate world and submit to its assigned role as enforcer of the status quo or it reassert its claim to leadership on society's intellectual frontier. With *Planet U: Sustaining the World, Reinventing the University*, M'Gonigle and Starke provide the rationale and inspiration for universities to break rank from the growth and globalization mainstream that is destroying the planet. Only by reinventing itself can the university hope to become society's champion for the locally-rooted global sustainability that is the quest of people and communities everywhere.

— Professor William E. Rees, School of Community and Regional Planning, University of British Columbia, and co-author of *Our Ecological Footprint: Reducing Human Impact on the Earth*

Planet U brought many topics together that are dear to my heart. Highlighting the experience of one campus, in one place, M'Gonigle and Starke give us a window on how we might use democratic practice to confront power, and become better stewards of the earth. The book offers an important challenge, including to my institution, and our project on the The City, Land, and The University. In that work we ask, "How can universities be responsible urban institutions — being true to their own mission *and* take leadership and responsibility in their own cities?" *Planet U* ask us to look both deeper into our core values and further out into the future. How can these institutions that are the stewards of our moral, intellectual, and cultural values not take leadership and responsibility for their campus, their city, and our planet? By grounding our actions in democracy and stewardship, M'Gonigle and Starke challenge us to reach for the stars.

— Rosalind Greenstein, Sr. Fellow and Co-Chair, Department of Planning & Development, Lincoln Institute of Land Policy, Cambridge, MA

This hopeful and insightful book sets out an irresistible challenge: for the university to become an "urban catalyst" for reinventing and invigorating the cultural and ecological fabric of our society. Following M'Gonigle and Starke's prescription, universities could lead the charge to meaningful action to protect our world.

— Elizabeth E. May, O.C., Executive Director of the Sierra Club of Canada

Smart, savvy and sassy, *Planet U* takes on big ideas in specific ways. M'Gonigle and Starke rightfully point out that the 20th century University is an artifact of the past, and if "the university" is to be sustained and to sustain, then dramatic changes need to take place. *Planet U* provides the blueprint — a must-read for engaged intellectuals.

— William G. Tierney, Wilbur-Kieffer Professor of Higher Education, and Director, Center for Higher Education Policy Analysis, University of Southern California

M'Gonigle and Starke deserve an A+ for demonstrating that universities could be, should be, and indeed *must* be transformative forces in the race for sustainable solutions, beginning on campuses and then radiating across the planet. This book should be mandatory reading for all university students, faculty, and administrators.

— David R. Boyd, environmental lawyer, Trudeau Scholar at the University of British Columbia, and author of *Unnatural Law: Rethinking Canadian Environmental Law and Policy*

This really is a terrific book! Universities are places where ideas start, and they can be at the forefront of social change. They can also be at the forefront of environmental destruction. *Planet U* shows exactly how to turn universities into a force for sustainability in a democratic society. It is full of good stories and great ideas. The world can be changed for the better, and the university is the place to begin.

— John S. Dryzek, Professor, Research School of Social Sciences,
Australian National University

Millions of people work and study in universities, yet precious few pause to consider their proper role in the wider society. This inspirational book reclaims the university from those sharp suits who would turn it into a corporation trading in intellectual property and credentializing future workers. *Planet U* recalls the great tradition of universities as change-making and precedent-setting institutions, as places of free speech, dissent, and the cultivation of wisdom. It identifies a gap: between what the university is, and what it could be. M'Gonigle and Starke have written a passionate, political book that enjoins us all to make universities the vehicles of global environmental sustainability they can be but are not yet. It is a privilege to recommend such a wonderful book which should be compulsory reading for everyone involved in higher education.

— Professor Noel Castree, School of Environment and Development,
Manchester University

Planet U gives a colorful introduction to how universities should conduct themselves internally and in their local environments to become working models of democracy and innovative change for global sustainability. This fascinating book challenges readers to rethink the concept, structures and mission of their own institutions of higher education, at the same time also offering to network for achieving the goal of global sustainability by activating the potential imprisoned in mechanistic, linear and far from democratic structures of contemporary universities.

— Elzbieta Goncz, Scientific and Education Associate, Chemical Faculty, Gdansk
University of Technology, Poland

For those of us who've been slogging away in the trenches of the environment movement for the past two or three decades, *Plant U* does two things. First, through its survey of the burgeoning campus-based sustainability movement, it reassures us that a new generation is in fact emerging, and one which will take over the movment — sooner rather than later, hopefully. Second, it introduces us to a new, very wide-ranging and yet practical way of experimenting with truly integrated sustainability, right in the "heart of the beast" of North American suburbanized, corporatised, consumer society. Only time will tell whether or not a transformative non-violent revolution can save the planet, but *Planet U* offers a vision of how this could be led by and through this ancient iconic institution of Western civilisation. Clearly, things are happening on campus, and M'Gonigle and Starke's book is an engaging call to sit up and take notice of the future as it evolves. Read it.

— Steve Sawyer was Executive Director of Greenpeace International (1988-1993) during which time he initiatied the organization's climate campaign. He presently serves as the organization's climate policy director.

As an academic who has been involved in treating the effects of industrial pollution on our population, I highly recommended this book. Anyone interested in what the university can do for the development of civil society will learn from this book. It will be most useful for universities in Eastern Europe.

— Dr. Lew Gerbilsky, President of Ukraine's Green Doctors (a national branch of the International Society of Doctors for the Environment), Ukrainian National Mining University, Dnipropetrovsk, Ukraine

PLANET U

SUSTAINING THE WORLD,
REINVENTING THE UNIVERSITY

Michael M'Gonigle & Justine Starke

ILLUSTRATED BY BRIONY PENN

NEW SOCIETY PUBLISHERS

Cataloging in Publication Data:
A catalog record for this publication is available from the National Library of Canada.

Cover design by Diane McIntosh.
Planet image: Photodisc. Gate image: Matthew Dula, iStock Photo.

Printed in Canada. First printing May, 2006.

New Society Publishers acknowledges the support of the Government of Canada through the Book Publishing Industry Development Program (BPIDP) for our publishing activities.

ISBN 13: 978-0-86571-557-8
ISBN 10: 0-86571-557-2

Inquiries regarding requests to reprint all or part of *Planet U* should be addressed to New Society Publishers at the address below.

To order directly from the publishers, please call toll-free (North America) 1-800-567-6772, or order online at www.newsociety.com

Any other inquiries can be directed by mail to:
New Society Publishers
P.O. Box 189, Gabriola Island, BC V0R 1X0, Canada
1-800-567-6772

New Society Publishers' mission is to publish books that contribute in fundamental ways to building an ecologically sustainable and just society, and to do so with the least possible impact on the environment, in a manner that models this vision. We are committed to doing this not just through education, but through action. We are acting on our commitment to the world's remaining ancient forests by phasing out our paper supply from ancient forests worldwide. This book is one step toward ending global deforestation and climate change. It is printed on acid-free paper that is **100% old growth forest-free** (100% post-consumer recycled), processed chlorine free, and printed with vegetable-based, low-VOC inks. For further information, or to browse our full list of books and purchase securely, visit our website at: www.newsociety.com.

NEW SOCIETY PUBLISHERS   www.newsociety.com

TO JANE JACOBS

whose legacy should inform and inspire those
who understand today the need for broad social change,
and who are ready to make it happen.

Contents

PREFACE

A S WE WERE PUTTING THE FINISHING TOUCHES TO THIS BOOK, a massive environmental conference concluded in Montreal. Reviewing this Preface at our desks,
we could imagine the nearly 10,000 official attendees jumping into their idling cabs
and heading through snowy downtown streets to the airport to jostle in the lineups at
the airline counters. For two weeks, diplomats, corporate executives, environmental
activists, union leaders, church groups, and municipal politicians from over 150 countries had been meeting in seemingly endless negotiations. As the departing delegates
waited to board their planes they could take comfort from the meeting's crowning
achievement: It had kept the Kyoto Accord alive (if barely), for the next decade.[1]

Compared with such a planetary event, one might wonder how much importance to sustaining the world can be attached to a book about the university. Yet
in light of the practical challenges facing us after Montreal, we can answer confi-
dently: A lot. The media spotlight is now dimming over the climate negotiations;
on the university, it has never shone. Indeed, the university is one of the world's
least examined institutions. But as we suggest in this book, the university may be
the globe's most promising new site for giving shape to the Montreal commitments, that is, for making transformation *real*.

This book began several years ago when we each found ourselves in the
abstruse, and almost invisible, world of campus planning. We were new members

(respectively) of the University of Victoria's Campus Development Committee and the student-based UVic Sustainability Project. From these positions, we watched while old trees fell to make way for new buildings, and parking lots to service them were squeezed out from student gardens. The very problems that Kyoto and Montreal were intended to counter were daily being created at our own institution, at a university.

Since those early days, we have come to understand that what happens at UVic — and at thousands of similar colleges and universities around the world — is not inevitable. Quite the contrary; if one actually stops to think about the university, one quickly understands its unique potential for innovation. As we will argue, the university holds a missing key to global sustainability — a locus for practical action. To date, few people have even noticed the university, let alone realized that something exists there to unlock.

When our work began in 1999, we thought that we were alone. Information about other campuses was difficult to find. Over time, however, we began to make contacts with what we gradually realized was an incipient movement emerging in other places at the same time as our local movement was developing. Today this diverse movement is taking shape worldwide out of countless local initiatives, self-assembling like a globe-spanning crystal of cooperative social action.

Planet U reveals the truly revolutionary potential of this campus sustainability movement and how to help it happen.

At the University of Victoria on Canada's West Coast, we began our work like everyone else in the movement, not as an abstract or academic endeavor[2] but as a practical on-the-ground initiative. Events happened quickly, and by the summer of 2002, what had been a closed process of updating our University's campus plan had evolved into an extraordinary flourishing of communal energy pushing for a new vision for the University. Facing ever more development and being asked to create a new plan for a contested future, students, faculty and neighbors started to interrogate the role of the university in addressing the huge challenge of global sustainability. The answers that came back were contradictory, confusing and unsatisfying.

Even to ask the question was to break new ground. In the process of debate, however, one thing was clear to everyone: huge gaps existed between what the university taught, what it did, and what it was capable of doing

In writing this book, and in the many campaigns that preceded it, we have benefited greatly from our association with a unique institution at the University, the POLIS Project on Ecological Governance. It is both an academic research center and an activist presence on campus and in the community. This institution helped the community to understand and articulate what was taking place, to research alternatives and to organize strategies for change.

This book grows out of a collaborative process, and we would like to acknowledge a large network of students, faculty, staff and neighbors that has shown great leadership in working for a new future for the University. We would like to thank the many members of the UVic CommUnity for a Sustainable Campus, particularly Jan Allen, Norm Mogenson, Noel Parker Jervis, Pierre D'Estrube, Ray Bull, Lyse Burgess, Bill Zuk, Alan Hedley, Lisa Surridge, Eric Seger, Nancy Turner, Anders Erickson, Gordon de Frane, Lucas Goris, Ingmar Lee, Magnus Bein, Ben Isitt, Stu Crawford, Stacie Harder, Maurita Prato, Glenys Verhulst, Krista Roessingh, Julien Perrier, Adam Mjolsness, Melissa Moroz, and Jeff Andrew. We would also like to express our appreciation to the many people who have led the UVic Sustainability Project over the years, especially Lindsay Cole, Jennifer Mutch, Graham Watt-Gremm, Jennifer Welsh, Sarah Webb, André Valillee, Moss Giasson and Kerri Klein.

From the POLIS Project on Ecological Governance, we are indebted to Shannon Macdonald and Emily McNair (especially for their initial research and production of *A Path Less Taken* in 2001), Nancy Klenavic, Anne Nguyen, Heather Johnstone, Tony Maas, Oliver Brandes and above all, the person who held it all together, Elizabeth Wheaton. We would especially like to thank Rae St. Arnault. Rae, in her activist work and in the preparation of this book, was there from the beginning. Rae spearheaded the initial visioning for the book with "A Celebration of Possibilities," the conference in the spring of 2003. We would also like to thank Karen Gorecki who contributed much inspiration and energy to the initial research; Jessica Boquist who was a dedicated project manager during a year of research; Britt Erickson for her research in this period; Rosemary Collard whose meticulous fact checking helped bring the project to a close; Jamie Biggar who juggled the logistics of tracking down the numerous sidebars throughout the text; and Jessie Cowperthwaite who helped prepare the final work for publication. We would also like to acknowledge the contributions of Sara Irvine, Jason Found and Eric Haensel. We are especially grateful to Wendy Wickwire for helping us uncover the rich history of the area where UVic now resides.

None of this work would have been possible without the financial support of VanCity Credit Union, Human Resources and Development Canada, the Endswell Foundation, the Real Estate Foundation of BC, the Vancouver Foundation, the McLean Foundation, the Institute for New Economics, and the Luna Trust. For this support, we are most grateful. And for their guidance, we are particularly appreciative of the work of Joel Solomon, Detlef Beck, Patrick Stewart, Vicky Husband and Dr. William Gibson.

We would finally like to thank many others who contributed to the manuscript, either through specific information or research or with comments on the draft: Julie Cruikshank, Elisabeth Sanders, Warren Magnusson, Jessica Dempsey, Serena Kataoka, Brad Morrison, Grant Keddie and Don Mitchell. In the preparation of the manuscript, we are indebted to our editors at New Society Publishers, Judith Brand and Ingrid Witvoet.

By opening up new spaces for cooperative dialogue and innovation, we hope that *Planet U* will make a tangible contribution to the quest for a sustainable planet. When we can reinvent the university, we will foster a new approach to global governance. As we do, venues for local discussion will increase dramatically, as will the topics on the action agenda. Great possibilities await.

THE REBEL

The University of Victoria, 2005.

Photograph by Sandy Beaman. Courtesy of the University of Victoria, 2005.

tree-sit

THE UNIVERSITY WAS CLOSED FOR THE HOLIDAYS, but two days after Christmas, the crew from Operations showed up in the campus forest, chainsaws at the ready. By the end of the day, a large patch of the forest was down and the site cleared for a new bio-medical building. Clearcuts are nothing new in British Columbia, but of the University of Victoria's once expansive Douglas fir forest, this was the last grove left within its academic core. And weren't universities supposed to be different?

The University of Victoria, 2005.

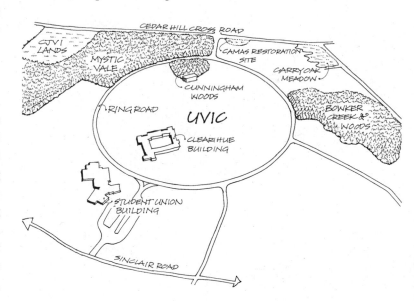

Visions in the forest

A lot of people certainly thought so. Two months earlier in the sunshine of a late autumn afternoon, some 300 students, faculty and neighbors had joined hands in a protective "ring around the woods," urging the administration to site the new building somewhere else. A hot topic that fall, the future of the woods sparked a larger public debate about the University's processes for campus planning. Why,

3

for example, couldn't UVic leave the woods alone and do something innovative, like put the buildings on nearby parking lots? This could even be part of a larger initiative to discourage car commuting and reduce the University's contribution to congested local streets and even to global climate change. Maybe, such an initiative could inspire the University to take a lead role in developing a more sustainable transportation strategy for the whole region.

But the University of Victoria's plans had long been set, and these were difficult, awkward ideas. Limit cars? No, everyone was assured that there were academic priorities that had to be met and operational constraints, good reasons for the choice of site. There were no acceptable alternatives. So the holidays came to an end with a hasty cleanup of downed trees, leaving a clearcut and an upturned forest floor to greet returning students and faculty.

UVic students set up camp in a tree to block the cutting of Cunningham Woods.

Sunday night, just hours before classes were set to resume, in the cool and wet of a West Coast January night, the students struck back. It was 2AM, but the grounds were alive as a group of Frisbee-golf players skirted the dark grounds, hitting target trees and lamp-posts as they made their nightly rounds. As they passed, another group of students worked in what was left of UVic's Cunningham Woods to hoist a banner into the swaying treetops. The banner depicted the University's motto "Challenge Minds, Change Worlds" below an ironic new slogan, "Cut Tuition, Not the Forest." Soon the wording was refined to "Cut Fees, Not Trees." The slogan reverberated throughout the University for the rest of the spring term.

Photograph by John McKay, *Times Colonist*, January 14, 2003, D1.

The next weekend, the students struck again. Hoisting planks, climbing ropes and a small tent, an invigorated student protest launched a platform into the branches of a large old arbutus tree — UVic's first tree-sit. A second platform appeared a few days later. For the next six months, Cunningham Woods hosted a permanent occupation in its canopy. From this perch, a rotating cadre of more than 100 students watched winter in the forest turn to spring while they protected the woods from further encroachment.

At the center of this action was Ingmar Lee, a dedicated environmental activist and student representative on the University's Board of Governors. Lee got the call as the forest went down: "I jumped on my bike and rode up there just in time to see the feller-buncher and the grinder eating up half of what was left of the Cunningham forest," says Lee. "There were trees lying around. Beautiful arbutus trees. Trees that people had put bird boxes in were all smashed on the ground."[1]

"People were poking through the refuse in shock," Lee recalls. "This was after we had blockaded the University for three hours one day to make our point about the Campus Development Plan during a wider provincial protest over government cuts. They'd seen hundreds of students and faculty out there concerned about the forest, and they snuck in when all the students were on holiday and mowed down the forest. We were outraged. We live on an island that has had 80 percent of its primeval forest destroyed. All the problems that result after clearcutting are here at UVic."

Ingmar Lee holds up a broken birdhouse found in the debris after the felling of Cunningham woods, December 2002.

Photograph by Bruce Stotesbury, *Times Colonist*, December 31, 2002, B2.

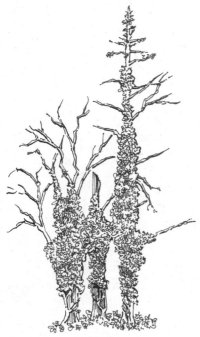

Ivy-choked trees.

"UVic's wilderness represents the largest unprotected Douglas fir ecosystem in urban Victoria," says Maurita Prato, another student organizer of the tree-sit. "This wilderness area has ecological significance for the entire Capital Region and should be preserved for all time."[2]

Protests like this have been happening in one form or another, in one place or another, for a very long time. It is an old story: ordinary citizens who have little power challenging big businesses and big governments that have a lot. And challenging them directly, with their bodies as well as their voices, bearing witness and being present. In Cunningham Woods, it was also about people protecting *place* and, in this case, not just any place, but the University. Of all society's institutions, students argued that the University had a duty to demonstrate wisdom in place. Indeed, many thought that, were the University more open to a collective vision, it could actually take a much needed lead in helping society address larger, but related, issues such as global warming and deforestation.

Outlaws and intellectuals

Students calling for a more responsive university is not a new thing, nor is their vision of a university working in the service of social justice. The university has often hosted struggles for social change as Alejandro Rojas knows firsthand. Rojas is a professor at the much larger University of British Columbia (UBC) across the Strait of Georgia that separates UVic from the mainland. In 1973 he was president of Chile's National Union of Students at a time of intense national reform under then-president, Salvador Allende. Under Allende, Chile's universities were incubators for political innovation as the government sought to make higher education accessible to all of Chile's social classes and to give students, faculty and staff the right to participate in the mechanisms of university governance.

"Chile was in the midst of radical change, radical redistribution of wealth, agrarian reform, nationalization of large companies that used to belong to foreign monopolies and nationalization of natural resources," explains Rojas.[3] In the early 1970s, Chile's universities were transforming their curricula and pedagogical approaches to address these broader social changes: "Universities were reacting to a situation in which the cultural identity of Latin America was being eroded and dismantled by the massive expansion of American culture."

"So our idea was that the university had to contribute to creating national dignity and sovereignty," remembers Rojas. "Our plans of study, our curricula and our research agenda should reflect mostly the demands of how to make the country a sovereign nation. We could enhance and defend what made us unique in the world rather than championing the wagon of worldwide homogenization." Every summer thousands of students were mobilized to volunteer with national literacy campaigns, teaching Chile's peasant population to read and write. In turn, the peasants instructed the students, sharing with them their direct knowledge and different understandings that come from working the land.

On September 11, 1973, the popular movement collapsed when Salvador Allende was assassinated, and General Augusto Pinochet took power in a coup d'état. Under the ensuing military dictatorship, thousands of people were murdered or forced into hiding to escape the purge. Rojas was blacklisted along with other political leaders on the Left, in trade unions, student groups and peasant associations. Political parties that did not support the coup were banned, as was the Chilean National Union of Students. "There was," says Rojas, "a price attached to our heads, alive or dead. Suddenly we found ourselves living underground, trying to secure a life somehow. I lived underground for about half a year, and then I was placed in an embassy as a political refugee and finally left for Europe. Many of my people were jailed and sent to concentration camps, and many of them executed. Democratically elected university chancellors were sent to concentration camps."

The allure of the ivory tower

Around the world, universities have long been centers for political discourse and catalysts for political action. Students were instrumental in the 1848 revolutions in Germany and Austria. In 1911 Chinese students led the struggle to overthrow the Manchu dynasty and later played a role in bringing Mao Zedong to power in 1949. In Japan student demonstrations in 1960 forced the resignation of the Kishi government. Student activism was omnipresent in the nationalist movements of former colonial nations such as India and Indonesia.[4]

Throughout the 1960s, countries around the world — from the United States to Vietnam, Britain to Brazil, Turkey to Canada — experienced an explosive student movement against nuclear armament, racial segregation, suppression of women's rights, environmental degradation, and war. In India, in 1964, over 700 demonstrations rocked the university system. Over 100 of the demonstrations turned violent.[5] In Paris, in May 1968, a student demonstration led to the now-famous general strike and national uprising. These were the famous "days of the barricades." Students called for a lecture hall to be made permanently available for political discourse, and their manifesto demanded an "outright rejection of the capitalist technocratic university."[6]

Throughout the world, opposition to the Vietnam War in the 1960s and 1970s was played out on dozens of campuses. At UBC Jerry Rubin, the radical American Yippie, addressed a protest rally (to which Rubin had brought a pig to symbolize repressive authority) then led a march that occupied the University Faculty Club. On the other side of the city of Vancouver, the founding in 1965 of Simon Fraser University created what quickly became a major hub of college activism in Western Canada.[7] Demonstrations were common as students sought to protect outspoken faculty, effectively stalling curriculum development in the University's early years. Through occupations and sit-ins, students and faculty propelled the administration into one initiative after another, erecting a whole faculty of interdisciplinary studies, creating one of the country's first institutional daycare centers, and much more.[8] In 1967 in the capital city of Victoria, a week-long occupation took place in the University of Victoria's administration building, as students unsuccessfully tried to reverse the University's termination of the contracts of three popular professors.[9]

Since the '70s, universities have been relatively quiet. But things may be beginning to change again as a new movement takes hold, a "sustainable campuses" movement. Like its predecessors, this movement is concerned about the most pressing issues of our time. But it also has a new role for the university — to be not just a site for making protests, but a place for creating precedents. This is

The protest encircled the globe

One truly amazing aspect of May '68 was the way the protest encircled the globe: Saturday May 11, 50,000 students and workers marched on Bonn, and 3,000 protesters in Rome; on May 14, students occupied the University of Milan; a sit-in at the University of Miami on May 15; scuffles at a college in Florence on May 16; a red flag flew for three hours at the University of Madrid on the 17th; and the same day, 200 black students occupied the administration buildings of Dower University; on May 18, protests flared up in Rome, and more in Madrid where barricades and clashes with the police occurred; on May 19, students in Berkeley were arrested; a student protest in New York; an attack on an ROTC center in Baltimore — the old world seemed to be on the ropes. On May 20, Brooklyn University was occupied by blacks, and occupations took place the next day at the University of West Berlin. On May 22, police broke through barricades at Columbia University. The University of Frankfurt and the University of Santiago were occupied on May 24. Protests in Vancouver and London in front of the French Embassy on May 25. On Monday May 27, university and high school students went on strike in Dakar .... On May 30, students in Munich protested, as did students in Vienna the next day. On June 1, protests spread to Denmark and Buenos Aires .... In Brazil, 16,000 students went on strike on June 6, followed by a large protest march in Geneva for democratization of the university. Even in Turkey, 20,000 students occupied the universities in Ankara and other cities. The chronology just keeps going as occupations, protests, scandals and barricades continued throughout the summer in Tokyo, Osaka, Zurich, Rio, Rome, Montevideo, Bangkok, Dusseldorf, Mexico City, Saigon, Cochabamba, La Paz, South Africa, Indonesia, Chicago, Venice, Montreal, Auckland.

— Len Bracken, *Guy Debord: Revolutionary: A Critical Biography.* Los Angeles, CA: Feral House, 1997, pp. 174–175. Available at <http://www.neravt.com/left/may1968.htm>.

They hated their universities for teaching it

1968 was, among other things, a moral revolt — it was a revolt of passion in the interests of humanity [against] what [protestors] perceived to be their alienation from dominant social values, from the values of the power elites, the Establishment, the "It." Why had the typically quiet 1950s suddenly burst forth with the student protest movement of the 1960s? .... A partial list would have to include: big business, capitalist technocracy and the rule by experts, the Vietnam War, the effects of a media-manipulated society and in general, all authority .... The year of the barricades served as a symbol of everything an entire generation of young people detested about the generation of their parents .... They hated the late 20th century hypocrisy of material, bourgeois, liberal, consumerist Western society .... They hated their universities for teaching it .... These students wanted their voices to be heard — they were not content to let their hearts and minds be controlled by [an] alien other .... So, these students marched, demonstrated, they occupied administration buildings across Europe and North America.

— Steven Kreis, "1968: The Year of the Barricades," *The History Guide: Lectures on Twentieth Century Europe*, Boca Raton and Davie, FL: Florida Atlantic University, 2000. Available at http://www.historyguide.org/europe/lecture15.html

Rojas's new mission. Though he left Chile, he did not lose his passion for social change, and he did not leave the university. Only today he has channeled it in a new direction, the burgeoning movement for campus sustainability. He is now a professor of agricultural science at the University of British Columbia. UBC is a big place, covering 1,000 acres (400 hectares) of land at the Vancouver campus where it is home to some 43,000 students and over 10,000 faculty and staff.[10] As UBC develops its campus, Rojas's students draw on community-based techniques like participatory action research to try to make its development an explicitly social, not just institutional, endeavor. Their special focus is the sustainability of the University's food systems.

The Planet and the U

Universities have long been special places, places of both innovation and resistance. From the "protestant" monk to the heretical stargazer, academics have been at the center of historical change in the West for the past millennium. But the challenges facing universities in the new millennium are arguably the greatest ones yet. "Material growth has shot up to almost inconceivable levels," says Rojas, "accompanied by unconscionable levels of hunger and poverty." Decades ago, the question of how to redistribute the wealth of society was at the center of Rojas's world in Chile. Today Rojas is as concerned about ecological wealth as social justice. "The cake is bigger than ever," says Rojas, "and it is redistributed more unfairly than ever .... But the cake is built from bad recipes ...."

For decades the environmental movement has worked to halt the momentum of planetary breakdown, and it has not succeeded. Instead, the breakdown has become systemic, scattered losses of individual species evolving into the wholesale decline in biodiversity, dirty air in industrial cities mushrooming into global climate change, inequities between developed and developing countries becoming entrenched as a globalized model of economic unsustainability. This book need not debate the severity of these problems — they are obvious.

Living beyond our means

Nearly two thirds of the services provided by nature to humankind are found to be in decline worldwide. In effect, the benefits reaped from our engineering of the planet have been achieved by running down natural capital assets.

In many cases, it is literally a matter of living on borrowed time. By using up supplies of fresh groundwater faster than they can be recharged, for example, we are depleting assets at the expense of our children. The cost is already being felt, but often by people far away from those enjoying the benefits of natural services. Shrimp on the dinner plates of Europeans may well have started life in a South Asian pond built in place of mangrove swamps — weakening a natural barrier to the sea and making coastal communities more vulnerable.

Unless we acknowledge the debt and prevent it from growing, we place in jeopardy the dreams of citizens everywhere to rid the world of hunger, extreme poverty, and avoidable disease — as well as increasing the risk of sudden changes to the planet's life support systems from which even the wealthiest may not be shielded.

We also move into a world in which the variety of life becomes ever more limited. The simpler, more uniform landscapes created by human activity have put thousands of species under threat of extinction, affecting both the resilience of natural services and less tangible spiritual or cultural values.

— Board of Directors for the 2005 United Nations Millennium Ecosystem Assessment, *Living Beyond Our Means — Natural Assets and Human Well-being: Statement from the Board*. The Assessment spanned four years and included 1,360 experts worldwide. New York: United Nations, 2005, p. 2.

We are certainly near — some would say past — the "tipping point," where self-reinforcing ecological decline is irreversible.[11] The demands today are even greater, and the issues even more urgent than those that inspired such campus activism 40 years ago. The focus of this book is a prospective one — how to remake a world whose survival is at stake — and how we might do so quickly.

In getting to this situation, our political and economic institutions have clearly failed us. Past actions have not halted, or even slowed, the trajectory of global ecological and social decline. Indeed, the pace has picked up. New approaches are needed. This book is about making more visible an incredibly important institution that, surprisingly, remains invisible. In so doing, it starts from a simple, but logical, realization: we cannot have a sustainable world where universities promote unsustainability. But neither can we change the university without also changing the world; the two are entwined. This realization is at the heart of this book, and it leads to an intriguing question: Which comes first? Yet despite this inextricable linkage, few people stop to ponder the relationship between the actions of the university and the trajectory of planetary change. A gap exists between what we learn for tomorrow and what tomorrow needs from us today. This situation is all the more significant when one considers how, in the past half-century, a massive "higher education industry" has emerged without anyone seeming to notice. Even though its scale and influence is arguably unmatched by any other industry on the planet, social critics pay it almost no heed, especially in comparison with the attention put on other sectors such as transportation and health.

Changing the world by creating a sustainable university is admittedly a strange idea, as if a university here or there could make much difference to these huge global problems, especially where only a scattered handful of people yet see its potential. Quite the contrary, the time has come round again for the university to take its place as a vehicle of social change. Indeed, one might ask how we could have overlooked it for so long. The possibilities for universities are enormous, and an increasing number of people believe that a collective responsibility exists to make them manifest. As forest activist Ingmar Lee notes, "UVic is one of the biggest consumers of forest products on Vancouver Island, a free-thinking university buying into the destruction of our magnificent forests. If we convert its actions in B.C., we can send our models to Alberta, Saskatchewan, right across Canada and around the world. That is what universities are for. We have to learn to overcome the forces of destruction, and we have to do it right, right here."

To appreciate what is possible, one must first take time to reflect on what the university *is*. Most importantly, the university is unique, and in many ways. For example, universities are rooted in local places, yet are well networked globally. With their departments of history and schools of planning, they are actively connected to the past but also shape the future. In space and time, they transcend boundaries. With their senior professors and junior students, they also connect society's elders with its youth. With their interdisciplinary studies and many

Considering place

When we fail to consider places as products of human decisions, we accept their existence as noncontroversial or inevitable, like the falling of rain or the fact of the sunrise. Moreover, when we accept the existence of places as unproblematic — places such as the farm, the bank, the landfill, the strip mall, the gated community and the new car lot — we also become complicit in the political processes, however problematic, that stewarded these places into being and that continue to legitimize them. Thus places produce and teach particular ways of thinking about and being in the world. They tell us the way things are, even when they operate pedagogically beneath a conscious level.

— David A. Gruenewald, "Foundations of Place: A Multidisciplinary Framework for Place-Conscious Education", *American Educational Research Journal*, vol. 40, no. 3, 2003, p. 627.

Pedagogue of place.
Professor Alejandro Rojas in the UBC Gardens.

Photograph by Elena Orrego, 2004

learned associations, they connect across intellectual and geographic boundaries and are thus participants across *space*. In this world, universities provide a relatively open public space. But they are also specific *places*.

The crisis of sustainability is at root a crisis of losing these places, that is, physical territories that are also emanations of local powers — local habitats, local neighborhoods, local cultures, local forests and fisheries, and rural communities. These individual losses add up to a threat of losing our collective place, the planet. Reinvigorating local places may just be the key to sustaining our global future. "Think globally, act locally" was the mantra decades ago, but we never learned how. It is time to do so, and for that we must go back to school. When we do, there are plenty of teachers to turn to.

Comparing notes.
During Pedestrian Sundays at the large, open-air Kensington Market in downtown Toronto, cars are kept out, and the community emerges to mix on the street. Here Jane Jacobs chats with another local.

Photograph by Robert B. Davis, 2005.

How dark is the age ahead?

One such teacher was Jane Jacobs, who died as this book was going to press. To those concerned about the future of civilized and sustainable cities, Jacobs is an icon. As a New Yorker and associate editor of *Architectural Forum* in the 1950s, Jacobs was struck by the lifeless nature of the conventional developments she was assigned to cover. By the 1960s, she was an active opponent of them, protesting the demolition of slum neighborhoods and the onslaught of cars and freeways. Instead, Jacobs proposed bottom-up, mixed-use approaches to city redevelopment. In 1961 she wrote the classic study *The Death and Life of Great American Cities*.[12] In 1968 she left the United States and took up residence in Toronto, Canada, where she continued her activism and her writing. Her books demonstrate a commitment to livable and vital cities, to an understanding of the role of cities in creating social wealth, and to resident citizens being allowed to create their cities through open dialogue and action. In 2004, then in her late eighties, she penned a dire warning about our collective future, *Dark Age Ahead*.[13]

Dark Age Ahead is a product of her rich experience, and its message is unsettling. We are, she says, losing our cultural memory, and without this memory, societies cannot survive. From the fall of the Roman Empire to Greenwich Village, from neighborhoods lost to freeways to families lost to political indifference, she asks a basic question about social adaptation: What dooms losers?[14] Jacobs suggests that several factors are presently at work that could well doom the West, factors that operate at a more fundamental level even than "racism, profligate environmental destruction, crime, voters' distrust of politicians and thus low voter turnout, and the enlarging gulf between rich and poor along with attrition of the middle class."[15] One of the most significant factors is the decline of higher education.

Jacobs's analysis of this decline informs our own. Harkening back to the Depression of the 1930s, Jacobs attributes to that period the Western world's obsession ever since with jobs. One effect of this was to displace the collective commitment to a social education with the individualized quest for a marketable "credential:"

> It has been truly said that the past lives on in the present. This is true of credentialism's origins. It emerged partly out of America's humiliation when the Soviet Union, with its Sputnik, had beaten America into space, and partly from the still-fresh ideas of the Depression. Credentialism emerged, mostly in California at first, in the late 1950s, when it dawned upon university administrators there that modern economic development, whether in the conquest of space or any other field, depended on a population's fund of knowledge .... It followed that development's most cultural valuable product — jobs — also depended on knowledge."[16]

Credentialism is linked to the other underlying causes that Jacobs identifies as leading to a new Dark Age — the erosion of community, the distortion of science, the centralization of government power and the loss of professional integrity. In her quest for a revitalized cultural memory, Jacobs hopes to address these in a future where "responsible government encourages the corrective practices exerted by democracy, which in their turn strengthen good government and responsible citizenship."[17]

This book is dedicated to the strengthening of such responsible citizenship. While it grew initially from our story at the University of Victoria on Canada's West Coast, it led us to encounter a broader movement that is growing in response to similar problems in other universities. Our story is thus a broad one; it is shared with other places throughout the world. Our perspective is limited, however, looking more at environmental than explicitly social issues, and at northern rather than southern countries. Different universities in different places will have other projects to focus on. But what we have learned through our experiences will, we believe, inform and mesh well with related investigations in other places. Our hope is to provide the emerging movement with a new awareness of the university — its dramatic potential to help create a sustainable world and its many strategies for doing so. We hope, as well, that it will contribute to a broad debate about the university — its character and its mission, its past and its future — at a time when the university is being channeled by social forces that are anything but advantageous to emerging generations of students and citizens.

This book is not a survey of everything that is being done in the campus sustainability movement worldwide. After all, our story starts in British Columbia, and B.C. is unique. A haven of environmental activism, it is home to some of the world's grandest — and most endangered — forests, such as the world-renowned Clayoquot Sound and Great Bear Rainforest. Greenpeace started here. David Suzuki lives here. Environmentalism is part of the culture. Yet the barriers to implementing a new vision here are comparable to hundreds of universities across the globe. Each has its special character, and particular issues to address, but all are invisibly networked by the long-shared history of the university. And all face a common set of obstacles to realizing a future for the university that must be radically more innovative, and more sustainable, than anything in its past.

Through writing this book, we have come to realize just how significant this new movement could be. For the story of the sustainable university is not just about more efficient light bulbs and fewer parking lots. Certainly, it is about numerous techniques of sustainability, and we will look at some of these. But it is also about institutional power and powerful mindsets that set the agenda for our modern world, and do so out of sight and out of mind. In the course of this story, we reconsider many important cultural and academic debates, including those of interest to today's social theorists. In these discussions, we suggest

An actor, invisible, at center stage

The university is a primary institution of postindustrial society. It is one of the chief innovative forces of the society, one of the chief determinants of social opportunity and social stratification and a focus of intellectual and cultural life. Its missions take on a new urgency and importance. In 1967 Daniel Bell wrote: "If the business firm was the key institution of the past one hundred years, because of its role in organizing production for the mass creation of products, the university will become the central institution of the next one hundred years because of its role as the new source of innovation and knowledge." The emergence of the postindustrial society moved the university's mission to centre stage.

— George Fallis, "The Mission of the University." Submission to the Rae Commission, in, *Postsecondary Review: Higher Expectations for Higher Education*, Toronto: Government of Ontario, October 2004, p. 21.

the need for broad engagement of such people. Out of their activity should come not just *passive*, but *active*, theory. Substantively, the book argues for a critical but constructive approach to social change in this age after modernism, an approach that can develop sustainability through what we call a more territorial strategy. The story we tell is a critical one, but it is not ultimately about us-versus-them as much as it is about common obstacles and collective opportunities. Despite the sometimes harshness of our judgments, this book celebrates the university for what it uniquely is — a place where society can think differently, act differently, and can do so right where its citizens live.

In the next section, we will reconsider the university, its general history and functions and its role in the specific places where it resides. We will then explore some crucial areas where universities can reform their practices. What we have chosen to look at — transportation, urban development and land use — are only examples of a much larger universe of possibilities. But these examples are ones that we have encountered at our university, and they are of wide concern in the emerging movement. They are also central to so many unsustainable practices today, and they are ripe with transformative possibilities. Lastly, we turn to the most difficult of all challenges to our modern institutions — who makes the decisions that direct the university and how we might make them better. From these pages, we hope to stimulate a dialogue long missing in our hesitant attempts to shift the trajectory of planetary erosion and cultural loss. Above all, we hope to propel a movement whose time has come, a movement that can reinvent the world, one university at a time.

PART I

THE TEACHER

genealogy of an ancient edifice

T HE BIG NEWS THAT DAY was not the new university but the temperature. Though sunny and bright, January 20, 1962, was one of the coldest "in local memory."[1] It was also sod-turning day for the University of Victoria, and faculty members wore gloves and stuffed their overcoats under their academic gowns, while local dignitaries and honored guests shuffled about to stay warm. Fitting to the historic tradition of the Western university, the presiding officer was a lawyer and judge, Justice Joseph Clearihue. His name still graces one of the most important buildings on campus, the home of the faculty of humanities. The judge was also chairman of the University's predecessor, Victoria College, that had been founded 60 years earlier in 1903, and that was now being replaced. Indeed, he had been one of its seven original students. With suitable pomp, but a very easy job of turning the frozen layer of grass and dirt precut for the occasion, he proclaimed for the crowd, "The university that we are going to produce is your university for the benefit of your children. I know that you will not fail us. Let this symbolic sod be a challenge to Greater Victoria."[2] Speeches followed, but not before the chilled assembly vacated the land for the warmth of the Victoria College gymnasium.

On that unseasonably cold day, the ground had been broken for a five-million-dollar development project for the new Gordon Head

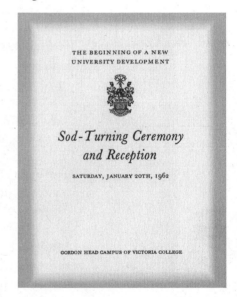

University of Victoria Archives.

campus. Work began immediately. The site had been used as an army base during World War II, but with prodding from Victoria's soon-to-be-mayor, Dick Wilson, it was identified for the new university and purchased from the Canadian government.[3] A master plan was already in place, and again with Wilson's leadership, a San Francisco architectural firm contracted to guide the development process. Soon the noise and bustle of construction echoed out over the neighboring farms. Almost a year to the day after the ceremony, the Clearihue Building was opened, and the university welcomed its first students. Many classes were held in refurbished army huts.

A new university coming to town should be a big event anywhere and especially in a small city like Victoria. In fact, it was a common occurrence in the 1960s, with the postwar economic boom creating huge demands for new jobs and technologies. Universities sprouted up in dozens of cities across the continent to meet that demand. In the sleepy provincial capital of Victoria, a new university promised new energy as professors and support staff took up residence, and thousands of new students arrived for classes every year. But Victoria was getting more than just an infusion of social life. With its university, it was gaining membership in an age-old fraternity. Even more, it was getting an almost ground-floor position in an emerging industry whose stellar future no one could yet foresee.

Turning the sod for such an institution is a strange phenomenon, not just because of the sight of people in fancy clothes and shiny shoes digging around in the dirt, but because of the sort of institution that is being inaugurated. Erecting and maintaining a university entails a huge investment of social resources, directing money (including taxes) that has to be raised from other traditional industries, like forestry and manufacturing, to pay the salaries of people who do unconventional types of work. Building a university entails a conscious allocation of a hard-won social surplus to create a place that does not churn out products that can then turn a profit in a distant market. Instead, the people occupying the university are paid to sit around and think and teach and produce, well, more thinking, and educated, people. The returns from this investment are different from other more tangible forms of production, yet it is not at all well understood just what sorts of returns society does get — or should — from these institutions and from the people connected to them. At a superficial level, it is a degree machine, a rite of passage into the job market. If this is what the university has become, according to Jane Jacobs it represents a tragic diminishment of past roles that were historically grander and more culturally ambitious.

Today, 50 years into the education boom, the university is a critical part of the social fabric, but its role is still not well understood, its functions usually just taken for granted, its social role and potential unappreciated. Although books continue to be written about the university, there are surprisingly few, especially compared with whole libraries that have been written about, say, the city. Yet the lineage of the university extends back over 900 years, long predating cities in anything like their current form and reaching back some five centuries before the rise of modern states whose taxes now support it.

Of the books that do exist, most take an insider's perspective and address administrative and organizational issues. When these insiders do touch on more sensitive matters such as the university's social responsibilities, they usually do so with great caution or at high levels of philosophical generality, discussing generic topics such as the "role of the university in liberal education." Outsiders concerned with global issues of economic well-being, environmental sustainability or social justice, simply give the university a pass. Rarely does the ordinary citizen or even university president consider critically the larger place of the university in society. Certainly the university produces technical experts, but what is its role in producing citizens? It produces research, but who decides what is studied? Today it responds to the corporate marketplace — supplying patents and high-tech machines, expert commentary and high-income customers — but how did its current preoccupations come about? The university also has a relationship to its immediate physical community, but what are its responsibilities to this community? There are many such questions but few answers because not a lot of people give the university a moment's attention.

Before the bricks and mortar

One who does is Marcus Ford, a professor of philosophy in the small town of Flagstaff, Arizona. Ford has written a trailblazing study of the modern university. Steeped in scholarship and history, Ford's book argues that the university is a global force that is intimately involved with, and implicated in, the profound changes shaping the world. In particular, Ford identifies a tension between the way the university works in practice and the critical ideas that emanate from it. These ideas should require society to rethink its roles and make choices about its future, but the practices of the institution prevent these ideas from being debated, let alone acted on.

Marcus Ford is a student of the great British philosopher Alfred North Whitehead whose philosophy of organism heavily influenced his thinking. If one approaches the university itself as organism, one might ask how it has developed over time, in its changing environment. "It's curious," he tells us from his office at Northern Arizona University "that people like me have been involved in universities for our whole lives without thinking about how it evolved and where it is going."[4] Ford's own consideration of this evolution was a gradual process that emerged from his thinking about global issues — especially environmental ones — until it dawned on him "how little the university was doing, even looking at those issues. I couldn't get my colleagues or the administration interested, so it got me to thinking about what sort of institution this is." Upon examination, Ford didn't like what he found. As he wrote in *Beyond the Modern University*:

> Higher education was part of the problem ... worse yet, the modern university was actively engaged in perpetuating and legitimizing the various cultural assumptions that undergird such problems. The very institution that I loved so much was neither an innocent bystander to suffering nor a salvific force in the world. Without giving any real attention to its purposes and processes, I had assumed that higher education, and more of it, would make the world a better place. I began to understand otherwise.[5]

Ford studied the university less as an insider concerned about efficient university operations and more as a citizen alarmed by the demise of planetary sustainability. With this perspective, he expected to find that the university was responding to this demise, but discovered that it was not doing so. Nevertheless his findings also generated some optimism that it could. Looking back, he saw that the university had indeed changed over time. In some periods, he notes, it would be "hard to imagine a more drastic transformation .... As long as it is assumed that the university has remained unchanged over the centuries, it is pointless to enter into a serious critique of the university with the aim of encouraging it to be-come something new .... [T]he university is a living institution."[6]

Scholars generally situate the beginnings of the university in the 12th century. It is associated with the great cities of the time — places like Bologna, Solerno, Rome, Florence, Montpelier, Aix-en-Provence and Paris. Ford puts Paris at the top of the list when trying to "visualize a University of the Middle Ages." Paris was:

that great overshadowing University on the banks of the Seine ... acknowledging no overlord but the Pope, and restive even of his control; ... a city within a city; ... a nation within a nation, with its own laws, government, customs, privileges, and immunities.[7]

Today's universities have roots that stretch back to that period. An ancient edifice, its line is unbroken

Universities	The Rest
70	15

About 85 institutions in the Western world established by 1520 still exist in recognizable forms, with similar functions and unbroken histories, including the Catholic Church, the Parliaments of the Isle of Man, of Iceland and of Great Britain, several Swiss Cantons and seventy universities. Kings that rule, feudal lords with vassals, and guilds with monopolies are all gone. These 70 universities, however, are still in the same locations with some of the same buildings, with professors and students doing much the same things and with governance carried on in much the same way.

— Clark Kerr, *The Uses of the University*, 5th ed., Cambridge: Harvard University Press, 2001, p. 115.

Medieval universities of Europe.

Universities were widespread in Europe throughout the Middle Ages. Many of the universities shown on this map are still thriving, making them some of the oldest living institutions in the Western world.

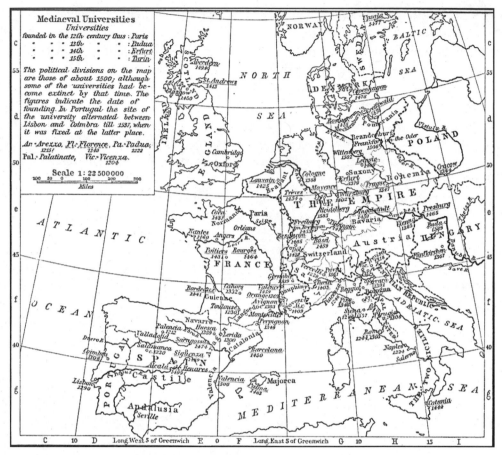

William R. Shepherd, Historical Atlas, New York: Henry Holt, 1923, p. 100.

over these centuries. The first universities arose during the Middle Ages, the so-called dark ages after the fall of Rome, and they were primary building blocks in the European quest to bring the civilizing light of high learning into that darkness. These universities did not, however, have any institutional or physical linkage to the previous age of high civilization of ancient Rome or Greece with its Platonic academy, although one can still trace many of their intellectual and philosophical aspirations back to these times. The original university started under the Roman Catholic Church (itself reaching back almost another millennium) and was enmeshed within the authority and dogma of Christendom. Neither an autonomous communal endeavor, nor a productionist one for economic ends, the early university's goal for humankind was to serve God. Specialization existed to some degree (for example, Bologna was known for law), and there were typically four faculties. Three were of a professional nature — law (canon, not civil), medicine and theology — and one was broadly educational: the liberal "arts" of grammar, logic, rhetoric, mathematics, music, astronomy. At the core of the liberal arts was theology. Indeed, philosophically, the university was held together by theology, the "queen of the sciences," that gave the enterprise a coherent and unified discourse.

The rise of modernism

Ford identifies a second state of evolution emerging from this religious institution that he places at about 500 years into the university's history. As part of the larger changes taking place during the Renaissance — the Protestant Revolution, the Scientific Revolution, the discovery of the New World — the university began to shift from a religious mission to one oriented to building the emerging nation state. This was the beginning of the university as the embodiment of modernism where its unifying mission was more to serve human progress than to fulfill God's will. At a basic level, this was manifest in a philosophical change, where the celebration of a human-centered reason (and science) gradually displaced the authority of a single religion. In its stead, a new humanism celebrated the power and intelligence of the rational individual.

Palace of Reason.

The architecture of the Sorbonne reflects a growing technical capacity developed during the Age of Reason and an aesthetics that mirrors the rationalism of that time.

"The Sorbonne in the Seventeenth Century," from Octave Gréard, *Nos adieux à la vieille Sorbonne*, Paris: Hachette, 1893, p. 94.

Attached to the glorification of a new reason were the hopes for a new era of peace. As John Ralston Saul puts it, "The philosophers of reason believed that nothing provokes violence as effectively as fear and that fear is the product of ignorance ... because they arrived on the scene after two hundred years of religious and civil wars."[8] If reason could allow us to know reality objectively, then reasonable people might be able to think their way past the historic conflicts and factionalism of competing dogmas and allegiances. Peace could be achieved through shared knowledge. Aided by new scientific technologies like the telescope and compass, new universal truths did emerge: the sun did not revolve around the earth, and the world was round, not flat. Through both the process of investigation and the substance of what was discovered, "man" not God became the center of a new universe. Science required physics and mechanics, not metaphysics and religion. Growing out of its discoveries was a new age of exploration, merchant trade and economic growth. This growth evolved into the Industrial Revolution that was itself made possible by a vast realm of scientific discoveries and new technologies, advances that again were engineered by the university.

Just as the university at Paris is seen as the embodiment of the medieval university, Ford argues that the founding of the University of Halle in Germany in 1694 marked the beginning of the modern university. Halle was opened less than 50 years after the signing of the Treaty of Westphalia in 1648 that ended the Thirty Years War, and that is also generally thought of as the beginning of the modern state. Although practiced in the heart of Lutheran territory, at the university:

> religious orthodoxy was soon renounced in favor of objectivity and rationalism, scientific attitudes and free investigation. At Halle, German took the place of Latin as the language of instruction, lectures were substituted for canonical texts, elective courses were offered instead of the formalized curriculum of the medieval university, seminars replaced disputations, and professors were given almost complete control over their work.[9]

In place of building cathedrals and religious orders, the new universities now built navies and colonial administrations. Human endeavors and social progress took center stage.

In a 2004 submission to an Ontario government commission on the future of higher education,[10] former Dean of Arts at York University in Toronto, George Fallis, highlighted the mission of the university in the 1700s as developed in Scotland. Scotland was a driving force in those days, as recently recounted in the intriguing book *How the Scots Invented the Modern World*.[11] During this period, Scotland's new universi-

The Order of Friars Preachers and the Foundation of the University of Glasgow, GUL Special Collections.

ties were closely associated with meeting the needs of government and the economy, and their collective mission was "universal public education" where accessibility, "not gentlemanly manners," was the primary virtue: "Wherever industrialization and nation building were interconnected national priorities ... the Scottish model was influential."[12]

Robe and Gown.
John Slezer's drawing of the University of Glasgow and the Blackfriars Church in 1693.

This populist mission also underpinned the creation of the system of land grant colleges in the United States that followed the same goal of state-building in the 1800s. The lynchpin moment came with the passage in 1862 of the Morrill Land Grant Act, legislation directed to facilitate national expansion and rural development. Cornell University and the Massachusetts Institute of Technology were created as land grant colleges. Indeed, the intention of the legislation was to establish a new college in every state or territory of the United States.[13] Original land grant colleges, such as the universities of Michigan and Wisconsin, would

Map of the System of Human Knowledge
UNDERSTANDING

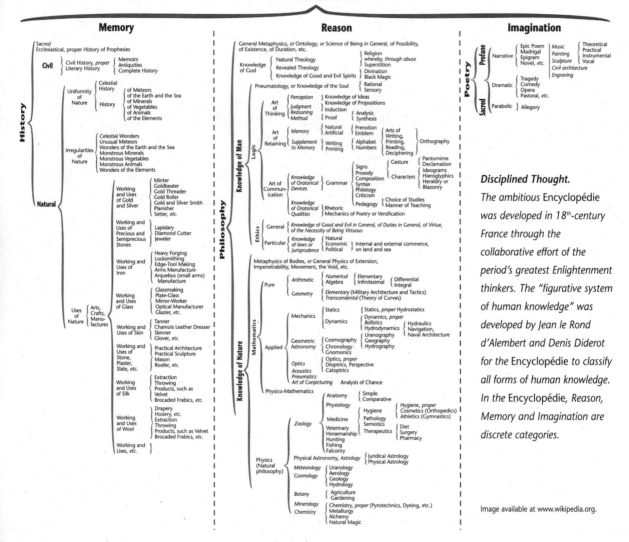

Disciplined Thought.

The ambitious Encyclopédie was developed in 18th-century France through the collaborative effort of the period's greatest Enlightenment thinkers. The "figurative system of human knowledge" was developed by Jean le Rond d'Alembert and Denis Diderot for the Encyclopédie to classify all forms of human knowledge. In the Encyclopédie, Reason, Memory and Imagination are discrete categories.

Image available at www.wikipedia.org.

"serve regional interests for social and economic development, by offering educational opportunities to the children of farmers and industrial workers as well as to the middle class, and by offering degree programs in applied fields such as agriculture, business, engineering, and home economics."[14]

Throughout the United States, these colleges were "inspired by democratic ideals [where] professors were common sights in the cornfields and in the barn as they worked with farmers on disease control and crop development."[15] With the rapid expansion of settlements across the American West, each state was offered 30,000 acres of federal land (taken after Native American territories were settled and their indigenous inhabitants relocated to reservations) if the state used the land, or the proceeds therefrom, to establish universities. Almost 200 new institutions of higher education were created in the United States in the years between 1880 and 1890, many of them land grant colleges and many of them in newly acquired territories.[16]

In fulfilling this function of national development, Ford credits the University of Berlin with a special innovation that continues to this day, shaping not just the university but the whole of modern consciousness. That innovation is the academic "discipline." Disciplinary thinking represented a profound shift in human intelligence by jettisoning the quest for a single unifying truth, a shared metaphysic that informed all thinking, in favor of a more experimental knowledge where truth was discovered only by taking the complexity of life apart, the better to study its inner workings. Increasingly universities applied a form of reason that could categorize reality so as to impose a human order on the seeming chaos of nature. In turn, notes Saul, society became ordered "around structures designed to produce answers. These structures have fed upon expertise and that expertise upon complexity. The effect has been to render universal understanding as difficult as possible."[17]

The rise of academic specialization in the 18th and 19th centuries had its parallel in the economic world where craft industries gave way to the division of labor in the production line. (This concept was first articulated in 1776 by one of those

Scots who certainly did shape the modern world, the philosopher and political economist Adam Smith.) Just as the growing industrial economy produced more goods, so too disciplinary specialization produced more rigorous research, the better for producing the conceptual clarity and technical precision that allowed for technological progress. But as Ford puts it, the results were not "synonymous with truth."[18] Specialization worked to build steel bridges and electric motors but did not get society any closer to answering the sorts of ultimate questions that had been at the core of the medieval university. Quite the contrary, the growth of the state-oriented university actively facilitated the displacement from society of a single, coherent worldview associated with a religious perspective. Knowledge organized into disciplines was — and is — knowledge as separate units, that is, units that operate in isolation from each other. As a result, the findings of one are not contradicted by the truths of another. Although the products of scientific enquiry might be argued to be true knowledge, the limits of this truth are confined within the scope of the disciplines themselves. Physics might tell an engineer how to build a warship, but it would not tell its sailors their purpose in battle. That would be within the realm of the department of politics. And in trying to evaluate this new, but fragmented, knowledge — part of what French theorist Bruno Latour referred to as the "purification" of knowledge[19] — one could no longer turn to the usual authorities, like the Pope. In this academic shift, Ford notes a cultural shift from matters of transcendent to those of utilitarian value. Whereas Paris attained preeminence for theology, Berlin was renowned for science and engineering. And so was born a new criterion for knowledge: if it works, it's science. That criterion is still with us, but the question remains, works for what?

Today universities continue to be organized into dozens of separate departments reflecting their disciplines, each doing their own thing, with limited communication between them. Even, bemoans Ford, where their basic beliefs are in conflict. Thus does the Department of Economics churn out students whose entire training is rooted in an assumption of unending economic growth — and the economy keeps humming. Meanwhile, earth scientists write about the immutable principles of thermodynamics that speak to the impossibility of such growth — and the Earth keeps getting hotter.

Ford's conclusion is stark: because "their 'truths' cannot be contradicted or modified by the truths uncovered by other academic disciplines, or by the events of the world itself," disciplinary thinking has become "harmful to the earth and to human communities."[20] Indeed, as Latour argues, a fundamental goal of modernity is to create a "purified" rationality that could be achieved only by completely separating the human from the non-human world.[21] And with its utilitarian justification, the modernist university now implicitly privileges the truths associated with the material progress of human society over spiritual or religious values, including any possible sanctity of nature. Steeped in these assumptions and possessed of a limited collective vocabulary and conversation, the university has taken limited notice of the consequences of the knowledge it produced and its role in producing them.

Enter the age of economism

As the nation-building university evolved, the usefulness of its knowledge and products began to transcend individual nations. Science became a global force, its truths universally accessible. This led to what Ford identifies as a third stage of the university's evolution, one of recent vintage. Emerging after WWII, the unifying mission of this period he calls "economism," a new way of life that is based on the belief "that future wars could be avoided if the economic

The Modernist University. The University of Victoria Campus Plan (1961) anticipated the replacement of the forest with buildings and grassed landscapes, and the physical division of the disciplines on campus.

University of Victoria *Campus Plan*, 2003, p. 13.

An alienated institution?

The university as a site of knowledge has often seen itself as something of an enclave, removed enough from the immediacy and demands of the modern life to produce the knowledge and information with which to better understand society and the science and technical inventions that ultimately transform it .... For others this meant an unresponsive, disconnected and alienated institution with a decidedly anti-urban bias.

— David C. Perry and Wim Wiewel, "Campus to City: The University as Developer," *The University as Urban Developer: Case Studies and Analysis*, edited by David C. Perry, and Wim Wiewel, Boston: M.E. Sharpe and Lincoln Institute of Land Policy, 2005, p. 4.

interests of individuals replaced the interests of particular nations. Economism would be the route to both *peace* and *prosperity*."[22] Economism entails a set of interrelated beliefs: from a faith in the social benefits of the market economy to a belief in the necessity of economic growth; from the promise of individual freedom to a suspicion of the very idea of collective interest. Ford's third stage is, however, still rooted in a collective cultural attachment to utility and an implicit truth that might be formulated in the equation: individual interest + material gain = social welfare. Says Ford, "[A] lot of the curriculum was based around job preparation, you know, teacher training or accounting, or jobs for chemistry or pre-med .... It makes perfectly good sense for people to go to university because they can come out and get a job."[23]

As in past eras, this third stage of the university is directly related to the evolving social context, which the university both reflects and creates. For example, the 1950s and 1960s were years of booming economic growth — and a huge expansion in the university system worldwide.

This growth over the past half-century has reshaped the university into an interrelated system of knowledge production so large and powerful that it can better be understood today as the higher education industry. The pattern of development was apparent even in the 1960s when the former chancellor of the University of California (Berkeley) Clark Kerr suggested a new name for the postwar institution, the "multiversity." Too big still to be considered a community (a *collegium*), the university was evolving more into a large-scale assemblage of "specialized factions, disciplines, students and research activities, united only by occupancy of a common territory called the campus."[24] (As we will see in the next chapter, this campus territoriality is one of the most important, yet neglected, aspects of the university's constitution.)

So successful has been this third-stage university that the economy that it serves has itself evolved into a reflection of the university. Thus is the knowledge economy the high point of national development today. At the same time, the university has evolved as an economic actor in its own right. The numbers are staggering. In 2004–2005, over a million students were registered in Canadian universities, a number that is expected to increase by 30 percent over the next decade.[25] In that year, Canadian universities performed research and development worth over Can$9 billion, 35 percent of the total national research and development (R&D).[26] This research sustained another one million jobs and contributed more to Canada's gross domestic product than "sectors like pulp and paper or automotive vehicles and [was] just as big as the combined arts, entertainment and recreation industries."[27] Two thirds of all new jobs to be created by 2008 will require postsecondary education. Already, over half of the population between the ages of 25 and 54 have postsecondary degrees.[28]

In the United States, the overall numbers are even more impressive. The US Department of Education counts 6,500 accredited postsecondary institutions.[29] As of 2001, 4,200 of these institutions granted university degrees where, overall, enrolment exceeded 16,000,000 full- and part-time students[30] supported by over 3,000,000 faculty and staff.[31] This higher education population in the United States is, at any one time, greater than the total population of Australia.[32] In 2001 direct expenditures by so-called Title IV institutions in the United States totaled over US$260 billion, and this is just 60 percent of the total number of its higher education institutions.[33] One study out of Georgetown University estimated the annual direct and indirect impacts of the American higher education industry at over US$1.2 trillion.[34] Part of this impact includes over US$27 billion in research in 1999, which translated into US$33 billion in the transfer of technology-related research, and the creation of 280,000 jobs.[35] Royalty payments back to Canadian and American universities from their patents and technologies are now approaching one billion US dollars every year.[36] Every American dollar of government money invested in higher education generates four dollars in economic activity.[37]

The rise of the higher education industry is one of the most important, and most overlooked, trends of the past half-century. And it is not just the macro numbers that are impressive, but the university's cultural impact: "The solutions to virtually all the problems with which government is concerned: health, education, environment, energy, urban development, international relationships, economic competitiveness, and defense and national security, all depend on creating new knowledge — and hence upon the health of our universities."[38] Thus, while the university is an "industry" in the new knowledge economy, it is more than that because the specialists of most other industries in this economy were trained at the university. In the knowledge economy, it is literally the mother of all industries! Yet, in the growing linkage of this one industry with all the others, the university risks being equated with the corporate goals of these industries. Indeed, with so many direct financial and intellectual ties between corporations and university departments, many universities have begun to take on the mission of corporatism as *their* mission. But, as Ford remarks, the university's graduates and the corporations they now serve have *not* solved these global problems and may well exacerbate them. Still others who come to university will find themselves becoming politicized. It is past time to reconsider the nature of this institution, and who and what it produces.

Cracks beneath the tower

That the university industry has escaped notice is, at least, partly because it doesn't fit the mental box we have of what constitutes an industry — something built on a primary resource like oil or timber, or around a product like a car or a computer,

Khalil Bendib, University, Inc., StudioBendib, March 28, 2005. Available at http://www.bendib.com/environment/new.html.

Corporate U

The media have ... missed the real story about academe. The real story is about university physics and electrical engineering departments being seduced by Pentagon contracts; molecular biology, biochemistry and medicine departments being wooed by drug companies and biotech firms; and university computer science departments being in bed with Big Blue and a few high-tech chip makers. The story about the university ... is that they will turn a trick for anybody with money to invest; and the only ones with money are corporations, millionaires and foundations. These investments in universities have dramatically changed the mission of higher education; they have led universities to attend to the interests of their well-heeled patrons, rather than those of students.

— Lawrence C. Soley, *Leasing the Ivory Tower: The Corporate Takeover of Academia*, Boston: South End Press, 1995, p. 9.

or even around a service like the professions of medicine or accounting. The university may supply business grads to run oil companies, engineers to design laptop computers, and doctors to staff hospitals, but its incentives and operations are different than normal industries. Where is profit, for example? And its products are vastly more diverse than those of a conventional industry, cranking out well-educated captains of industry but also well-researched monographs on the Dead Sea Scrolls.

Despite these differences, a symbiotic relationship exists between the growth of the global economy and the newly minted higher education industry. In this symbiosis, the university is changing in new ways. For example, in a recent study entitled *No Place to Learn*,[39] two Canadian professors argue that universities are moving beyond even credentialism to the point where they are no longer oriented primarily to teaching, but to corporate- and government-driven research. Pharmaceutical companies cut countless deals with the world's medical schools, while those who raise doubts find themselves out of research funds or out of a job.

Meanwhile, as the university develops as a self-directed entity, its internal momentum grows and becomes more difficult to challenge and redirect. Propelled by privatization, commercialization,[40] and government downsizing, the university is itself increasingly driven by its own corporate agenda, its mission steered by development officers (whose numbers exploded in the 1990s) and assisted by outside consultants who help them to create their own brand. In this new university,[41] dissent is a threat to fundraising and to good corporate relations. As George Fallis puts it, "If the university is to resist giving priority to research which promotes economic growth and to the task of commercializing research, it must resist its two greatest patrons — government and industry."[42]

For higher education, today is the time of its greatest success and authority. It is also a time of an emerging crisis that mirrors the disparate ecological and social crises enveloping the globe. As its power grows, the seemingly scientific truths at the core of the modern university are open to question, rife with contradictions between faculties, and challenged by the very expertise housed within it. This is what that poorly understood term "postmodern" is all about — taking apart (or deconstructing) the claims to truth embedded in the mission of modernism. As one of the intellectual giants of postmodern philosophy, Michel Foucault has demonstrated that the seemingly rational knowledge that is the university's claim to legitimacy is not absolute.

Like its forebearers, the rationality of the modern university is a stepchild of institutional power, the claim of Western science to universal truth "a mirage associated with economic domination and political hegemony."[43] Or as Saul puts it, "The Age of Reason has turned out to be the Age of Structure, a time when, in the absence of purpose, the drive for power as a value in itself has become the principal indicator of social approval. And the winning of power has become the measure of social merit."[44]

The historical context of which the university is itself a part provides the bounds of true knowledge — religious truth giving way to the truth of state-building, the truths of scientific and technological discovery underpinning a progress that is now coming face to face, perhaps catastrophically, with the real global limits of that progress. Meanwhile, fragmented into its disciplines, having jettisoned an explicit commitment to a shared truth, the academy is unable to act. Thus is the crisis of the Earth also a crisis of the university that is itself both a product of the Western culture that brought on this crisis and an instrument of that culture's self-justification. As another famous French postmodernist Jacques Derrida puts it, "The white man takes his own mythology, Indo-European mythology, his own

Mute languages

Postmodern thinking suggests that the academic community is a kind of fiction and that *difference* is the hallmark within and between institutions which bear the title. The growth of specialization has become so complete that colleagues even within a faculty often cannot discuss their areas of expertise without misunderstanding. It has become impossible to defend any particular hierarchy of subjects in the modern university today, let alone any notion of authoritative knowledge.

— Anthony Smith and Frank Webster, *The Postmodern University? Contested Visions of Higher Education in Society*, Bristol, PA: Taylor and Francis, 1997, p. 5.

logos, that is the *mythos* of his idiom, for the universal form of what he must still wish to call Reason."[45]

And so, we are stuck — without a truth that has been rejected, and quite properly so — and wondering what to do. In this conundrum, Marcus Ford argues for a new university rooted in a constructive postmodernism. Generally today, postmodernism has an unpalatable popular image of people who speak in an incoherent language with which they deride the inherited beliefs that so many hold dear. Meanwhile, "constructivists" are often criticized for potentially repeating the mistakes of the past. Postmodernism seems to lead to a radical relativism where there is simply no objective truth at all, anywhere. Ironically, this critical perspective has no impact whatsoever in the departments of computer science or genetics, let alone in the professional trades like health information science or advanced accounting that continue to pump out their seemingly true (i.e., useful) research. Yet there is no denying the essential postmodernist insight that institutional power precedes cultural knowledge. What we know as true is as much a function of our particular experience, culture and language as it is a claim to objective, let alone universal, reality. Over the centuries, scientific discoveries and technological advances have shown us how to make cars that move and airplanes that fly. But if, in so doing, they are costing us the Earth, what sort of truth is that?

With the limits of progress becoming ever more obvious, the advent of the postmodern critique of modernist truth is more than mere coincidence. We are discovering (but not acknowledging) that the assumed truth of unending growth and progress is also killing the context for all our many truths: the planet. Yet, closing the loop of our own intellectual prison, as Michel Foucault again puts it, the university maintains a "sort of de facto — and de jure — monopoly, which means that any knowledge that is not born or shaped within this sort of institutional field is automatically, and from the outset, if not actually excluded, disqualified a priori."[46] Thus does so much of the university today not even discuss, let alone respond to, problems that consume us as a whole. Perhaps, however, many do not want to reflect critically on the university for fear of undermining the institution that has shaped our thinking for so many centuries, and thereby engendering a demise of the civilization it has built and a return to the chaos that preceded the Age of Reason. Ironically, by not doing so at a time of unparalleled individual freedoms, humanity strides into Jacobs's new "dark age," into a prison of its own making — of the university's making — never even seeing its walls until, perhaps, it is too late.

Yet, even this is, in the end, a sterile debate. As Marcus Ford tells us, it is certainly no longer possible to be premodern, but "being modern is going to be the death of us all."[47] And so the real question for sustaining the world in an age after modernism is, as it always has been, what is to be done? How can our new understandings after modernism not just be deconstructive, but reconstructive?

And, for an institution with a millennial history, an unequalled intellectual richness, a role as a de facto innovator in society and an unrecognized level of economic and social power, the important question for the postmodern constructivist is, where to start. In response, we might suggest a new approach that offers a different perspective than that of the global economism of the modern university, a response that reconstructs by going *down* not *up*. We suggest that the university, every university, begin in a place where it can truly act, which is to say, in a place where the university actually *is* — the place where the sod's been turned.

A messy concept

The fact that "sustainability" is a messy, ill-defined concept gives universities an opportunity to grapple with the concept and develop new ways of thinking about the concept. Sustainability provides colleges and universities an opportunity to confront their core values, their practices, their entrenched pedagogies, the way they program for student learning, the way they think about resources and allocate these resources and their relationships with the broader community.

— Arjen E. J. Wals and Bob Jickling, "Sustainability in Higher Education: From Doublethink and Newspeak to Critical Thinking and Meaningful Learning," *International Journal of Sustainability in Higher Education*, vol. 3, no. 3, 2002, p. 230.

Society Must Be Defended — Michel Foucault

THE GROUND IS CRUMBLING

I would say: for the last ten or fifteen years, the immense and proliferating criticizability of things, institutions, practices and discourses; a sort of general feeling that the ground was crumbling beneath our feet, especially in places where it seemed most familiar, most solid, and closest to us ... the astonishing efficacy of discontinuous, particular and local critiques ... I think that the essentially local character of the critique in fact indicates something resembling a sort of autonomous and noncentralized theoretical production, or in other words a theoretical production that does not need a visa from some common regime to establish its validity .... P. 6.

SUBJUGATED KNOWLEDGES

When I say "subjugated knowledges" I am also referring to a whole series of knowledges that have been disqualified as nonconceptual knowledges, as insufficiently elaborated knowledges: naïve knowledges, hierarchically inferior knowledges, knowledges that are below the required level of erudition or scientificity. And it is thanks to the reappearance of these knowledges from below, of these unqualified or even disqualified knowledges ... it is the reappearance of what people know at the local level, of these disqualified knowledges, that made the critique possible ....

What was at stake in both cases, in both this scholarly knowledge and these disqualified knowledges, in these two forms of knowledge — the buried and the disqualified? .... We can give the name "genealogy" to this coupling together of scholarly erudition and local memories, which allows us to constitute a historical knowledge of struggles and to make use of that knowledge in contemporary tactics .... Pp. 7–8.

INSURRECTION OF KNOWLEDGES

It is therefore not an empiricism that runs through the genealogical project, nor does it lead to a positivism, in the normal sense of the word. It is a way of playing local discontinuous, disqualified, or ☞

nonlegitimized knowledges off against the unitary theoretical instance that claims to be able to filter them, organize them into a hierarchy, organize them in the name of a true body of knowledge, in the name of the rights of a science that is in the hands of the few. Genealogies are therefore not positivistic returns to a form of science that is more attentive or more accurate. Genealogies are, quite specifically, antisciences. It is not that they demand the lyrical right to be ignorant, and not that they reject knowledge or invoke or celebrate some immediate experience that has yet to be captured by knowledge. That is not what they are about. They are about the insurrection of knowledges. Not so much against the contents, methods, or concepts of a science; this is above all, primarily, an insurrection against the centralizing power-effects that are bound up with the institutionalization and workings of any scientific discourse organized in a society such as ours .... P. 9.

LIBERATION OF KNOWLEDGES

Compared to the attempt to inscribe knowledges in the power-hierarchy typical of science, genealogy is, then, a sort of attempt to desubjugate historical knowledges, to set them free, or in other words to enable them to oppose and struggle against the coercion of a unitary, formal, and scientific theoretical discourse... To put it in a nutshell: Archaeology is the method specific to the analysis of local discursivities, and genealogy is the tactic which, once it has described these local discursivities, brings into play the desubjugated knowledges that have been released from them. Pp. 10–11. ■

— Michel Foucault, *Society Must Be Defended: Lectures at the Collège de France, 1975–76.*
Edited by Mauro Bertani and Alessandro Fontana; translated by David Macey.
New York: Picador, 2003, pp. 6–11.

archaeology of a buried landscape

T HE ORGANIZER WENT EARLY TO THE CAMPUS MEADOW and started digging. Unsure of how many people would turn up to gather the camas bulbs and tend the cooking pit, Cheryl Bryce decided that a couple of days of preparation with her sister and nephews were in order. "It was amazing," she recalls, "to just dig in and get our hands back into the soil. We reconnected to the earth and to that place, but also we connected in a different way as a family."[1] Lands Manager for the Songhees First Nation, in June 2005 Bryce led a camas harvest in a Garry oak meadow at the University, a Songhees event that was layered with significance. Cutting into the soil, flipping over the sod and digging out the bulbs, this was "the first time in well over 150 years since our hands went back into that soil."

Bryce is a member of the Chekonein family of the Lekwungen (or, today, Songhees) Nation. Her people had tended these local meadows for countless generations before the arrival of white colonizers. Victoria archaeologist Al Mackie estimates that down the hill from where the University now stands at nearby Cadboro Bay, a village had existed for "at least the last 2,500 to 3,000 years but probably longer."[2] The onion-like camas bulb, an excellent source of carbohydrates, was long an important local staple. The bulbs were steamed in cooking pits until they darkened and turned sweet. Residing at the northern end of the plant's geographic range, the Lekwungen also traded camas for other foods and goods from coastal and inland peoples. In the camas meadows that still exist throughout the region, its wild purple flowers provide a stunning sight in spring.

"Harvest Time."

UVic sits in the heart of the Songhees (Lukwungen) territory, where camas has a long history as a plentiful source of carbohydrates and an important resource for trade. Songhees lands manager Cheryl Bryce holds a bowl of camas bulbs freshly harvested from a campus meadow at a traditional pit-cook hosted by the Lukwungen Nation in June 2005.

Photograph by Jon Corbett, *The Ring*, 2005, ol. 37, no 7, <www.ring.uvic.ca/05jul07/features/camas.html>

Despite her concerns, Bryce's harvest was a huge success. She had hoped for maybe 20 people, but 100 turned up. "It felt amazing having the drums and the singing, and to have all those children there. It was exactly what I had prayed for," says Bryce. "It's not just the restoration of an ecosystem, it's the restoration of a culture." That restoration extended widely. "We had students coming in, schools coming in, lots of people from the University, people from the Songhees community. There were some Elders from the Nuu-chah-nulth territory, a lot of First Nations students attending at UVic, a Metis youth, students from our schools." Building on the event, Bryce would now like to conclude a formal agreement with the University and work with local governments throughout the region to support the harvesting of camas, salal, swordfern and other plants from other ecosystems. Bryce would like to see traditional management techniques applied in Victoria's major downtown park at Beacon Hill. She even hopes to "get the fire department onside to do traditional burns so that it can restore the camas ecosystem and, with it, the Songhees culture." Her mission, says Bryce, is "to teach in a different way. It is a way of decolonizing and of identifying with the land."

As if in a magic landscape

Like so many places, the natural history of the lands around the harvest meadow has been made all but invisible by more than a century of development and change. Yet buried beneath the landscape of buildings, lawns, roads, parking lots and exotic gardens is a storied past. It remains unremarked in the official histories of the university because it is not seen as relevant. As education theorist William Tierney puts it, "If knowledge production is impartial and shared within a disciplinary community of scholars, then the physical locale of where one conducts knowledge is relatively unimportant."[3]

Occasionally the invisible presence that motivates Bryce's work surfaces. At UVic, it is evident in the obligatory opening ritual at official ceremonies, such as academic conferences and convocations. At such events, lead-off speakers will acknowledge the Songhees people and thank them for their "permission" to be on their land, a respectful, though often awkward, gesture. It is certainly ironic. Nevertheless, the acknowledgment conveys an emerging awareness and obligation and, however subtly, imparts a complexity to the place where the university resides. Recent occupations rest on deeper histories. To some, however, the yearning for a sense of place is but a nostalgic, even reactionary, celebration of parochialism and exclusion. In this view, place is not really local at all but another site where a hybrid host of cosmopolitan influences converge over long-distant spaces.[4] Thus a place today is as much a product of the architectural trends in San Francisco and the consumer fads in London as it is the fading memories of locally born residents or the rekindled enthusiasms of amateur natural historians. There is no going back to the local. In this hybridization, however, important possibilities are lost to memory and experience.

Dig a little, and any suburban campus has remnant roots with stories to tell. Bryce doesn't need to dig very hard. "Our ancestors created that landscape," she explains, harkening back to the burning, digging and other practices that sculpted the land through use. She traces her lineage back some five generations to a noted ancestor, Cheetlum. In Cheetlum's time, the landscape was so blanketed with camas and Garry oak meadows that the first colonizers described it as if it were "tended like an English park."[5] Mixed in with open landscapes were towering forests of ancient fir and cedar, diverse wetlands and numerous springs, a bountiful seashore and sheltered ocean waters.

One of Canada's preeminent anthropologists of the 20th century, Wilson Duff characterizes the local peoples as:

never in any political sense a single tribe. They were comprised of a large number of more or less autonomous household groups, whose sprawling plank houses were clustered in a number of winter villages, and who moved regularly from place to place in the course of their annual round of activities. Specific resource use areas and house sites were owned and used by specific households; other places within what was regarded by themselves and outsiders as Songhees territory were utilized more or less in common.[6]

Curator of Archaeology at the Royal BC Museum, Grant Keddie points to seasonal rounds with a "wide range of fish and bird species .... Deer and elk would have been hunted in the open parkland and Douglas fir forests above Cadboro Bay [the area around the University], and harbor seals and sea lions hunted in nearby waters."[7] Although the archaeological work on what is now University grounds has been minimal, the early historical record indicates that within a mile (two kilometres), the village sites on the bay were of substantial size. One early colonial observer, the chief commissioner of "lands and works", Joseph Trutch, wrote to the Colonial Secretary that the Songhees "possessed by occupation the whole southeastern portion of Vancouver Island, including Saanich Peninsula, their principal village being at Cadboro Bay."[8]

The canoes returning from gathering camas to Esquimalt.

Watercolor by Paul Kane, 1847 (April 8 – June 10), courtesy of Stark Museum of Art.

The relations of Bryce's ancestors to the rich world around them were very different from those of today. For one thing, boundaries were fluid, fluid between places in different seasons, between families and larger social groupings and between "owners" of resources and users. After 1842 this fluidity fell into catastrophic decline. In that year the Chief Factor of the Hudson's Bay Company, James Douglas, landed in the bay where the Chekonein family group was centered. Coming to map the landscape in advance of settlement, Douglas named the bay after his schooner, *Cadborough*. Legend has it that Douglas was quickly accosted on his disembarcation by a local chief who warned him of the importance of an oceanside spring. Said to have mystical qualities, the spring was presided over by a huge maple tree that grew beside it. The hillside above the bay [including the campus of the University today] was covered with springs. This was a landscape of great power and importance to the whole Lekwungen peoples. Douglas decided against building his fort there, however, and in the next year established Fort Camosun a few miles away in what is now the heart of downtown.

Moving around

Their line of travel was centered at Cadboro Bay. Coming from Cordova Bay cedar forest after making their annual canoe supply, they crossed Telegraph Trail to Cadboro Bay, where a few shacks were situated — say, between the present hotel and the high ground east. From here during early July the passage was made to San Juan Island, where salmon fishing was done. By September 1 sufficient dry food and grease was put up to carry them over the winter.

The next move was back to Cadboro Bay, but their camp was made on the south side of the Bay just east of the present clubhouse. Dancing, feasting, berry picking and the burying of salmon eggs was their principal play and work during these few weeks ....

From here the natives crossed overland to the Gorge, one trail ending at the old Finlayson house and the other further up the arm .... From the upper end of the arm Esquimalt Harbor was reached, and in this location most of the deer, ducks and geese were procured for Fall and Winter.

— From Charles French, in his letter to Hudson's Bay Company archives, in Wilson Duff, "The Fort Victoria Treaties", *BC Studies*, no. 3, Fall 1969, p. 49.

Douglas drew the name Camosun from the name of a Songhees landmark ("Camossung") that was located nearby. Camossung was an important spiritual

Mystic Spring

As he stepped ashore and prepared to follow the Indian trail that led to Camosun [now Victoria] his attention was arrested by a huge maple tree ... [at the foot of which] was a spring as clear as crystal .... The Indians were proud of the spring and used its water freely. They said it possessed medicinal properties. They also claimed that it was bewitched ....

"The tree is a god. It guards the spirit of the spring, and as long as the tree stands the water will creep to its foot for protection and shade ...."

Later the vandal hand of man ... held an axe within its grasp and before its sharp strokes the monarch was laid low .... With the tragic end of the old tree the Mystic Spring disappeared and was seen no more.

— D.W. Higgins, *The Mystic Spring and Other Tales of Western Life*, Toronto: William Briggs, 1904, pp. 11–12, 20–21.

figure, a young girl who had been anointed as the guardian of the area's natural resources and then transformed into an underwater rock possessed of magical power. Local youths gained spiritual strength by diving to the rock. The name is still important in the region, but its historic role in cultural and ecological stewardship has long since been forgotten. At the time, Douglas himself seized on another level of significance. Watching the tide rush over Camossung rock, Douglas noted that it possessed "a degree of force and velocity capable of driving the most powerful machinery if guided and applied by mechanical skill."[9]

For the Songhees, these newcomers with their maps and fort and exceeding curiosity might as well have arrived from another planet. It is not possible that these local inhabitants could have conceived of what lay ahead — fixed plots, bought and paid for in writing; indeed, whole landscapes with lines across them where one's movement was blocked, and one's presence not to be allowed. Yet Fort Camosun was certainly a novel place of tangible interest, and soon families began to congregate around it. People from all around converged to see what was up, to trade and get in on the new opportunities it provided. While relinquishing their territories was not in their lexicon of considerations, a new social landscape was imposed in the blink of an eye. Symbolically, within a year of establishing Fort Camosun, Douglas renamed it after his monarch, Queen Victoria.

Up on the farm

Less than a decade after Douglas landed at Cadboro Bay, the area was formally designated as a colony, thus opening it up to settlement. As the newly designated Governor, Douglas quickly concluded what have come to be known as the Fort Victoria Treaties with the local groups. Actually "concluded" is a stretch. Notes historian Arthur Ray, Douglas "persuaded the chiefs to show their approval by making their signs on the bottom of a blank piece of paper."[10] In the 1950s, anthropologist Wilson Duff interviewed elderly locals who were one step removed from those whose names appear on the treaty. He concluded that the chiefs did not actually sign the document as their names were "listed in a neat column obviously written by an experienced clerical hand. The x's, all equal in size and form, lie to the right in a neat vertical column."[11] He suggested that the text was added

Wealth and a different kind of power

After the Flood when Raven, Mink and the Transformer Hayls (X€ls) were travelling around teaching the people how things were to be done, they came to this place and found a young girl and her grandfather. The girl, q'ama'sə? [Camossung], was sitting in the water, crying. "Why are you crying?" asked X€ls. "My father is angry with me and won't give me anything to eat." "What would you like?" he asked, "Sturgeon?" "No." "Berries?" "No." She refused a lot of things, and that is why these are not found along the Gorge. "Ducks?" "Herrings?" "Cohoes?" "Oysters?" These she accepted, and that is why they are plentiful here.

"You will control all of these things for your people," said X€ls. Then he turned her into stone, sitting there under the water, looking up the narrows. Her grandfather's name was Snukaymelt (snək'€'məlt) "diving." Since she liked her grandfather to be with her, he was also turned to stone, as if jumping in carrying a rock to take him to the bottom.

— Told to Wilson Duff by Jimmy Fraser (Songhees man) in an interview, 1952, in Wilson Duff, "The Fort Victoria Treaties," *BC Studies*, no. 3, Fall 1969, p. 36.

Conveyance of land

Know all men, we, the chiefs and people of the tribe or family of Che-ko-nein ... do consent to surrender, entirely and for ever ... the whole of the lands situate and lying between Point Gonzales and Mount Douglas ....

The Condition of or understanding of this sale is this, that our village sites and enclosed fields are to be kept for our own use, for the use of our children and for those who may follow after us; and the land shall be properly surveyed hereafter. It is understood, however, that the land itself, with these small exceptions, becomes the entire property of the white people for ever; it is also understood that we are at liberty to hunt over the unoccupied lands and to carry our fisheries as formerly.

We have received, as payment, Seventy-nine pounds ten shillings sterling.

[April 30, 1850]

(Signed) CHAYTH-LUM his x mark, and 29 others.

Done before us,

(Signed) Alfred Robson Benson, M.R.C.S.L.

Joseph William McKay.

— Richard Wolfenden (Government Printer), Che-Ko-Nein Tribe: Point Gonzales to Cedar Hill, *Papers connected with the Indian Land Question 1850–1875, 1877*. Victoria: Government Printing Office, 1987 (orig. ed. 1875), p. 8.

Fences of freedom

Ownership was secured by action rather than word, action that made use of the land in ways that English people could appreciate — planting and tilling, gardening, building a house, bounding a space .... A properly fenced garden was property .... [T]hose that did not plant gardens, or did not fence them or did not create landscapes that bore imprints familiar to the English did not possess the land and could not have property rights to it ....

The French philosophers Gilles Deleuze and Felix Guattari suggest that the spatial energy of capitalism works to deterritorialize people (that is, to detach them from prior bonds between people and place) and to reterritorialize them in relation to the requirements of capital itself (that is, access to land conceived as resources and freed from the constraints of custom ....).

— Cole Harris, *Making Native Space: Colonialism, Resistance, and Reserves in British Columbia*, Vancouver: UBC Press, 2002, pp. 48, 53.

after the "signing," adapted to local circumstances from the documents "that the New Zealand Land Company used to buy tracts from the Maori."[12]

Nor were these treaties such a great deal for the inhabitants. Notes Ray, "The cost to the [Hudson's Bay Company] was nominal."[13] But in three days in the spring of 1850, Douglas concluded nine "purchases" of land that, with two later purchases, gave Douglas "the agricultural land he would require" to establish major settlements in the area.[14] In Douglas's colonial mind, ownership of property was exclusive, and "shared territories had no place." This, wrote Duff, led to "ethnographic absurdities in the treaties" that completely ignored the existing basis of land management in "shared areas."[15] Bryce's great-great-great-great-great grandfather Cheetlum appears as the first name, "Chayth lum," on the Chekonein treaty.[16]

With the treaties in hand, a long process of displacement began. Whole communities were shifted from one location to another, the locations and boundaries of designated "Indian reserves" changing with the colony's evolving needs. Practitioners of the old ways faced enormous pressures; promises of continued hunting on open lands quickly succumbed to farm fences and industrial development. Local Saanich lore has it that their peoples temporarily stopped loggers in 1850 from cutting huge trees at Cadboro Bay for ship masts.[17] Within four years, however, the Hudson's Bay Company (HBC) established its 1,100-acre Uplands Farm (including land now occupied

Rationalization of a landscape.

Within a decade of the first arrival of Douglas at Cadboro Bay in 1842, lines of land ownership began to be laid on the local landscape. The entire area was divided up by 1859.

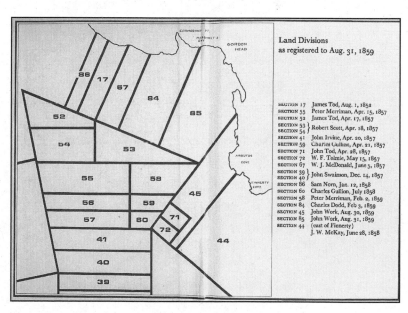

Land Divisions
as registered to Aug. 31, 1859

SECTION 17   James Tod, Aug. 1, 1852
SECTION 55   Peter Merriman, Apr. 15, 1857
SECTION 52   James Tod, Apr. 17, 1857
SECTION 53 } Robert Scott, Apr. 18, 1857
SECTION 54 }
SECTION 41   John Irvine, Apr. 20, 1857
SECTION 59   Charles Gullion, Apr. 21, 1857
SECTION 71   John Tod, Apr. 28, 1857
SECTION 72   W. F. Tolmie, May 15, 1857
SECTION 67   W. J. McDonald, June 5, 1857
SECTION 39 } John Swainson, Dec. 14, 1857
SECTION 40 }
SECTION 86   Sam Nom, Jan. 12, 1858
SECTION 60   Charles Gullion, July 1858
SECTION 58   Peter Merriman, Feb. 2, 1859
SECTION 84   Charles Dodd, Feb 3, 1859
SECTION 45   John Work, Aug. 30, 1859
SECTION 85   John Work, Aug. 31, 1859
SECTION 44   (east of Finnerty)
              J. W. McKay, June 28, 1858

Ursula Jupp, *From Cordwood to Campus in Gordon Head 1852–1959*, Victoria: Ursula Jupp, 1975, inside cover.

by the University).[18] By 1859 over 2,200 acres in the area had been parceled out to 13 families.[19] While the Chekonein people at Cadboro Bay and the adjacent islands were not displaced all at once, the Songhees were established in an informal reserve in what is now downtown Victoria in 1850. Over the following decades, many Songhees agitated to return to Cadboro Bay. They came close to achieving this objective when, in response to a Songhees petition, the HBC offered its farmland in the area to the Department of Indian Affairs in 1881 for $56,250, but the offer was turned down.[20] After many forced displacements, by 1911 the whole of the Songhees Nation was moved to its present location in Esquimalt, some distance from the city center.

In place of the Songhees, a new farming community emerged. It was to thrive in the area for the next 100 years. The Uplands Farm was Vancouver Island's first official farm, its last acreage now lying fallow at UVic. Although life today is remote from a connection to these places, signs of their presence can still be found. One of the early settlers of what became the Gordon Head neighborhood was Michael Finnerty who by the 1870s owned a 330-acre (134-hectare) property, Spring Bank Farm. Its farmhouse was located near to where one now finds the university's central quadrangle. To clear the land, Finnerty is reputed to have felled "mighty trees ... monsters up to ten feet in diameter."[21] He also had a "magic spring at his disposal ... whose marvelous curative properties were attested to by many leading citizens."[22]

Old trail, new cart.
Trees 10 feet in diameter once grew along the Henderson Road entrance to the University of Victoria.

Photographer unknown. BC Archives, 1910.

Visitors from Victoria prized the mineral water from this spring well into the next century. Finnerty Road is now a main access road to the University, and an old apple tree and small sapling from his orchard still stand in the University's central quadrangle in silent recognition of a forgotten past. The springs beneath the parking lots are similarly unremarked, except to the extent that they may emerge as obstacles to new building construction.

Even more remarkable was the spring at the top of what is today called Mystic Vale. Historical records indicate that this spring was located on the farm of J.W. Mackay, one of the HBC signatories of the Chekonein Treaty. The spring was said to be highly productive, at one point being dammed to create a large irrigation pond, and later supplying water to power a generator near Cadboro Bay. In the 1880s, the maple tree that guarded Mystic Spring down at Cadboro Bay was reportedly felled, and with "the tragic end of the old tree, the Mystic Spring disappeared and was seen no more."[23] Quickly, however, the name was transferred to Mackay Spring at the head of Mystic Vale. Today whatever flow might remain from this spring is engulfed by a large storm sewer that empties into Mystic Vale.

In Gordon Head's early days, the landscape was dotted with wooden-frame farmhouses, a one-room schoolhouse, dairy herds, poultry farms, orchards, market gardens and berry crops. For almost a century, what was to become the UVic campus was home to pioneers, farmers, greenhouse growers and entrepreneurs. Until the postwar boom in suburban development, an established agricultural community thrived, European farmers mixing with Chinese market gardeners whose greenhouses dotted the countryside. Algernon Pease was one of those farmers who, in 1911, built a house

History forgotten is history deconstructing.

This water tower on the edge of the University of Victoria's campus, photographed in 2005, was constructed for the Pease family farm built in 1911. The house itself was moved many years ago, and it is still used by the University.

Photograph by Justine Starke, 2005.

on top of the hill now traversed by Sinclair Road. In 1914 Pease was instrumental in launching the Victoria Public Market downtown. On their Hamsterley Farm, the tower that once supplied water for the bathroom and kitchen of the Pease's 14-room house still stands as a derelict building on the edge of campus. In 1964 the Pease house became home to the University of Victoria's first president, Dr. Malcolm Taylor. The old house was then moved and is still used by the University today.

Building the burbs

UVic's landscape history is typical of many North American universities — the displacement of aboriginal occupation, the subsequent entrenchment of a family farming community and the more recent colonization by the city. Local Saanich councillor Bob Gillespie looks back over much of the past century and remembers the changes. When he was a boy in the 1930s, his father would shoot pheasants from their front porch: "He'd wait until two lined up, so he could get them with one bullet."[24] Meanwhile, Bob trapped muskrats down the hill in the local Bowker Creek, a creek that has its headwaters at UVic.

"So when I was 15, I would come down with my traps, and I would set them in there. There was wild watercress and celery that the muskrats would live on," he recalls. "I would come back early, 5:30 in the morning, to find out how many I got, then kind of sneak them all the way home because at 7:30 some of my friends were going to school, and I didn't want them to see what I was doing. I'd get two or three a day — I made over $300 during the wartime, which was quite a bit of money!"[25]

But changes came, gradual development that clogged the creek: "Bowker Creek was a lovely creek, years and years ago when the Chinese fields were all through there. And it was beautiful, and it survived, but they put in these nine-foot culverts where the Post Office is, and Bowker Creek runs right underneath it .... It goes right through the shopping center." Before his time, says Gillespie, the construction of a straight-line road in 1915 started to change what was predominantly an agricultural community. Until then there were only a few twisty roads, cart trails really, built along old Indian paths. With the construction of Shelbourne Street, however, motorized vehicles moved in, and the economics of the area began to change with easier access for more people, large farms being broken up and lots of smaller ones appearing. The area and its greenhouses were, says Gillespie, "nationally known for selling their tomatoes. The Lum family was recognized as the biggest producer all across Canada." Gillespie has lived all his 75 years on the same street near the University. While he doesn't regret the changes, there are things he doesn't like.

An active farming community continued into the 1940s. When World War II broke out, however, the Department of National Defence established an army camp at Gordon Head. At the end of the war, a battle ran for four years over a proposal to create an airport on the land. By that time, a local ratepayers association existed to fight the proposal. Though an airstrip was built, only two planes ever flew from there.[26] A few huts used by the military still stand and function as university labs and offices. To old-time inhabitants like Gillespie, the memories of that base are still fresh, especially training exercises that went "right down to the Cedar Hill golf course .... They had a mock war right where I lived on Epsom Drive."

After World War II, the pace of change accelerated exponentially. From trapping muskrats as a kid, ever the entrepreneur, Gillespie as a young adult "got into the trades, into the electrical. And then the boom was on." Going on now 50 years, this period of development has become the standard to what is considered normal today. But this period started out as anything but normal; the explosion of growth coming after decades of self-reliance, a decade of global economic depression and then war. The suburbanization that followed had a special impact — the sweeping imposition onto a once active and diverse landscape of a homogeneous infrastructure that was largely unrelated to local self-provision. Suburban development rendered functionless the ecological features of the local landscape: trees cut down, meadows paved over, streams channelized, food crops turned to lawns.

"I was working seven days a week, night and day, wiring because there were not that many tradesmen," says Gillespie. "And then Saanich and the developers started to push in the roads and then the sewers. After the sewers it was like a prairie fire right up until UVic was built — that made another change by commercializing the whole area." Like so many North American universities built in the past half-century, UVic was constructed during this phase of landscape colonization that drove local farms further and further from the center of town and its fast-spreading pavement. Gillespie's Bowker Creek succumbed to the effects of residential septic tanks and ditching. Where once there had been a dairy on Rendell Farm, Shelbourne Plaza was built in the 1960s, the first strip mall in Victoria.[27] Lum's greenhouses were replaced by a Kmart. As local historian Ursula Jupp explained, "In 1952 an outbreak of new house building spread like an epidemic over Gordon Head, stunning residents used only to the coming of scarce a handful of arrivals each year."[28]

Man with cauliflower.
This photograph was taken in Gordon Head, Victoria, in 1926.

Photograph by John William Clark, BC Archives.

In 1959 the Council of Victoria College purchased the Gordon Head army camp to use as an ancillary site for the nearby Lansdowne campus that was located where Camosun College is today. After evaluating the site, UVic's first architects, William Wurster and Don Emmons from San Francisco, suggested that Victoria College move the whole school to the Gordon Head site.[29] As UVic took root in the 1960s, buildings sprang up like mushrooms in an autumn forest. Access was provided with the construction in 1964 of Ring Road, a one-way, two-lane road that circles the academic core. With its wooded setting, it resembled the parkways built in the same time period in parts of the United States. The Ring still defines the university, the road and its adjacent parking lots dividing old farming fields, camas meadows and (second-growth) woods outside the Ring from the more organized academic spaces on the inside. Only a small fragment of these woods are left within Ring Road, the so-called Cunningham Woods that was the site of the 2003 tree-sit. The empty airfield was transformed with planted trees, ornamental shrubs, lawns and gardens.

Landless planning

Like that of so many new universities built worldwide in the '60s and '70s, UVic's birth was embedded in the paradigm of limitless growth that Marcus Ford calls economism. This paradigm molded the physical shape and function of the region occupied by the campus. But it also shaped the university curriculum, if subconsciously, embedding the experiences and values formed by an ever-extending detachment from place. A new vision of progress was progressively enshrined within postwar modern life. Fruits and vegetables, shoes and shirts, oil and electricity came from elsewhere, following long production lines, some many thousands of miles in length, bringing goods to the local shopping center, itself an innovation of the late 1950s. With disappearing local producers and the shifting tastes of suburban consumers, the downtown Victoria Public Market closed in 1959; the site soon occupied in part by a parking lot. That same year, to open up the Gorge Waterway, that symbol of aboriginal stewardship, Camosun Rock, was blown up.[30] In the decades since, the lines of supply have become more numerous and longer. In contrast to the farms that once sat where the classroom sits today, it is almost impossible to find a single item that can be identified as having been produced locally, by known local hands with known local materials. Such commodification instills an experiential remoteness and abstraction that erases personal consequence or responsibility.

In 1965 the local municipality's planning department in Saanich produced *A Plan for the University Area* that explicitly sought to separate the future of the University

A restless and hollow feel

There is a growing sense of frustration and placelessness in our suburban landscape; a homogeneous quality which overlays the unique nature of each place with chain-store architecture, scaleless office parks and monotonous subdivisions. These qualities are easily blurred by the speed we move and the isolation we feel in our cars and in our dwellings. At its extreme, the new forms seem to have a restless and hollow feel, reinforcing our mobile state and perhaps the instability of our families. Moving at a speed which only allows generic symbols to be recognised, we cannot wonder that the manmade environment seems trite and overstated. Americans moved to the suburbs largely for privacy, mobility, security and ownership. Increasingly they now have isolation, congestion, rising crime and overwhelming costs. Meanwhile our city centers have deteriorated as much of their economic vitality has decanted to the suburbs.

— Peter Calthorpe, *The Next American Metropolis*, New York: Princeton Architectural Press, 1993, p. 18.

area from traditional land uses. This document recognizes that a profitable market for land development would be created by concentrated growth of capital infrastructure amidst the agricultural community:

Although the use of this land is fairly intensive with regard to the production of a variety of vegetables, flowers and nursery plants, the land is vulnerable to small lot subdivision whenever the price offered for real estate exceeds the returns of the farmer .... it is assumed that virtually all farming as an economic use of land will disappear.[31]

From a complex landscape embedded with active physical functions, the land became real estate to be managed for esthetic appeal. The rural production of local food was replaced by housing developments planned for the area's "amenities." The 1965 *Plan* reflects the quintessential suburban vision of the "garden city." The University itself evolved from a hub of development amidst disappearing farmers' fields into an ornamental island of green amidst sprawling suburbs. As the municipal planners saw it:

The university district should represent the ultimate of beauty in the design of buildings and urban spaces. The area is endowed with pleasant natural features which should be judiciously explored in the overall design and landscaping of urban spaces. In developing areas with outstanding natural features, such as fine trees, outcrop and rolling view topography, every effort should be made to preserve the quality of the natural environment and make the best use of these features.[32]

Now that's a phrase worth pondering: "natural environment."

Over the 40 years of UVic's existence, every farm in the local area has been abandoned, and almost all the lands turned into subdivisions for a growing population. Saanich has gone from being a community of 25,000 people in 1946 to become a sprawling residential community of 103,654 residents in 2001.[33] Fifty years ago, farmers produced 85 percent of Vancouver Island's food supply, while today less than 10 percent of the Island's food is grown locally.[34] Correspondingly, between 1974 and 1999, Vancouver Island lost 42,008 acres (17,000 hectares) of agricultural land.[35] The story is similar across Canada and around the world. Although Canada's rich farmlands today make up only five percent of its land base, between 1971 and 2001, 9,445 square miles (15,200 square kilometers) of land was lost to suburbanization.[36]

As land-based functions succumb to real-estate-based functions, driven by rezoning and rising prices, food production becomes less viable with

Suburban trends in several world cities, 1965–2000.

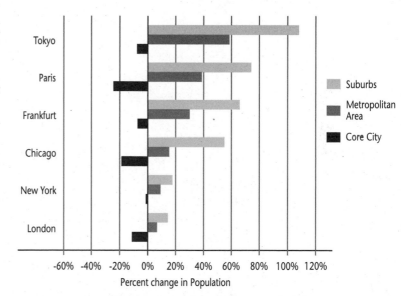

Joel Kotkin, *The New Suburbanism: A Realist's Guide to the American Future*, Costa Mesa, CA: The Planning Center, November 2005, p. 7. Available at <www.planningcenter.com/resources/index.html>

each new subdivision. This process enshrines a new, modern rationality that takes its truth from the values of the market and the zoning rules of its legal system. In the process, it displaces earlier aboriginal and agricultural rationalities that, however different, were both rooted in the immediacy of doing what the land could sustain. The University was itself a prime motivator of these changes as was the area's "proximity to waterfront, golf courses, Mount Tolmie Park."[37] But with the need to staff the University, and house its thousands of students, the municipality saw the University increasingly as "the nucleus of the district; it will have an important bearing on the future land use and major road pattern" in the area.[38]

As the airport proponents had discovered, development was not always a smooth process. In the early 1960s, property owners successfully protested the rezoning of some local University lands for the construction of high-rise apartments.[39] In later years, Mystic Vale was also purchased to thwart more high-rises. At the same time, the University erected numerous buildings and parking lots in the headwaters of Bowker Creek. Throughout the municipality, growth followed the typical suburban pattern of low-density planning, single-family housing and wide streets. Thus has an economistic vision been entrenched in the land, the loss of local physical function an unnoticed corollary to growth and progress over a seemingly limitless global frontier.

The distance from here

UVic's suburban development reflects the quintessential character of postwar economism. Its circular Ring Road projects an especially ironic metaphor of the times, as some critics put it, a freeway to nowhere. UVic's growth was part of the rise of the higher education industry in that period. Between 1950 and 1971, total government expenditures on postsecondary education in Canada increased 35-fold, from Can$67 million to Can$2.4 billion.[40] In that same period, postsecondary enrollment increased more than 600 percent.[41] In the United States during the 1960s alone, over 500 new higher education institutions opened, a 26 percent increase in one decade, with annual college enrollment increasing by over 120

Enrollment in Canadian Institutions of Higher Education: 1951 to 1975

Total Expenditure on Post-Secondary Education in Canada: 1951 to 1974

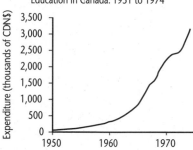

United States Land in Farms: 1950-1990 (millions of acres)

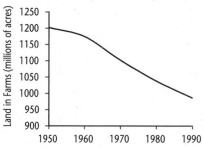

Population Distribution in the United States by Suburbs, Rural Areas, and Central Cities: 1940-1990

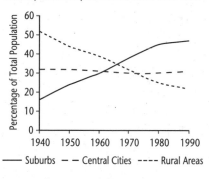

—— Suburbs — — Central Cities - - - - Rural Areas

Higher Education Institution (HEI) Growth in the United States: 1940-1990

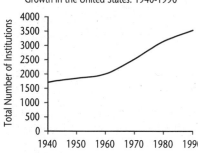

Adapted from M. Wisenthal, *Historical Statistics of Canada, Section W: Education*, Statistics Canada, F.H. Leacy, ed., available at <http://www.statcan.ca/english/freepub/11-516-XIE/sectionw/sectionw.htm#Post>; Land in Farms, adapted from USDA National Agricultural Statistics Service, Quick Stats U.S. & All States Data, Land in Farms, available at <http://151.121.3.33:8080/QuickStats/PullData_US>; Population Distribution, adapted from Suburbs and Suburban Sprawl, a report by Land Use and Cover Change at Michigan State University, available at <http://www.landuse.msu.edu/related/sprawl_report.pdf>; HEI growth was adapted from Thomas D. Snyder, ed., *120 Years of American Education: A Statistical Portrait*, Table 23: Historical Summary of Higher Education Statistics, National Centre for Education Statistics, U.S. Department of Education, 1993, available at <http://nces.ed.gov/pubs93/93442.pdf>.

Booming university, changing landscape.

The 1950s marked the onset of a period of unprecedented growth in the number of expenditures on and enrollment in higher education institutions. At the same time, large-scale changes in land use began to occur as suburban populations skyrocketed and enormous tracts of agricultural land were lost to accommodate the boom. Although it is difficult to quantify the relationship between these two growth patterns, a dynamic interplay existed between university growth and suburbanization. Thousands of universities in North America stand on what was once productive land, and suburbs developed around the new universities being built on the urban fringe.

percent from 3.6 to 8 million students.[42] To match that enrollment, instructional staff doubled in that decade. Between 1960 and 1990, staff levels increased by 280 percent, from 660,000 to 2.5 million.[43]

Today's higher education industry is thus situated in a period of unprecedented economic growth and landscape colonization, quite unlike the more contained urban character of the historic university. Between 1960 and 1985, New York City expanded by 65 percent, yet the population grew by only 8 percent.[44] From 1950 to 1990, Chicago's land mass swelled by 124 percent, while its population grew by 38 percent.[45] Over that time period, the population living within the American central city shrank from 65 to 35 percent, with the reverse happening to the suburbs where 65 percent of the total population lived in 1990.[46]

In these figures one can detect a correlation between the intellectual detachment of the academy from the natural world, and its own physical detachment. An insulation is built right into the structure of the university, hard-wired into its physical and intellectual life. In recent years this historic process has been at the center of concerns for ecological and social sustainability, what political economists call "distancing." The term usually refers to our dependence on remote locations — tomatoes in snowbound Canada arriving fresh from sunny Mexico in January. This type of distancing is, however, accompanied by another distancing — that between people and the places where they live. When our goods come from afar we stop using — and needing — the places at home. While seldom remarked on by mainstream historians of economic progress, this displacement is in fact at the heart of the modernist project — local farmers and artisans being "dis-placed" by urban merchants and traders, who are in turn displaced by multinational agribusiness and chain stores.

Today these far-reaching spatial relations so shape the structures of everyday experience that some critical geographers now deny the existence of "local" at all. Over the past century, with increasing mobility and trade, the geography of place has increasingly given way to what James Kunstler calls the "geography of nowhere:"[47]

It is, of course, the opposite of somewhere, that is, of a place, of a milieu …
a space devoid of symbolic expressions of identity, relations and history: examples include airports, motorways, anonymous hotel rooms …. Never before
in the history of the world have non-places occupied so much space.[48]

At the university, *nowhere* is evident in the sprawling acres of parking lots filled
with mass-produced cars, the cafeteria food delivered via an exclusive servicing
contract with a nameless multinational, and the standard-issue buildings heated
and lit by energy from the void. In this history, place-as-local is but a nostalgic
concern because the land has progressively lost its sustaining function, and thus its
"agency" in shaping human affairs. This process is not economic only, but cultural,
redefining our social nature from its historic connection to the locales where we
live. Students glued to the screens in the university computer lab were, as children,
similarly stuck to the video play station. Meanwhile, with no one mucking around
in the creek down the street (which had long since ceased to have fish in it, let
alone clean water), it went unnoticed as municipal engineers buried it in the cul-
vert. Where no one digs in the camas meadow, the richness of that meadow
declines. But who sees it? What Bryce's ancestors experienced as collective places
collectively cared for have now become institutionalized spaces — privatized, corporatized, bureaucratized — to be managed for other ends. The result is what one
scholar calls a landscape that embodies a "private ecology" where "those who own
and control the material and mental means of … the production and consumption of wealth concretize new inequalities on an environmental scale."[49]

This fracturing of place is the physical corollary of the disciplinary divisions
that accompanied the rise of the modern university. Without a coherent worldview to shape these disciplines, many instead reflect the economism in which the
university is situated. Thus do the world's faculties of forestry teach the "scientific
forestry" of "maximum sustained yield," that is, the science of producing lumber
for housing starts. Meanwhile, the agricultural sciences develop new chemical fertilizers and pesticides, the better to replace small-farm labor with agribusiness

Change and memory

The values that I have as I get older — you know the natural values that we have — I love to try to learn to live with nature, and I learnt it through my father. If you're in the bee business you get to know nature. And when they came with tanks on their backs spraying DDT, my father was screaming! He was 50 years ahead of his time. They were killing off the little bees that do all the pollination. So I got to really appreciate where I am living. How I learnt that is easy. I lived on the same street for 70 years. Okay, if you live on the same street for that length of time you can see the environment slowly change around you. You can see it going from the bigger farms to the small farms to the smaller subdivisions, then you start to see the old trees go, the old barns go, the owls go, the pheasants go ….

— Robert Gillespie, Saanich Municipal Councillor, *Interview*, January 10, 2005.

capital and feed a disproportionately urbanized world. And, of course, the science of medicine provides drugs to treat the symptoms of industrial affluence — from heart failure and cancer, to obesity and diabetes — but does not address the nature of the "dis-ease" of a body disconnected. In the modern university, natural science itself has increasingly turned into what might better be called "artificial science." The more "natural" sciences — from ecosystem forestry to biodynamic agriculture, from ecological economics to naturopathic medicine — find no place in the university curriculum. Quite the contrary, they are actively excluded from virtually every campus. It is all of a piece — the long history of this edifice that is the Western university, the buried landscape on which it sits, the fractured sciences that it generates and the planetary consequences that it does not see.

Physical education

Even where they are no longer connected to their place as a source of food or fuel or entertainment, people are still creatures of the local, collectively breathing its air, sharing its water and its weather, and engaging in the thousand chaotic interactions of membership in the ecology of everyday life. As the environmental and social subsidies that everywhere underpin the geography of nowhere decline, reinvigorating the nature and quality of the experiences of place is critical to the quest for a more sustainable world.

Thus is place deeply pedagogical, as the renowned educator David Orr noted over a decade ago in his book *Ecological Literacy*.[50] This pedagogy is, however, not just about a green building here or a student garden there, but about the whole structure and trajectory of higher education itself. What is demanded of the end of economism, notes David Gruenewald, is a *critical* pedagogy of place that identifies not just the ecological underpinnings of each place, but the political and economic relationships that link local and global geographic landscapes.[51] These relationships shape the globe and what counts as its acceptable knowledge. Which raises questions as to the university's future role in physically remaking places of lived and grounded experience that might, in turn, transform its thinking. In so doing, argues one political economist, the university might then confront those unsustainable global spaces of "material flows of commodities, money, capital and information" that render insignificant the "sensual experience and representational meaning" of place.[52] In the process, the university will help these places now without history find a new history. And it will give these places now without power a new agency.

PART II

THE INNOVATOR

Chapter 4

leaving carbon city

Next stop, the University.
GO BY STREETCAR *has become a landmark sign for the Nob Hill area of Portland.*

UNDER A BLUSTERY OVERCAST SKY, the rail lines glisten from the overnight rain as a few early morning passengers downtown climb aboard Portland's new streetcar. Only six years old, this inner city system winds throughout the city center where it overlaps with the MAX, the light rail system that serves the suburbs. Thousands of commuters and central city residents ride this transportation network daily. If Portland has a reputation as one of the most livable cities in the United States, this system is a big reason why.

"People love it," says the streetcar driver as she closes the door, watching in the mirror while the passengers get seated, "and it's free in the downtown core." Gliding noiselessly through the area's trendy Nob Hill district where the lines do a complete loop, its impact is evident. Development is compact, streets are quiet and the atmosphere is lively but unhurried. Shops and cafés line the route. One stylish new condo development

Photograph courtesy of Portland Streetcar, n.d. Available at <www.portlandstreetcar.org.>

71

even boasts a large neon sign that promotes the system. The streetcar benefits more than just its passengers.

At another stop, a young couple boards the car, accompanied by an immaculately dressed elderly parent and, it seems, the parent's friend who is visiting the city. As the doors close, their conversation turns to the tramline and how they "never have to use the car." "It's wonderful," says the mother as she describes the route, past the hospital, more shops, the downtown offices and the intersection with the MAX. "I am a believer," says our newfound tour guide. "I am a transit believer."

The light rail system was created in 1986, with the streetcar completed for service in the downtown in 2001. At one end of the line is Portland State University, and as the driver notes, "Probably the majority of our passengers are students either at the nursing school or at the Portland State University." The University generates a big ridership, as would any college, leading one to wonder how other universities might follow Portland's lead. What would it take for universities everywhere to take the initiative in a broader transportation revolution that could benefit cities and regions across the world? In this chapter, and the two that follow, we will ask such questions — for transportation, urban development and land use — to understand how universities might be innovators in creating a more sustainable world and how they could do so by acting locally.

A world at stake

To call for the university to spark a transportation revolution is a bold, but fitting, objective. Given their size and numbers, universities generate serious transportation headaches almost everywhere. Like huge vacuums, universities every morning draw commuters from all over the region onto the roads, clogging urban arteries as students and staff make their way to campus. At the end of the day, they deflate and empty thousands of cars back onto the urban road network. This ebb and flow produces one of the least desirable aspects of urban life, traffic congestion. However, some cities manage the job of moving people with more grace than others. In

Portland, the combination of streetcars, light rail transit and buses make public transit an easy choice for commuters. But in cities that don't have efficient or comprehensive transit options, the car remains king of the road. Noisy streets, traffic jams, exhaust fumes and sprawling pavement are the inevitable result.

In fact a lot more is at stake here than urban congestion. For decades pollution has stained yellow the skylines of cities, and smog has been a lethal health problem. But now human-induced

Transportation overkill

In Vancouver, the car population is growing faster than the human population. In the US, there are more motor vehicles on the road than there are people of driving age.

— Ray Straatsma, Better Environmentally Sound Transportation, Vancouver, B.C., *Interview*, January 15, 2005.

climate change is generally accepted as the 21st century's biggest environmental challenge. Even though the car is the No.1 climate culprit, the auto industry is also the unassailable key to a nation's economic "health." Yet the road ahead is a rocky one for this industry, as new studies suggest that production from existing oil reserves will soon peak, at which point the world will begin to run out of oil, a trend that will be exaggerated where demand keeps growing.[1] Some analysts disagree with the peak oil hypothesis (and suggest that global oil production capacity will continue to increase for a few years yet[2]), but even if more oil can be found, it will be costlier to develop and more damaging environmentally than occurred with the past exploitation of more accessible supplies. And it will continue to fuel global warming. This situation prompted even the cautious International Energy Agency to suggest that such growth must be seen as "calling into question the long-term sustainability of the global energy system."[3] The world clearly faces an oil/auto conundrum. As a result, continued oil dependence ensures a predominant national security objective of "access to supply" that actually produces insecurity, oil wars and terrorism. The result is a spiral of economic and ecological decline, and military instability. Underlying this spiral is a simple fact: our sprawling infrastructure subsists on ecological debt, and the ecological capital we are borrowing against is fast falling to empty.

The shape of today's auto-centric cities is a product of the postwar boom economy that also spurred the growth of the higher education industry to which many car users now commute daily. Both remain rooted in the economistic values and vision of the 1950s; both have outgrown the smaller world of that time. A full two thirds of present US consumption of petroleum now goes to transportation, and over 50 percent of this is used for personal vehicles.[4] One billion barrels of oil are consumed every 11½ days, feeding between 600 and 700 million vehicles powered by internal-combustion engines.[5] Oil has also transformed food production (particularly with oil-based fertilizers), industrial manufacture (evident especially in the proliferation of plastics), trade (through shipping and accessible airplane travel), and international politics. Despite the prospect of peak oil, this energy-hungry economy means that the demand for oil is forecast to increase by over two thirds in the next ten years.[6] Considering all the negative side-effects of the

Alarm bells.

"[This graph shows] the gap between consumption and discovery, which has been growing since 1981. It also shows that drilling more does not help. There was a huge surge in drilling in the early 1980s, driven by high oil prices giving high tax charges against which exploration expense could be offset, but it delivered little. Exploration drilling [wildcats] is declining because there are fewer viable prospects left, and advances in technology mean that the industry drills fewer dry holes. The alarm bells should begin to ring when the finding rate falls below the consumption rate. The world can eat into its inheritance from past discovery for only so long. Sooner or later the consumers have to find out how to consume less. They have no other option."

— Quoted from Campbell and Sivertsson.

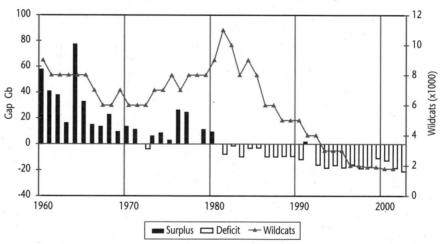

Growing Gap between Discovery and Consumption

Colin Campbell and Anders Sivertsson, *The 2003 Update of the ASPO Oil & Gas Depletion Model*, presented at the 2nd International Workshop on Oil Depletion, Paris, France, May 26–27, 2003, p. 5.

auto/oil industry, finding new reserves to meet projected demand could well be worse than running out of oil! This is the conundrum of the carbon city — can't live without it, can't live with it. And so what alternative is there?

Rather than addressing this conundrum head-on to redirect economic growth, the '50s-style model of development-as-unending-growth is now exported to emerging superpowers like China and India. The United States and China now account for one third of the world's oil consumption.[7] In 2004 China's consumption soared to 6.6 million barrels per day, while the United States consumed 20.5 million barrels per day.[8] In China the one-car family has become the new national goal, the bicycle an artifact of a "less-developed" past. So while Portland turns to the tram to undo its congested history, General Motors celebrates a 300 percent rise in car sales in one year in China, an alarming achievement for a country of 1.3 billion people.[9]

These multiple contradictions are rooted in a profound power bind. Put simply, the macro-economy that underpins the world's continuing prosperity also generates the world's slow-motion march toward ecological collapse. In this economy, the oil/car complex is the global super-industry and employer. Every year for decades, car manufacturers and oil producers have occupied all but one or two of the ten largest Fortune 500 corporations in the world.[10] The result is policy gridlock — lots of rhetoric, but no change. One lesson of this stalemate is that global dependence will not be undone at the macro level alone, a level that is itself enmeshed in the very structures of economic wealth and power that must be reconfigured.

Where local leadership can be mobilized, greater flexibility exists at the community level to initiate change and create new models of a sustainable economy. Building a network of local alternatives will help wean us off this dependence by creating alternatives more suited to the post-oil economy. Hundreds of places like Victoria — places not dependent on automobile manufacturing — could do this in a comprehensive regional way, from the bottom up. Portland has begun to move in a different direction, and it is only one model among others. Even in countries

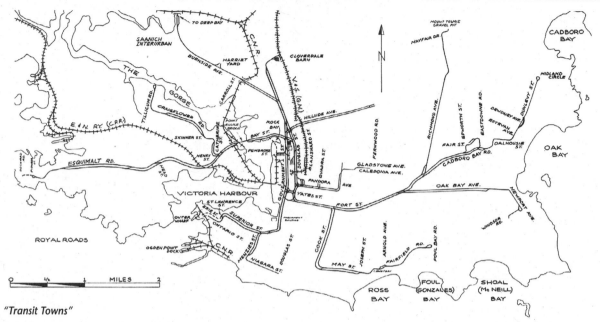

"Transit Towns"

As in dozens upon dozens of small cities across North America at the time, residents of Victoria in the first half of the last century could easily get around their region with trams and trains.

Memories of youth

"Victoria College had a lot going for it," he said. "The fees were very low and you could live at home and you could bicycle to the campus, such as it was. We lived in Oak Bay, on McNeill Avenue, which wasn't even paved, about three blocks from the water, from Shoal Bay — or McNeill Bay to give its proper name. We got all our firewood from McNeill Bay off the beach, and we spent a lot of time there. Few people were affluent enough to drive cars in Victoria," Berton said. "Victoria was a town of streetcars; there were streetcars everywhere … from Oak Bay to the Gorge."

— Sandra McCulloch, "Pierre Berton Dies at 84," *Times Colonist*, December 1, 2004, A1.

less wealthy than the United States and Canada, middle-sized cities have retrofitted tram systems into car-congested streets. The effects are evident, as in Portland which has announced that its central core has seen CO_2 emission levels drop below 1990 levels, rendering it compliant with the Kyoto Protocol on greenhouse gases. The county office cited the "creation of two more light rail lines and a 75 percent growth in public transit" as the leading reasons.[11]

And like Portland State, a key social proponent of such change would be the university.

Something old, something new

In the late 19th and early 20th centuries, electric streetcars were the backbone of transportation in every Western city of any significant size. They were built because construction of rail

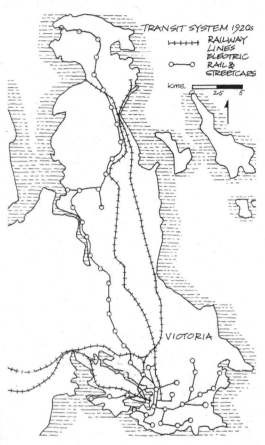

Photograph by Franklin, BC Archives, 1900.

Riding in style.
Well-turned passengers board streetcars lined up on Oak Bay Avenue in 1900.

infrastructure was very efficient in its use of energy, materials and land (especially in comparison with road infrastructure that uses about four times as many resources[12]). In comparison to automobile production and operation that "now consumes more resources than any other industry," trains and trams were also relatively cheap to produce and operate.[13] Even small-town Victoria began installing a streetcar system in 1890, and by 1900 streetcar lines extended from the Royal Naval Base on the outskirts in Esquimalt, up Fort Street through downtown and out past Royal Jubilee Hospital. At the time, Victoria's population was just 32,600, yet it sported a streetcar system 29 miles (47 kilometers) long, and toward the end of its life, the system carried over 13 million riders annually.[14] In 1903 the line was extended down Cook Street. That extension a century ago left its legacy in Cook Street Village, Victoria's best example of mixed-use new urbanism with a dynamic blend of apartments, cafés, restaurants and food markets. At the time, Victoria's famous artist and writer Emily Carr described the route as lined with skunk cabbage and mud puddles. But as the streetcar system expanded (for example, with double-tracking up and down Fairfield Road) so did the neighborhoods.[15]

By 1913 British Columbia Electric and the Vancouver Tramway Company had built interurban electric railway systems in the Lower Mainland of southwestern British Columbia and on Vancouver Island, linking the lines to the streetcar systems of both bustling port cities.[16] Throughout the region and into much of the countryside, you could get almost everywhere by tram or train. Vancouver's interurban line linked the old B.C. capital, New Westminster, with the quickly growing center of Vancouver — spurring the growth of many towns and neighborhoods in between. In Victoria, the *inter*urban (not *sub*urban) linked small village nodes along the Saanich Peninsula as the train meandered through the rural and forested countryside. Many people remember the familiar whistle and comforting rattle of the old Interurban as it trundled from station to station. People (nostalgic ones of course!) still talk about the convenience of the streetcars that linked these regional commuter trains to each neighborhood along the way.

After World War II, however, as Councillor Gillespie's boom took hold, all this changed. And rapidly. In a 1947 referendum, Victoria voted to decommission its streetcar system in favor of a gas-powered fleet of buses.[17] The decision meant widened roads, street thoroughfares and highway-oriented development. As Geoffrey Castle notes in *Saanich: An Illustrated History*, "The whole country turned to automobiles. Cars were the big deal …. It was like riding an aeroplane, it was a thrill. Cars and buses steadily eroded the traffic from the railways."[18] Vancouver lost its streetcars shortly thereafter, as did almost every city in North America. City after city saw its transit lines ripped up, rights-of-way sold and built

Photograph by Duncan Macphail, BC Archives.

Railway blues

In choosing the automobile as the engine of growth, the highway and automotive planners scrapped mass transit. General Motors, Exxon (then Esso) and the Goodyear Tire Company bought up the San Francisco trolley, tore up the track and replaced it with Esso-drinking buses rolling on Goodyears. In the name of progress, GM, Firestone and Standard Oil of California ripped up the Los Angeles interurban train system.

— Richard J. Barnet, *The Lean Years: Politics in the Age of Scarcity*, New York: Simon & Schuster, 1980, p. 23.

Ripping up the tracks.
A bus drives past a Victoria streetcar line being dismantled on Cook Street in 1948.

over. Private cars proliferated. This shift was not the result of a force of nature or economic law, but of a conscious campaign by car companies, oil producers and tire manufacturers to replace public electric mass-transit systems with gas-powered cars and buses. In a couple of decades, 146 rail systems were dismantled across the continent.[19]

What may have been a corporate campaign for market share evolved into an entire model of urban and national development, which became a way of life and a vision of progress. As Jane Jacobs notes, the expansion of the American interstate highway system in the 1950s was less about its stated goal of national security than it was about creating a new economy in the shadow of the Great Depression: "full employment, guarantee of jobs: jobs building roads, jobs designing, manufacturing, servicing and repairing automobiles, jobs refining and transporting oil and filling gasoline tanks."[20] Of the many impacts of the new automobile economy, however, one of the most important was on the city itself. Historically, streetcar cities generated compact patterns of growth. With the car, however, came the suburb, and with the suburbs came sprawl. And as we have seen in the last chapter, many universities were built on the urban fringe, where suburban neighborhoods in turn grew up to accommodate the growth these new universities brought.

Some North American cities resisted the pressure and retained their streetcar systems. When Ottawa and Montreal abandoned their systems in 1959, the only city in Canada left running streetcars was Toronto, which had been operating a system since the 1860s. However, like most places, Toronto's streetcars came under attack. In the 1970s, under the leadership of

The jolly trolley.
A disused streetcar finds a new life as a children's playground as it slowly dissolves into the woods.

Photographer unknown, BC Archives, 1955.

Jacobs and the "Streetcars for Toronto" committee, citizens succeeded in blocking a massive expressway expansion through the residential center of the city and also convinced the transit commission to drop its streetcar abandonment policy in 1972.[21] Today just one of Toronto's articulated streetcars replaces 90 private automobiles from the morning rush hour. Toronto's streetcar system is among the biggest in North America today.[22]

It is no coincidence that some of North America's favorite cities have streetcar systems, making their streets walkable and friendly. San Francisco put streetcars back on its main shopping street and added a new streetcar line to its commuter train station. Like other successful systems, San Francisco's streetcars are linked with other public transit modes such as subways and light rail, creating an integrated public transportation system and contributing to the vitality that San Francisco's colorful streets are famous for.[23] And, of course, there is Portland.

The streets of many European cities were built well before even the idea of motorized vehicles had been conceived, and the scale of their streets reflects this. This livable scale is often augmented with expansive streetcar and tram systems. Trams are found in Brussels, Rome, Milan, Cologne, Amsterdam and Vienna (to name a few). In 1972 Freiburg, Germany, preserved and

Andy Singer, *CARtoons*, Prague: CARBusters, 2001, p. 75.

expanded its streetcar system, creating a downtown pedestrian district that is complemented with an extensive network of bicycle trails. Since 1976, where other cities have seen car use explode, car use in Freiburg has declined from 60 percent of all trips made around town to 46 percent, while bikes are up to 28 percent from 18 percent and transit is up from 22 to 26 percent.[24] In Melbourne, Australia, old-fashioned streetcars form the nucleus of a great urban transit system. Dozens of small European cities maintain expansive tram systems. These systems are so much a part of the urban fabric that it is not uncommon to see men in dinner jackets and women in evening gowns step unselfconsciously from the streetcars into the local concert hall for an evening performance.

Car junkie or car-free?

Dumb growth, smart growth

But having the kind of efficient and sustainable transit networks that streetcar cities offer is only part of the solution. From his office in downtown Portland, Rex Burkholder leans forward in his chair to express his concern that, as a transportation planner's favorite example of a multi-modal transit system, Portland's achievements are only a beginning. "The biggest challenge is you have a built environment set up in ways where you can't get there from here unless you have a car," says Burkholder, "and the car is like a gas, it fills up every space."[25] Burkholder is a community cycling activist who is now also an elected councillor within METRO, Portland's regional government. "We have had some successes, yet still 85 to 90 percent of some trips are made by car in the region as a whole, because we still have these suburban areas where people really don't have choices," says Burkholder.

Portland's MAX lines and its streetcars are an important means to an end that is still a long way off — a region where residents do not depend on the private car. This ambitious goal demands remaking both the central city and the suburbs as part of a new movement with the rather jarring moniker of "smart growth." Advocates of smart growth foresee infilling and densifying urban and suburban areas to create "complete communities" that can reduce the need for people to drive. Overall they want to see an end to suburban-oriented development. At the broadest level, smart growth is a new vision of an urban form explicitly situated within local ecosystems, where the environment is not just treated as an add-on. Such a vision demands that planning be more open and participatory so as to be able to elicit workable new urban strategies. It is, however, still about growth — but growth that creates the new infrastructure that is everywhere needed to repair and replace the infrastructure that will no longer work in the age of climate change and peak oil.

The intellectual justification for urban smart growth is similar to that for the planetary university; that is, the university that *consciously shapes itself as a model of planetary sustainability.* This will require that it address the institutional character of unsustainability. When it does, it will confront today's dependence on a flow economy of high throughputs of energy (e.g., oil) and resource (e.g., cars) that supports a model of development that is both *inequitable* and *hierarchical.* These inequities and hierarchies are diverse in their manifestations — corporate, bureaucratic, urban, Northern, white, male. Combined, however, they are also *centralist* because the throughputs needed to keep such resource-intensive and highly organized structures of power afloat necessarily come from exploiting less-powerful groups and distant places. The displacement of native communities from Cadboro Bay was a classically centralist development that, in the process, also "rationalized" the landscape with surveyed boundaries, private properties and commercial functions.

In contrast, a smart growth strategy should yield a more *territorialist* economy that can use resources more equitably because they sustain much less-hierarchical social systems. Such an economy necessarily means a much-reduced dependence on non-local inputs except where these are exchanged on a just basis as in, for example, "fair trade." Enhanced territoriality also means different types of human experiences, ones that are connected more directly to the life forces emanating from the local place where one is. Center and territory are, in other words, diversely manifested forces, and neither fixed geographic designations nor self-contained polarities. Historically, territorialist tendencies have always existed in "dialectical" tension with centralist ones, evolving in different forms and different ways in various contexts. The challenge of sustainability is to bring these tensions overall into greater balance.

Sustainable transportation is thus about replacing cars (and the systems that produce them) with more efficient alternatives (trams and buses) and more human energy (bikes). Such alternatives are more rooted in the territorial community than

Between center and territory

At one dialectical pole, center is manifest in hierarchical organizations built around the imperatives of concentrated power, sustained indirectly by non-local resources (or flows of energy). In contrast, territorial forms of social organization are rooted in forms of social power which are dispersed and on-the-ground, and are maintained by local resources and direct production ... center and territory have both a physical component (geographic spatial relations), and a social component (institutional relations).

It would, however, be inaccurate to reduce them to discrete, concrete, either/or dichotomies. Quite the contrary, unlike the largely physical concepts of "cores and peripheries" that are utilized by dependency theorists, center and territory are social tendencies that intermingle in various degrees and manifestations in the many places and acts of everyday life ... That is, they exist as omnipresent tendencies in all forms of social organization and cultural consciousness ... [and they] describe not specific structures but dynamics that exist at all scales ....

Overall, a basic contradiction can be seen to beset all forms of centralist growth. In short, the rise of central power is, and always has been, sustained by the territorial structures that precede that rise, and it cannot survive without them .... Center is not equivalent to "bad," and territory to "good" ... political centralism can be useful for fostering inter-regional equity. Certainly, the black poor in rural Alabama were grateful for the federal Civil Rights Act in the 1960s, and the peacekeeping force that was deployed in East Timor was a product of a "centrist" institution. Nevertheless, the legitimacy of centrist structures can ultimately be assured only when their own successes also support, not erode, territory ....

— R. Michael M'Gonigle, "A Dialectic of Center and Territory: The Political Economy of Ecological Flows and Spatial Relations," *Nature, Production, Power: Towards an Ecological Political Economy*, Fred P. Gale and R. Michael M'Gonigle, eds., Northampton: Edward Elgar, 2000, pp. 4–6.

in the centralist corporation or competitive nation state. Indeed by fostering new patterns of territorial development, we will necessarily also create new sources of counterbalancing power — the livable region versus the corporatized globe. And we do this in an integrated way by fostering new practices, new experiences, new values and new businesses to serve these places. In this way (and in the language of the geographer), *place* becomes not just a site where multiple systems of power come together across *space*, but one where life is the product of the coming together of locally generated power.

This shift is a huge one. But it *is* what sustainability is necessarily about and why it has been so difficult to achieve. It is not just about political intransigence or bad policies, but about the inherent problem of waiting for change to come from state or corporate structures that are themselves enmeshed in the centralist growth that underlies unsustainability. In the face of this macro-level gridlock, the university in all its aspects — its expertise, its regional impact, its political heft, its economic muscle — can initiate micro-level alternatives. In doing so, change would not entail an old-fashioned revolution of one class against another, but a gradual transition by *people in place* against an inherited *structure of spatial dependency*. In this way, the challenge of global sustainability is unlike any social struggle of the past.

To make this happen on the ground, possibilities abound. No one knows this better than Todd Litman, founder of the Victoria Transport Policy Institute. He has been pressing transportation alternatives locally and internationally for a decade: "If the University really wanted to make a difference, the University could then start challenging jurisdictions to say, 'Okay, we've done it, look at us, we've accomplished this.'"[26] Universities can discourage the car and encourage people to use the bus or ride a bike, but these options rely on adequate transit service and safe bike routes. With the exception of on-campus residents, the viability of alternatives is ultimately determined by the regional infrastructure and the services that commuters must rely on outside of the university. And here the universities of the 21st century could truly come into their own as the prime motivators for regional sustainability.

Longer shadow, larger footprint

As economic globalization deepens, some shadows grow longer and some footprints grow larger. The allocation of ecological responsibility to the geographic location of production is increasingly a distortion of both responsibility and the capacity to change .... [T]he production cycle located in a specific place cannot be isolated from choices and market conditions both upstream and downstream. In many cases — those Nike tennis shoes made in Southeast Asia — what we are seeing is a shift of power downstream, in which US or European consumers and the large retailers, advertisers and marketers that stimulate and feed their demand have most of the power to define what happens upstream at the production end of the commodity chain of athletic footwear.

— Ken Conca, "Beyond the Statist Frame: Environmental Politics in a Global Economy," *Nature, Production, Power: Towards an Ecological Political Economy*, Fred P. Gale and R. Michael M'Gonigle, eds., Northampton: Edward Elgar, 2000, p. 149.

"My experience at UVic is that you don't have to convince people that they want to cycle, or even to ride transit. It's a matter of providing quality service and getting those people who may be tempted but haven't really followed through," argues Litman. As in campuses around the world, thousands of UVic students and employees drive their vehicles to the University because it is easy, parking is cheap and the transit system is infrequent and not well routed. The campus is a major destination for traffic in the city, with some 7,000 cars passing through it daily.[27] In Portland, Burkholder has the same experience: "We forget that we have made the roads really easy to use. Everywhere we make them big enough so that you can drive around a lot. We provide huge amounts of parking, and then we say, 'Well why aren't people taking the bus?'" To make a successful transition to a "car-free" future is again something for which the university has a competitive advantage over almost any other institution given its ability to draw on its population, land area, expertise and economic and regional clout to take a comprehensive approach.

Integrating strategies

Like smart growth, one of the catch phrases of transportation planners is "transportation demand management" or TDM. TDM provides incentives to use alternatives to single-occupancy vehicles, involving diverse strategies such as higher parking charges, park-and-ride schemes, car-share co-ops, mass transit, support services for cycling, Internet support for telecommuting and traffic-calming road design (i.e., road bumps or narrowing to slow vehicle speeds).[28] Instead of searching out new resource *supplies*, strategies to manage *demand* can be applied to reduce resource throughput not just in transportation but in home heating, lawn watering, new product manufacturing and other sectors.

One simple TDM solution pioneered by universities is the U-Pass. More than 50 colleges and universities have unlimited-access U-Pass programs that provide fare-free transit service to more than 825,000 students and staff.[29] Ideally the U-Pass should make public transport essentially free to pass-holders, taking them out of their cars by shifting the costs of the pass onto parking charges for those who still drive. Locally, even the partial introduction of the U-Pass for students (not staff and faculty) has had a dramatic impact. In Vancouver bus ridership to Simon Fraser University (SFU) and the University of British Columbia (UBC) has increased 63 percent, with a 10 percent drop in car traffic.[30] Following the introduction of the student U-Pass at UVic, traffic to campus declined 13 percent since 2000, cycling rose by 12 percent and transit ridership increased 33 percent (representing over one quarter of the trips made to campus).[31] One study reported that the number of occupied parking spaces declined by 30 percent.[32] Yet without a corresponding increase in the regional commitment to enhanced public transit, students often watch full buses pass them by. Noted one UVic student, "It's very frustrating to pay over Can$300 a course and be late for class because full buses pass you on the road." By staggering the start times of classes, UBC was able to spread demand for buses over a longer morning peak period, resulting in a 12 percent increase in the riders who were accommodated by the same number of buses.[33]

The promise of such TDM initiatives is a more sustainable regional economy with a higher quality of life and a changing set of cultural values. Cities and universities with good bus or tram systems for commuting, "blue bike" programs for getting around campus throughout the day and walkable villages for evening shopping encourage less energy and resource consumption and more communal living.

Integrated urban transportation designs will reduce resource use and CO_2 emissions, preserve greenspace by mitigating the need for parking, reduce traffic congestion, revitalize neighborhoods — and cost less. As Toor and Havlick note in *Transportation and Sustainable Campus Communities*, adding a new parking space is 2.5 times as costly as shifting one person to transit.[34] An integrated TDM strategy also reduces the huge costs to individuals that are associated with the purchase, maintenance, insurance and parking of a car. Similarly, public costs fall as new road infrastructure and maintenance are not needed, and accident rates decline. The issue is not whether society can afford a new transportation infrastructure of trams and light rail, buses and bicycles, but the reverse — how we can no longer afford the resource misallocations of the system we have. Changing the cultural values associated with 50 years of economistic growth will, however, require committed leadership.

Such leadership is possible at the local level. In conjunction with the City of Boulder and the local transit agency, the University of Colorado has given 60,000 people in the community access to passes,[35] leading to a 200 percent increase in student transit use in the first year[36] and overall to date an increase of 600 percent![37] When the University offered free bus passes to faculty and staff who didn't purchase a parking pass, ridership went up 85 percent in one year.[38] Stanford University offers cash rebates to people who use alternative modes of transportation, helping to pass along the University's savings to those who make the savings possible.[39]

Since 1997 the University of British Columbia has been working to change travel patterns to and from campus. Through the TREK program, UBC introduced the U-Pass in the fall of 2003 and has implemented a range of TDM strategies that reflect its mission of "trip reduction, research, education and knowledge" (TREK). One study reports that Cornell University in Ithaca, New York, was able to reduce the construction of new parking spaces from 3,100 to 350 by investing in TDM, saving US$12 million in the first six years of the program.[40] Cornell is also reported to have raised parking fees and expanded the capacity of the public transit system by working with city and county authorities.

To augment this, Cornell offers reserved parking and discounts to people who participate in ride-share programs.[41] Overall Cornell has saved US$37 million over 12 years in avoided construction, infrastructure improvement and transportation costs.[42]

As we will discuss in later chapters, the long-term commitment to such initiatives also depends on embracing more open processes of decision making that can take the university beyond technical solutions to a wholesale change in values and commitments. At the same time, when a university commits to a serious long-term TDM program, notes Todd Litman, "everything cascades from the parking." Managing the demand for parking opens up land for other uses, such as infill development and greenspace preservation.[43] Such a cascade effect means that one change spurs a series of iterative changes, a common pattern in many smart-growth strategies. Such linkages augur well for rapid changes where comprehensive strategies are initiated.

De-carbonated cities

Where diversified and sustainable transportation systems exist, they often become a defining part of the urban experience. For example, Copenhagen has a car-free zone in its center on Stroget, a pedestrian shopping area. It is not a single street, but a series of interconnected avenues that create a very large pedestrian center, although it is crossed in places by streets with vehicular traffic. Copenhagen also has a public program that provides bicycles for general use (with a 20-kroner returnable deposit) throughout the downtown area. Bicycle paths are often separated from the main automobile lanes and have their own signal systems. A number of islands have even banned motor vehicles, including Borkum in the North Sea, Sark in the Channel Islands and Paquita Island in Rio de Janeiro, Brazil. In the Italian city of Siena, the central city (population 30,000) is almost car free. Ghent, Belgium, has an 86-acre (35-hectare) car-free area that encompasses the city heart. Giethoorn, Netherlands, is a car-free town with a population of 2,500. The main form of transportation is by canal boat. Geneva, Switzerland, has ten car-free streets in the heart of its city, Perhaps the most significant initiative in recent years was the very successful congestion charge for cars entering central London initiated by the city's mayor, Ken Livingstone, over the vigorous opposition of both business and the national government.[44] Fort Collins, Colorado, has a commercial district in its old town that allows no traffic except for maintenance crews. Charlottesville, Virginia, has a free trolley that connects the main street to the University of Virginia campus.

In the car-controlled city, an alternative transportation future will be diverse, from small-scale technologies (e.g., bicycles) to medium-sized strategies (e.g., buses) to large-scale systems like light rail transit (LRT). All these systems represent a huge increase in efficiency over the private car, whether that efficiency is measured in terms of money, resources, social equity or just plain human well-being. Some systems promote new nodal centers (as does light rail) while others promote the linear, shop-lined main street (as does the tram), while still others promote a whole different carbon-free way of living in the city (as does the bicycle).

Photograph by Stephan Horlak, 2001.

At the top end, rail-based systems are the most energy-efficient mass-transit option available, driven by electric power coming from overhead lines or the rail itself. New tracks can be laid down in the center of existing highways or along existing rail rights-of-way and do not require expensive elevated railbeds. They contribute mightily to the ambience and flavor at the heart of many European cities, large and small alike. "The benefit of LRT is that it can leverage land-use changes in a way that other systems, particularly bus systems, don't seem to achieve," points out Todd Litman. Many planners see LRTs and streetcars more as development tools than as transportation modes.[45] "You are creating these walkable neighborhoods that a lot of people seem to like. You're gaining a lot of property value, you're providing mobility for non-drivers, you're doing all these things you want to do," says Litman.

Car junkie or carfree?

TAKE THE TEST

Calculate your very own
Single Occupancy Vehicle Factor

1. How did you get to/from school/work today?
   a) In a vehicle BY MYSELF = 10 points
   b) In a vehicle with ONE OTHER PERSON = 5 points
   c) In a vehicle with TWO OTHER PEOPLE = 3 points
   d) In a vehicle with THREE OTHER PEOPLE = 2 points
   e) NO car—took a BUS, BIKED, WALKED = 0 points.

2. Find your daily score by adding the points for your trip TO and FROM your destination. For example, one day, one return trip in your car alone = 20 points; with 2 passengers = 6 points.

3. For your weekly score, add all your daily scores (assuming a five-day work week).

4. What's **YOUR SOV** Factor?

   0-19: Be proud, you're a **Self-Propelled Superstar!**
   20-39: Better than most, you're a **Transit Trooper!**
   40-59: With a little effort, you could be **Cleaner'n Greener!**
   60-79: Caution! You're driving a road to a **Fumin' Future!**
   80-100: Seek help, you're a **Fossil Fool!** Consult your local transit guide or cycling coalition.

And the technology is just getting more efficient. In our transition away from fossil fuels, a variety of alternative energy sources will need to be employed by the carbon-free city. As an example, Calgary, Alberta, advertises its system as the first wind-powered public transit system in North America. Through its financing mechanisms, it claims that its system reduces CO_2 emissions by 26,000 tonnes a year, equivalent to eliminating 7.5 million vehicle trips annually.[46]

The most famous example of integrated urban thinking is Curitiba, Brazil, which merges social and environmental initiatives into urban planning. Its bus system is a part of this thinking, with 35 miles (56 km) of two-way lanes reserved for its buses, the first city to design a "surface subway."[47] This Bus Rapid Transit (BRT) system includes articulated buses that can seat up to 270 passengers and are hinged in two spots to take corners easily. It carries 20,000 passengers an hour in each direction, with a bus arriving each minute during rush hour at bus stops that are in tube-shaped shelters and raised off the ground for easy loading. The character of the buses is akin to a tram, but more flexible as they are not track-based, offering perhaps a useful hybrid model. The whole system is regulated by the city that sets routes and fares. For about 30 cents, one can transfer as often as one wants throughout the system. The buses are owned by private companies, and the whole network is self-financing.

And now the carbon-neutral campus

"Transit is not one thing; it is a whole variety of services ranging from taxis to shuttle buses or shuttle vans to small buses to big buses to street cars, light rail transit, heavy rail transit, freight transit," maintains Litman. At the center of it all are the age-old technologies of walking and cycling that create health in both the local population and its environment. A healthy socio-ecosystem must be inviting to pedestrians and bike-users, with high-quality sidewalks, paths and bike lanes, enjoyable routes and easy linkages to buses and trams. Smart cities and planetary universities should be on a building boom right now. The important thing is to make sure that all these different modes are interconnected and that a system

evolves that is mutually reinforcing and supportive. "One of the things to empha-
size is that we are really not talking about a very radical change," Litman says.
"What we are saying is that the growth rate in car use should be eliminated by
incremental shifts." And, one must ask again, where better to begin a coordinated
approach than with the university? Not one in particular, nor only one, but in as
many places as the university can be convinced to act.

   In considering how the university might lead by example, one must think
about it in new ways. As we have discussed, the university teaches as much by the
nature of its physical existence — the pedagogy of place — as it does explicitly in
its seminars and research papers. A serious commitment to innovative transportation would entail new topics for teaching and research at the university, expanding
departments of civil (and mechanical and electrical) engineering into centers of

social innovation, faculties of medicine into centers for healthy communities, schools of planning into regional educators, and business programs into facilitators of local entrepreneurship. And as the university reduced its greenhouse gas emissions to the levels set by the Kyoto Protocol, it would also work to take its region not just to the modest levels set by Kyoto. To respond seriously to the pace of ecological deterioration entails what some call a "factor 10" reduction in resource throughput.[48] Managing demand to meet that challenge would take the planetary university to where it should be — at the center of social education and innovation, and the cutting edge of a new cultural trajectory.

The potential of seizing such an opportunity is exciting — intellectually, physically, politically. "To me I am having the perfect life, and it is in the middle of an urban area. My world is within 30 blocks of my house. It is rare that I travel more than 30 blocks away, and most of it is within ten blocks, my kids' schools are there, my wife works a mile away, the swimming pool, the grocery store, and my work are in walking, cycling or transit distance. I think that is why people come to live in cities, because they are efficient, they make life easier for everybody," says Burkholder.

"When I compare that to the richness of my life and think that I have an hour to two hours a day to interact with other people instead of being in my car, it's just a richness and a value that is so great that I don't know why you would ever want anything else …. You know our lives would be immeasurably richer if we could say, 'Hey guess what, I don't really need a car.'"

taking the high street

THE TRAFFIC NOISE FROM THE ROAD DROWNS OUT ANY CONVERSATION while walking along the edge of campus. Sinclair Road is a busy commuter route taking well-heeled residents of suburban Saanich to their downtown offices or to the local shopping centers. The road cuts through UVic, separating residences and non-academic buildings on one side from the library and academic offices on the other. But this municipal connector may not actually be such a bad thing. With a bit of vision, it could become something else entirely.

"High streets have long been places where people congregate," Paul Merrick shouts out over the din of the cars.[1] One of Western Canada's most distinguished architects, Merrick is referring to the main streets that have been the center of village and city life for centuries. "The social structure that these streets foster is fundamentally valid," Merrick proclaims. "From long ago, the urban fabric was structured around paths and places. It's all about intersections and the exchange of goods and services."

Merrick knows whereof he speaks. A fourth-generation British Columbian, he has watched his community evolve firsthand. He grew up in an area of West Vancouver where, in the 1940s, cars were only just arriving. The bridge across the inlet to his community was built the year he was born. "Growing up in my village, I could name every shop. You knew everybody, their kids were in my school, there was completeness to each of us, providing goods and services to each other. As Jane Jacobs puts it, there were 'eyes on the street.'" He chuckles now about how, as a student in architecture school, he found himself working in a section of City Hall called "special projects" where he drafted routings for freeways that were being considered for Vancouver's development, but ultimately were blocked. Later, he apprenticed in one of Canada's leading firms in Toronto, where he helped design one of the new postwar universities, Trent University in Ontario, still regarded today as one of Canada's architectural gems. But in the piecemeal approach taken to planning in universities today, there is, he says, a feeling of "unwholeness."

Along Sinclair Road, no path leads his journey. Instead, on this cool October day, he shuffles through the wet grass and around scattered ornamental trees, with the cars passing a few feet to his left. Even though he is on University property, no bicycle lane separates him from this flow. A few feet to his right are acres of parking lots — potential building sites. As he walks along the roadway, Merrick considers how UVic might reclaim this mini-freeway. If it were redeveloped into a new high street, it would gradually refashion the University from a suburban to an urban form. And if it changed the University, then it would change the municipalities in which it sits.

If getting control of the car is critical to the sustainable city of the 21st century, one place to start would be with this conveyer belt that fractures an anonymous landscape, dividing the University into isolated fragments. In combination with its promotion of serious transportation alternatives, the University could turn this commuter route into a still moving, but vital and alive, main street where the sounds of conversation replace the roar of engines, drawing together both sides of the University rather than breaking them apart. Such a vision, however, raises the larger question of the responsibility, and potential, of the University as one of today's de facto city planners.[2]

The new city planners

Higher education is the industrialized world's top industry for many reasons beyond its size and its role in supplying employees and ideas to other major industries. With perhaps 10,000 individual institutions in North America alone, it also has an unparalleled geographic reach. Colleges and universities are found in virtually every city of any size in every northern country, and many of these individual institutions are economic powerhouses in their host communities. No other industry has this local penetration. For example, although a relatively small university with a student population of 18,000,[3] UVic employs almost 4,000 people, is the fourth-largest employer in the region and its largest non-governmental employer.[4] Its direct revenues were over Can$350 million, with an estimated indirect impact of Can$1.7 billion in a city of 300,000 people.[5] On the B.C. mainland, the much larger University of British Columbia has direct expenditures of Can$1.2 billion, an estimated economic impact in its region of Can$4.6 billion, and is ranked as the province's third largest employer.[6] Meanwhile, Canada's largest university, the University of Toronto, is said to have an economic impact in its region larger than the gross domestic product of the whole province of Prince Edward Island.[7]

In the United States, the numbers are far larger. Another relatively small university with a student population of 11,250, Yale University is the largest employer in New Haven (total population, 123,630) with a payroll of US$900 million.[8] A recent survey of the 20 largest American cities found that nearly "550,000 or 35 percent, of the 1.6 million people who work for the top ten private employers are employed by eds and meds,"[9] that is, universities and medical schools/hospitals. Washington DC's top four private employers are universities and university hospitals.[10] Columbia University and New York University rank among New York City's top five private employers.[11] After the city government and the Catholic Church, Columbia University is New York's third-largest landowner — and it

Under construction.
The crane building UVic's Engineering/Computer Science building is visible through the trees that were once the front line of the tree-sit erected to block cutting and construction.

Photograph by Justine Starke, 2005.

is just one of New York's many universities.[12] On a regional basis, higher education in the state of Texas alone is estimated to generate over US$33 billion of economic activity every year,[13] while the annual figure for the University of California's ten campuses is between US$14 and US$17 billion, generating over US$4 billion in state and local taxes and nearly 370,000 jobs.[14]

This pattern of economic dominance is repeated in city after city around the world where these institutions have enormous spin-off effects on local industry. In 1996 more than half of the US$100 billion gross domestic product of the Silicon Valley economy came from companies started by Stanford graduates and faculty.[15] Companies related to the Massachusetts Institute of Technology would, if they had formed a country a decade ago, have ranked as the 24th largest world economy in 1994 with US$232 billion in sales, a total that was roughly equivalent to the whole of South Africa's economy that year.[16] Universities are "employers, purchasers, engines of economic growth, innovators, cultural meccas, branders of place and, increasingly, major real estate developers."[17] This economic impact is not widely noted. For example, one of the first books written on the impact of universities on city planning was published in 2005. It notes that there is "neither a rich professional pedagogy, nor a core body of urban research, nor a well-developed professional practice [that addresses] the significance of the university presence in urban development."[18] This presence is often quite negative given the resource consumption and suburban developments that have accompanied university growth over the past decades. In this regard, if UVic has a two-lane roadway to contend with, "University America" confronts a ten-lane freeway.

But it doesn't have to be this way. Just as the University could reshape regional traffic and development patterns, it could also help the built environment evolve in very different directions. To see what is possible one inevitably turns to Europe and to cities like Barcelona, Lyon, Strasbourg, and Freiburg that are famous for their calm atmospheres and livable architecture, scaled for walking and talking, wandering and looking. Pedestrian cities like Venice and Copenhagen are world destinations that integrate historic pasts with vital presents, manifested physically in flourishing street life and livable scales. Central Copenhagen's main street went car-free over 40 years ago, and its planners continuously study the way people interact with the street in order to integrate new designs to encourage even more walking and cycling.[19] Venice's charming winding streets are packed with artisan shops, cafés and restaurants, above which sit historic apartments where the family laundry hangs to dry and where children spill into the car-free streets to play.

These cities are the inspiration for a new kind of development — a "new urbanism" movement that has its roots in both academic analysis and social activism. Ironically, new urbanism reflects a desire for a past era when community and tradition were still valued and were built into the whole urban form, including its architecture. In North America, new urbanist designs harken back to an era when houses had front porches where people put their feet up and chatted with others passing on the streets, and where they could walk to shops where local owners knew their customers. This movement seeks a new scale of development that is intensive, not extensive, so that community can flourish again. And it can work not just in Europe but in younger cities like Portland, Oregon; Curitiba, Brazil; and Melbourne, Australia, that have their own strategies to make their streets lively and that promote pedestrian-friendly development and the revitalization of public spaces.[20]

The university is often prominent in the city center. Many of North America's most renowned universities are found in the urban core, with little physical division between city and collegiate life. Where there are gates, from Columbia in New York to UC (Berkeley) in California, the main street beckons right outside. In smaller towns, such as Eugene, Oregon, the design of its main street suggests what is possible in the transformation of suburbia. What is the character of these streets? Diversity — coffee shops, laundromats, book stores, delicatessens, walk-up apartments, travel agencies. Dynamism — where the stuffy world of the public institution spills out into the chaotic throng of small business. Interaction — old people and children, students and office workers jostle on the sidewalks, shoppers and residents emerging from street-level doorways, buses pulling in and out. These are public spaces where private conversation is a collective act. Instead, notes Rex Burkholder, "suburban universities particularly have a hard time because they provide people with a very restricted experience with other people."[21] Where students have to get into their cars and drive downtown in search of some happening venue, they leave behind a campus that is empty and still.

Again the University's potential for making the central tenet of smart growth — densification — happen is unequalled. "What has happened in the last 50 years," notes Paul Merrick as he looks at the buildings scattered over UVic's campus, "is a sloppiness that results from how easy it has become for people to get around. Before the car, people wanted to be close to one another." Ironically, to bring people together, it is important to create boundaries, boundaries that divide the urban from the rural by containing building activity, and boundaries that foster living spaces where the buildings are. "Walk down a lane between two colleges in Oxford, and, bam, you come to the border of the town and walk into a farmer's field, and the cows are right there," he notes. Meanwhile in the University, "each building is seen not as an object *in* space, but an object that *defines* space." Looking around at the University and the suburb, he says the task today is "to correct, repair and even mutate the patterns of settlement that simply don't work."

Looking over the parking lots, Merrick's conversation casts back to a "timeless way of building," the phrase coined by the noted architect Christopher Alexander in his classic study of the universal rules of living architecture, *A Pattern Language*. One of Alexander's rules applies directly to the university: "If you spend eight hours a day at work, and eight hours at home, there is no reason why your workplace should be any less of a community than your home."[22] In the pursuit of just such an objective, smart growth advocates talk of creating "complete communities" that can reduce car dependency because, like neighborhoods of the past, they are designed on a human scale. In keeping with traditional neighborhood design, a complete community is one that includes residential housing, public schools, grocery stores and shopping districts, healthcare facilities, families from diverse income and ethnic groups, and basic services accessible to all by walking, cycling or public transit. "An urban village would provide housing on campus for walkable access to classes and should contain amenities such as shops and transit stops so people can access their needs without having to leave the university,"[23] says Cheeying Ho, executive director of Smart Growth B.C.

The benefits of this new form of growth are not just social but economic. Notes Patrick Condon, James Taylor Chair in Landscape and Livable Environments at the University of British Columbia, smart growth policies at the University help to stimulate "a diverse economy and provide jobs within the student community that would allow additional work opportunities that don't require people to go too far."[24] Adds Ho, "To me, smart growth means a more sustainable and equitable way of accommodating how our communities grow, while ensuring preservation of our natural environment, access to transit and affordable housing, efficient use of land and infrastructure and meaningful public participation."

Andy Singer, *CARtoons*, Prague: CARBusters, 2001, p. 73.

The university as urban catalyst

One of the outcomes of the tree-sit at UVic was a revised Campus Plan that encourages the University to create a "village core." Unfortunately this could mean anything from a homogenous shopping-center-style development to a diverse and charming village center with synergistic possibilities for suburban revitalization in the municipality as a whole. So what should be built in a new village core? And where will it go? Who will decide? Will there be any consideration of smart growth principles? What services will be offered? Will it be McMall or High Street? Will it be institutional and anonymous, or creative and alive? Will it inspire aesthetic

Urban ecosystems

By city ecology I mean something different from, yet similar to, natural ecology as students of wilderness address the subject. A natural ecosystem is defined as "composed of physical-chemical-biological processes active within a space-time unit of any magnitude." A city ecosystem is composed of physical-economic-ethical processes active at a given time within a city and its close dependencies .... The two sorts of ecosystems — one created by nature, the other by human beings — have fundamental principles in common. For instance, both types of ecosystems — assuming they are not barren — require much diversity to sustain themselves. In both cases, the diversity develops organically over time, and the varied components are interdependent in complex ways. The more niches for diversity of life and livelihoods in either kind of ecosystem, the greater its carrying capacity for life. In both types of ecosystems, many small and obscure components — easily overlooked by superficial observation — can be vital to the whole, far out of proportion to their own tininess of scale or aggregate quantities .... And because of their complex interdependencies of components, both kinds of ecosystems are vulnerable and fragile, easily disrupted or destroyed.

— Jane Jacobs, Foreword, *The Death and Life of Great American Cities*, New York: Vintage Books, 1992 (orig. ed. 1961).

appreciation and foster economic dynamism? More generally, will that adoption of new urbanism mean not just an architectural style, but a set of values that prizes sustainable and equitable urban forms?

How these questions are answered will depend on the processes used in the planning. Central to good planning is a single principle — the willingness to accept creative tension between inclusive public processes that draw on the local knowledge that can generate a general community vision, and the expert knowledge of planning professionals who can craft technical solutions. The historic failure of the technocratic urban (and suburban) planning that characterized much of the postwar period has been a reliance on too much of the latter. Such top-down planning yields decisions that provoke more conflict after the decision, and take more time, than is generated by the use of inclusive planning processes in advance of a decision. Smart growth advocates point to many state-of-the-art public processes — from broadly inclusive design charrettes to community-based idea forums — that generate the most innovative design solutions. The adoption of such processes requires a shift in thinking about how the university is governed. This is, however, a Catch-22. To achieve transformative development first requires a transformed decision-making paradigm to let it happen. But this is a topic for later chapters.

In the meantime, one can imagine a range of alternative scenarios to draw on the expertise and diversity available in the university and the surrounding community and on best practices from around the world. To tackle sprawl, the suburban university could, for example, establish a building containment boundary to require new buildings to be built in a smaller defined area, utilizing areas of grass and parking lots within the boundary. To integrate with the community, the area should be a mixed-use development with retail and other services at the street level and housing, offices and classrooms in the upper levels. At UVic, a linear main street that runs along Sinclair Road could turn that problem into an architectural

opportunity that could also generate new transportation linkages into the municipality and throughout the region, possibly even developing a tram line as part of a new regional rail system adapted to the end of the age of oil. In the process, this linear development would be an early stimulus to new forms of neighborhood economy.[25]

Socially, there would be mixed income and cooperative housing arrangements, for students but also staff, faculty and community members. At the commercial level there would be a variety of (fair trade) coffee shops and specialty bookstores. Health food stores would sell local organic produce, and community services would be provided that draw on the talents (and services and faculties) of the university, such as dance and art studios, graphic design shops, multicultural centers, physiotherapy, or storefront student legal aid clinics. Any development would be built in a gradual, evolutionary and entrepreneurial fashion to allow for self-correcting feedback.

Some models for a new urban process are now emerging. Out of necessity, Simon Fraser University (SFU) in Vancouver has embarked on such a path. Incredibly, SFU was built in the suburbs in the early '60s on the top of an uninhabited mountain; at the time, no consideration was given to the huge transportation implications of doing so. In the late '90s, SFU secured rezoning approval to build the *UniverCity Highlands* in exchange for the dedication of much of the mountain as a municipal park. The Highlands is the first of several neighborhoods planned for the UniverCity. It will have 4,500 new homes, a stylish commercial district, elementary schools, recreation centers, offices, boutiques, shops, parklands, bicycle paths, public transit and traffic-calmed roadways.[26]

SFU's UniverCity is intended to be a model of sustainable community development, indeed, of a "new suburbanism,"[27] built on the four cornerstones of *environment, equity, economy* and *education*. "Part of the objective was to try to create a more active community, an around-the-clock community at SFU that could provide housing for faculty, staff, students and make this a more vibrant place," explains Michael Geller, president and CEO of the SFU Community Trust.[28] In the promotional literature, it features a high street where the pedestrian shopper will encounter only independent businesses, no retail chains. "You can go anywhere in North America and see the same businesses," says Geller, "so we made the decision right at the beginning that you wouldn't find Starbucks or Kentucky Fried Chicken on our Main Street."[29] Despite such good intentions, SFU's proposal faces many dangers from attempting to create an "instant community." Even with a progressive vision, any planned community runs the risk of homogeneity and sterility. Indeed, the massive high-end residential developments that have been built by the University of British Columbia completely overwhelm the University's achievements in sustainable operational practices. In any event, "real" communities are socially diverse and evolve over time. As with the universities of the past, the revitalization of urban community will require today's universities to take the long view and engage with their regions over the long term.

New suburbanism

We see New Suburbanism as a practical and beneficial way to address fundamental issues facing suburbia and support the nurturing and development of semiautonomous villages throughout the expanding periphery. In promoting the village concept, we share some common objectives with the new urbanists, notably the importance of public and open spaces as well as cultivating community.

— Joel Kotkin, *The New Suburbanism: A Realist's Guide to the American Future,* Costa Mesa, CA: The Planning Center, November 2005, p. 1. Available at <www.planningcenter.com/resources/index.html>.

Our stock in flow

A few weeks after Merrick's stroll along Sinclair Road, several hundred people crowded into Victoria City Hall to witness the sort of creativity and thoughtfulness that Merrick espoused, but from a local developer. The vast expanse of the high-ceilinged Council Chambers shrank before the standing-room-only crowd, the imposing royal red carpet invisible beneath the feet of people standing shoulder to shoulder. All were here to listen to green developer Joe Van Belleghem's pitch to reclaim an 11-acre (4.45-hectare) industrial site in the urban core, Dockside.[30]

For the city, a lot was at stake. After the creation a century ago of the Inner Harbour — which hosts the provincial legislative buildings and the grand Empress

Hotel — and the founding of the University of Victoria in the 1960s, the proposed Dockside development would be the region's "third major planning statement."[31] If the principles of "green building" were embraced by the city, this would be the city's chance to "lead the way in Canada, and throughout the world," argues Van Belleghem.[32] At Dockside, all the visible amenities that could be envisioned of an urban village for the university were there. But its hidden physical amenities evoked the real enthusiasm from the assembled citizens, however seemingly prosaic the topic. From building materials of low-emission concrete and sustainably harvested wood, from onsite energy sources and sewage treatment to the use of recycled wastewater, from car-share cooperatives to mini transit systems, from the collective composting of food wastes and to the use of non-toxic cleaning products, Van Belleghem had seemingly thought of everything in his quest to reduce harmful material throughputs.

Green building is now well established at many campuses across North America. Its goal is to reduce, reuse and recycle material inputs. As we have seen, the goal of reducing throughput is *the* basic physical challenge of environmental sustainability. Just half a dozen years ago, green building was a marginal concept, yet it is actually relatively easy. "There is a fundamental assumption that environmentally sustainable building is going to cost you money," Van Belleghem told the adoring crowd. "This is just not right. If we reduce our water use, we can actually save money. We can make good business cases for all these innovative practices."

The benefits of green building can be realized because so much waste is built into recent patterns of development. Just as the automobile has led to wasting land in patterns of sprawl, intensive use of under-priced energy and water — indeed, all manner of resources and environmental services — has led to technologies and building practices that are unnecessary and wasteful. Parallel to smart growth's message to the urban planning movement, a new school of thinking has emerged that is only now beginning to be heard in the schools of business. Variously called "natural capitalism"[33] and "ecological modernization,"[34] the thinking is that economy and environment need not conflict where the regulatory space is open to innovation. There is, as well, an important social component here. As Van Belleghem told the crowd: "What is 'affordable' is not just what it costs someone to buy a unit, but what it costs to operate it. If energy and water costs are low, it's more affordable. And if you don't need a car, it is so much cheaper. This is our goal — to achieve the triple bottom line of economic, environmental and social sustainability." "Live-work" arrangements are part of this mix.

With significant cost benefits, building green has begun to catch on at many cost-sensitive universities. At UVic, green innovations are making inroads with lighting retrofits, low-flush toilets, more energy efficient buildings, water recycling, permeable paving for groundwater recharge, even composting food waste from the campus cafeterias.[35] The University of British Columbia (UBC), the third-largest university in Canada, funds its campus sustainability office with the money it saves through energy reduction savings. UBC's energy and water retrofit program also enables UBC to reduce CO_2 emissions by 16,535 tons (15,000 tonnes) each year.[36] The State University of New York at Buffalo has managed to keep its energy costs to 1993 levels and has saved US\$65 million by implementing creative strategies for saving energy.[37] By replacing existing toilets, water fixtures and light fixtures, Columbia University's lighting retrofit and water conservation programs are saving US\$2.7 million annually.[38]

Those economic savings translate into environmental savings. For example, buildings are the

Building a green island downtown.

Dockside Green came to life after the City of Victoria's unprecedented requirement that potential developers of the Dockside land meet triple bottom line criteria that integrate economic, ecological and social goals. Achieving this objective will have a synergistic effect on the project as a whole.

Image courtesy of Busby Perkins+Will, Windmill Development Group and VanCity Enterprises Ltd, 2005.

largest contributors to greenhouse gases on campuses. Using 33 percent of the world's energy and producing about 10 percent of the world's greenhouse gases, buildings are huge consumers and polluters.[39] But while most universities address this by building a green building here or retrofitting an old one there, few universities have taken a comprehensive and integrated approach. The University of California (UC) is an exception, crafting the strictest green building and clean energy standards of any university in the United States. Implemented in July 2003, the standards require all new or newly renovated buildings to meet, at a minimum, silver-level certification by the United States Green Building Council's Leadership in Energy and Environmental Design (LEED). UC's Green Building Policy applies to all of its ten campuses across the state.[40] The University's Clean Energy Standard mandates a zero increase in fossil fuel consumption and stipulates strict goals for energy efficiency improvements and renewable energy production. All new buildings must exceed the energy efficiency standards of the state building code by 20 percent, while existing buildings must increase efficiency by 10 percent by 2014. Also by then, 10 megawatts of renewable energy must be generated on or near each campus, while ten percent of grid-purchased electricity must be shifted to renewable energy sources, with that percentage increasing to 20 percent by 2017.[41]

Given their size and reach, were universities to make green building a comprehensive mission, they could transform the entire fabric of engineering and construction. Were they to do so while actively phasing out automobile dependence and revitalizing the urban and regional communities, the ripple effects would be enormous. One of the campus sustainability movement's icons is Middlebury College in Vermont because it is doing just that, consciously working to strengthen the local economy while minimizing the campus's environmental throughput. It will, for example, buy 20 percent of its building materials from manufacturers located within 500 miles (800 kilometers) of the school, half of those to be extracted, harvested or recovered from within the same area. To minimize the destruction of old-growth forests, 50 percent of wood products must receive certification from the Forest Stewardship Council.[42] And the examples go on. In

Ashland, Wisconsin, Northland College has a residence hall that is 50 percent more efficient than a standard building and incorporates two greenhouses, a wind tower and photovoltaic solar panels.[43] Meanwhile, Duke University in Durham, North Carolina, has saved US$800,000 over ten years through student-initiated energy conservation measures. In February 2003, Duke University agreed to match US$25,000 for the purchase of wind-power technology. Students, faculty and staff then began a campaign to collect US$25 pledges that would see the University purchase 1,250 kWh of wind-powered electricity.[44] Similarly, the University of Colorado-Boulder provides 35 to 40 percent of the energy consumed by three of its buildings with wind power.[45]

Vancouver, B.C., will soon be home to the Centre for Interactive Research on Sustainability (CIRS), which promises to be the "greenest building in North America" once it opens in 2006.[46] Owned by the University of British Columbia, the CIRS Great Northern Way Campus will produce more energy than it uses. As importantly, the building will be jointly managed with several regional postsecondary institutions and technical schools in order to create educational partnerships, incubate new innovations and provide working space for diverse government agencies, private partners and non-governmental environmental organizations.[47]

CIRS follows in the model-building tradition established by the Adam Joseph Lewis Center for Environmental Studies at Oberlin College, Ohio. The Lewis Center is a net energy producer, and it discharges potable water instead of waste. It was conceived and developed by David Orr, author of *Ecological Literacy* [48] and a pioneer in the sustainable campus movement.

Universities worldwide save millions of dollars annually through the implementation of sustainability programs that focus on energy efficiency, waste reduction and recycling, transportation management and food production and consumption. The University of Michigan's large savings result from a dramatic reduction in energy use on campus.

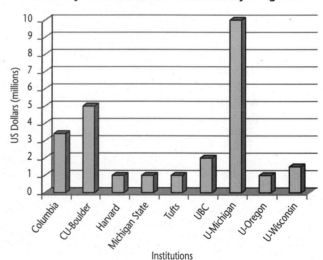

Annual Savings by University Environmental Sustainability Programs

Rosemary Collard, "Annual Savings by University Environmental Sustainability Programs," adapted from Garrett W. Meiggs, *Campus Sustainability in Higher Education*, Ithaca: Cornell University, 2005.

Mimicking nature

"A central philosophical and methodological underpinning of ecological design is the notion that natural ecological systems should serve as a template for human designs. In contrast to most contemporary architectural endeavors, and in keeping with this principle of ecological design, the Center was explicitly conceived as an *integrated building-landscape system* that would continue to change and to improve in performance over time."

— John Petersen, Professor of Environmental Studies and Biology, Comment on college website, Oberlin, Ohio: Oberlin College, 2003–04. Available at <http://www.oberlin.edu/ajlc/design_4.html>.

Integrated design.

Conceived by David Orr, author of Ecological Literacy, the Lewis Center at Oberlin College boasts a long list of integrated green features. For example, the Lewis Center's Living Machine combines conventional purification technology with a mini-ecosystem that mimics the water-purification processes of a wetland. After passing through the Living Machine, the buildings' wastewater can be reused in the Center's toilets and irrigation systems.

Photographs courtesy of Oberlin College.

"On college campuses people can begin to see and envision things that otherwise are just giant global problems," he says. For Orr, the idea is to understand "the campus as a microcosm. It's big enough to be interesting and small enough to be manageable."[49]

The Lewis Center was intended not only as a place where students attend classes, but also as a way of reconceptualizing the relationship people have with their environment. For Orr, architecture *is* pedagogy, and the Lewis Center is not only an integrated physical system, but also a tool for instruction and a part of the curriculum. "When Thoreau said he went to Walden to drive some of the problems of living into a corner where he could study them, that's what I've tried to do here," says Orr. "On this acre-and-a-quarter site we address all of the problems of sustainability: ecological restoration, horticulture, food production, harvesting solar energy, even purifying waste water — it's our standard here in the building: drinking water in, drinking water out." The center was developed through Oberlin's Environmental Studies program, drawing on a design team with experts in education, design and renewable energy, as well as on input from students and faculty.

These local sites of sustainability need to grow and seed the culture they are embedded in until whole institutions, neighborhoods and regions have been transformed. The day after Van Belleghem's presentation, the headline in the local newspaper read, "Radical Dockside plan wins plaudits."[50] The plaudits were there for sure, but "radical"? In reality, its radicalness is more a reflection of the nature of contemporary values and practices than the proposal itself. As the great historian Walter Prescott Webb commented in 1951, ever since Europe's discovery of the New World, the rise of Western society has been "founded on boom conditions."[51] As the negative costs of this boom mount, redesign will become standard fare, while past excesses will be seen as radical.

A path less taken

Again we come back to the university as a contested site for experimentation and incubation of innovation.[52] To go beyond incremental green developments, the planetary university will take the space freed up by increased efficiencies, not just to squeeze in more old-style growth in the future — growth that will overwhelm any savings from gains in efficiency — but to redirect that growth in fundamental ways. Historic patterns of *linear* growth must give way to all manner of life that is rooted in *circular* sustainability. This is the meaning of Herman Daly's call for a "steady state" where institutions are built to maximize the longevity of the *stock*

The Copenhagen Principles

1. Convert streets into pedestrian thoroughfares
   The city turned its traditional main street, Stroget, into a pedestrian thoroughfare in 1962. In succeeding decades they gradually added more pedestrian-only streets, linking them to pedestrian-priority streets, where walkers and cyclists have right-of-way but cars are allowed at low speeds.

2. Reduce traffic and parking gradually
   To keep traffic volume stable, the city reduced the number of cars in the city center by eliminating parking spaces at a rate of 2–3 percent per year. Between 1986 and 1996 the city eliminated about 600 spaces.

3. Turn parking lots into public squares
   The act of creating pedestrian streets freed up parking lots, enabling the city to transform them into public squares.

4. Keep scale dense and low
   Low-rise, densely spaced buildings allow breezes to pass over them, making the city center milder and less windy than the rest of Copenhagen.

5. Honor the human scale
   The city's modest scale and street grid make walking a pleasant experience; its historic buildings, with their stoops, awnings and doorways, provide people with impromptu places to stand and sit. ☞

(e.g., buildings) and minimize the *flow* (e.g., heat and light) required to sustain that stock. In the process, the quest for more physical growth gives way to institutions that maximize qualitative human development.[53] To achieve a steady state at the university, and to do so as part of a steady state in the city and region — this goal is definitive for the planetary university, a university that is truly taking the high street.

6. Populate the core

    More than 6,800 residents now live in the city center. They've eliminated their dependence on cars, and at night their lighted windows give visiting pedestrians a feeling of safety.

7. Encourage student living

    Students who commute to school on bicycles don't add to traffic congestion; on the contrary, their active presence, day and night, animates the city.

8. Adapt the cityscape to changing seasons

    Outdoor cafés, public squares and street performers attract thousands in the summer; skating rinks, heated benches and gas-lit heaters on street corners make winters in the city center enjoyable.

9. Promote cycling as a major mode of transportation

    The city established new bike lanes and extended existing ones. They placed bike crossings — using space freed up by the elimination of parking — near intersections. Currently 34 percent of Copenhageners who work in the city bicycle to their jobs.

10. Make bicycles available

    The City introduced the City Bike system in 1995, which allows anyone to borrow a bike from stands around the city for a small coin deposit. When finished, they simply leave them at any one of the 110 bike stands located around the city center and their money is refunded. ∎

— Paul Makovsky, "Pedestrian Cities: Copenhagen's 10-Step Program," *MetropolisMag.com*, August/September, 2002. Available at <http://www.metropolismag.com/html/content_0802/ped/index.html>.

locating the commons

To enter onto Kyushu University's new campus in suburban Fukuoka, Japan, is to enter into a complex experiment of ecology in action. Perhaps this is why the world's leading scientific journal, *Science*, has taken such an interest in it.[1] Rather than seeing buildings sprawled across the terrain, the visitor will encounter a large-scale habitat of restored ponds and marshes, lush hillsides and clustered development. The site for the new campus was previously a rolling landscape of abandoned rice paddies, orchards and commercial forests. University planners intended to bulldoze the hilltops into the valleys and create a level surface for easy construction.

But one faculty member, biologist Tetsukazu Yahara, had a different idea: to "convert more than 40 percent of Kyushu's almost 600-acre (275-hectare) campus into a conservation experiment."[2] As recounted by Dennis Normile in *Science*, the master plan was dramatically revised to "maintain existing contours, concentrate the buildings along a curving central spine, and leave the flanks of the campus for preservation."[3] Some areas are being turned into "a refuge for plant species displaced by construction."[4] When construction is completed, the result will be a university campus created with a process of "transplantation" that will have protected oaks and pines, turtles and salamanders, even ponds, by moving them into a reconstructed landscape. With 270 species of plants and animals identified on the site, several of which were listed as endangered, the University also adopted a "no species loss" policy.[5] These novel strategies were incorporated into new courses and dissertation topics. Engineering models developed for the construction are already being applied to dam construction and riverbank restoration throughout Japan. One hopes that the building development will be as imaginative.

Kyushu U's initiative is important not because the place was unique. Indeed, the site was "very ordinary,"[6] says Yahara. But the University was able to see beyond the ordinary and was willing to act on its vision. Extraordinary ecological features survive beneath the bland face of so many suburban universities, says Victoria ecologist Briony Penn: "What is lacking these days is historical imagination. People don't ask questions about place or historically what has gone before it."[7] Penn is a local, her connections dating back five generations to the time when the Pease family developed its strawberry fields long before UVic occupied the land.

Kyushu U weaves through its environment.
In a densely populated country, Japan's new Kyushu University campus is being designed to fit within a radically restored local environment.

Image courtesy of Kyushu University.

An award-winning environmental educator and journalist, and former host of the local television show *EnviroMental*, Penn is also a co-founder of The Land Conservancy of BC (TLC). Leaning against the porch railing of her Salt Spring Island home near Victoria, Penn observes, "that what North Americans have utterly and completely lost is a sense of place. UVic could have a real opportunity to try and be with its place through everything it does."

"The biggest problem in the world today is incremental loss of habitat," remarks Penn. "It is even bigger than secondary sources like pollution or climate change. If you lose the natural world, you've lost everything. If a university cannot understand that notion of incremental change and the impact it has over time, then we've had it." Before colonial development, the ecosystems that are now the grounds of UVic were characterized by dry-to-moist Douglas fir forests that transitioned into more open and dry areas of Garry oak and arbutus forests, with cottonwood, alder, cedar and grand fir growing in the wetlands around streams and rivers.[8] Now heavily fragmented by development that paid no heed to the historical landscape, the campus is a microcosm of a larger global problem and thus a potential laboratory for a different future.

"It used to be that UVic had an incredible population of owls. That was before Operations made the decision to chop down dead and decaying trees. If you cut down all your dead and decaying trees then you have just lost your woodpeckers and all your owls, and if you spray pesticides to keep your sports lawns green then you've lost your butterflies and your moths and then your bats," Penn says. "Eventually you have a collapsing, unbalanced, unfunctioning ecosystem which is essentially where it is now."

Over the years, the forests and meadows have been eroded to make space for new buildings, roads and parking lots. What may have been well-intended landscaping initiatives in the past have compromised the integrity of the fragments that remain. Pesticides applied to maintain lawns and gardens have poisoned biodiversity; English ivy, a non-native decorative species planted to green up concrete buildings, has invaded wild spaces — taking over the forest floor and choking the trees it climbs. Old trees taken down to reduce the risk of liability have displaced a diversity of insects, owls and woodpeckers.[9] To rehabilitate this landscape calls for new forms of ecological knowledge, but also new ways of thinking about the *social* form of the urban landscape.

Cherry Orchard Mall

In the Middle Ages, the village green was a useful piece of turf in the center of town. Used for all sorts of endeavors — feeding sheep, practicing archery, occasionally grazing livestock — the green was a collective space, a *commons* for common use.[10] As with many of the agricultural fields around the village, the use of the green inside the village was cooperatively organized by the community. Through collective norms and historic traditions, the resources of the commons were shared equitably and their health carefully maintained. The land, the communal institutions in which it was embedded and the "common" knowledge passed down through the generations comprised an integrated system that was the glue of medieval society. In England access to collective pastures and grain fields meant food security for poor and property-less peasants.[11] The growth of merchant trade and market systems affected this physical and social landscape, large landowners *enclosing* (i.e., privatizing) once expansive common pastures, and driving peasants off the land and into the cities.[12] Over the centuries, agricultural villages turned into market towns, and market towns into industrial cities, and the village green into a soccer field in the middle of the metropolis.

The village green.
Located at East Witton,
Pennines of North Riding,
this historic village green
is embedded physically
and socially in the heart of
community life.

Photograph by J.K. St. Joseph, Cambridge University Collection of Air Photographs, Unit for Landscape Modelling, 1952.

The story of private growth through public enclosure continues today in various forms throughout the world. In North America, it has manifested in centuries of colonization of aboriginal societies, but it exists as well in the ongoing sprawl of housing tracts and shopping centers that engulf yet more farms and forests on the edge of town. Sprawl has contributed mightily to the rise of placelessness, one suburb like another, one city's Cherry Orchard Mall is erected on the same clearcut as the next city's Spring Garden Villas. In the municipalities that surround UVic, as in virtually every suburb in North America, grassy urban parks are commonplace,

The nature of the commons

Despite its ubiquity, the commons is hard to define. It provides sustenance, security and independence, yet (in what many Westerners feel to be a paradox) typically does not produce commodities. Unlike most things in industrial society, moreover, it is neither private nor public: neither business firm nor state utility, neither jealously guarded private plot nor national or city park. Nor is it usually open to all. The relevant local community typically decides who uses it and how .... More fruitful than such attempts to define commons regimes through their domains are attempts to define them through their social and cultural organization: for example, local or group power, distinctions between members and non-members, rough parity among members, a concern with common safety rather than accumulation, and an absence of the constraints which lead to economic scarcity.

— "The Ecologist," *Whose Common Future? Reclaiming the Commons.*
Gabriola Island: New Society Publishers, 1993, pp. 7–9.

A world turned upside down

Enclosures have appropriately been called a revolution of the rich against the poor. The lords and nobles were upsetting the social order, breaking down ancient law and custom, sometimes by means of violence, often by pressure and intimidation. They were literally robbing the poor of their share in the commons, tearing down the houses which, by hitherto unbreakable force of custom, the poor had long regarded as theirs and their heirs'.

— Karl Polanyi, *The Great Transformation: The Political and Economic Origins of Our Time,*
Boston: Beacon Press, 2001 (orig. ed. 1944), p. 37.

although they perform minimal ecological function. Meanwhile suburban growth has meant continuing encroachment on peripheral lands, with the accompanying demise of rural social and physical function — lost forests, lost farms, dry springs and absent fruit.

As each local habitat disappears and another farm is paved over, the result is more incremental contributions to the worldwide loss of local "carrying capacity" where cities survive only because they *import* sustainability. This historic pattern of developer-driven urban growth is not unique, however, but is commonplace in a whole host of industries. The factory trawlers that have depleted over half of the world's commercial fish populations and the feller bunchers that still chew their way through the world's forests work with the same logic. These industries entail the privatization, commodification and erosion of natural and social processes that provide clean water, productive land, genetic biodiversity and ecosystems rich in plant and animal life.[13]

Being lost in these developments is something without which the world cannot survive, *healthy socio-ecosystems*. This phrase describes self-maintaining places where human and natural communities coexist in rooted, mutually sustaining relationships. These socio-ecosystems are the cells that make up the planetary body. As they succumb to disease and displacement, the Earth's health declines. The history of the university is implicated in this long decline, in the unidirectional construction of a conquering city seemingly immune to the natural world. It is also present in the creation of the artificial sciences so useful to this growth, embedded within their exclusivity that allows them to push aside other social knowledges of this larger world. Thus does center triumph over territory, the human mind fixed on the macro-structures of economic globalization, everyone's gaze casting *up* at the apparatus of placeless power. Few even notice the quiet passing of the socio-ecosystems where they live, yet if such places are the essential building blocks of a sustainable world, it is time to focus *down*.

Matching its ability to reduce energy and resource throughputs, and to build a livable city, the university can also help collar the sprawl of development over wild and productive lands. In the process, the university could challenge the millennial history of urban conquest and of professionalized science over communal knowledge. As today's agricultural science embodies this privileging of a particular way of knowing, the time is ripe to reinvigorate the village green and reverse the colonizing pattern of rural displacement. Thus does the compact and efficient village of the last chapter provide an opportunity for a new approach to the land, not just as a lawn in the center of town, but as a functioning "green infrastructure"[14] in which the region, the city, and the university are all re-embedded.

Natural tensions

For many people the loss of habitat is so incremental that it goes unnoticed. For others it is a constant source of frustration and vigilance. The ongoing fragmentation of UVic's natural areas led to the tree-sit in Cunningham Woods. In other locales, it means letters to the editor in the local campus newspapers and the formation of student and community groups with such names as the "Friends of ..." or the "Community for an Environmentally Responsible Campus." Saving Mystic Vale from development in 1993 is a good example. A local developer owned the land and had plans for subdivision.[15] In response, a student-led group, the Friends of Mystic Vale, took people on tours, held vigils and information sessions and collected over 1,500 petition signatures in support of saving Mystic Vale. The group lobbied UVic to purchase the Vale, pointing out that under the provincial legislation of the University Act, a university has the right to expropriate land in order to be used for public purposes.[16] With the early support of the visionary University President Howard Petch, the Friends of Mystic Vale generated enough concern for the forested ravine that an agreement was eventually made between the provincial government, the Municipality of Saanich and the University of Victoria to buy the Vale for Can$2.7 million and to protect it in perpetuity by a legally binding covenant.[17]

Ten years later, when students rallied to protect Cunningham Woods, the last forested area within the Ring, they lost. But while the two buildings went ahead, the controversy led to a ten-year moratorium on some of the University's most remarkable landscapes, such as its Garry oak meadow and the headwaters of Bowker Creek. The new *Campus Plan* explicitly recognized a variety of new concepts from smart growth to ecological restoration. "There is so much potential," notes Penn, linking such activism to the traditional mission of the university. "If a place becomes an actual place, then everything is pedagogy. Every decision made on that landscape affects a particular commitment to sustainability, and this will change how people learn because it's going to affect everything they do. So they can't just simply drive their car and park it. That value system now affects how they see the world."

The argument for densification rests on the assumption that, by concentrating growth within a specific area, the need for sprawling development is minimized and the potential ecosystem revitalization maximized. This follows, however, only if the land that is saved is managed for its ecological values, not just left fallow to be overgrown with invasive species and held for future development. In doing so, lessons can be learned directly from the university's physical, as well as its intellectual, assets. "There are," says Penn, "virtually no institutions in Canada that are teaching people the elements of where they live. In biology there is increasing emphasis on microbiology and genetics; I get fourth-year biology students who can't tell the difference between a red cedar and a Douglas fir." This is where high street and the commons intersect. For example, with future building growth largely directed inside a building containment boundary, as in Kyushu University, the restoration and enhancement of its remaining natural areas is possible, and the pursuit of education outside the classroom an opportunity for the new planetary university.

Restorative ecologies

The field of ecological restoration is large and growing. And it is replete with techniques — decontaminating toxic soils, removing invasive species and propagating and planting native plants. Restoration also involves watershed-based initiatives to retain healthy creeks and rivers, and ecosystem inventory and recovery programs. All involve a transdisciplinary approach using skills and knowledge found in ecosystem management, environmental dispute resolution, geographic information systems and remote sensing, land use planning, landscape architecture, landscape ecology, sustainable agriculture, urban agriculture, urban design or permaculture.[18] At UVic, faculty and students now collaborate with staff from Facilities Management to identify and map exotic plants and shrubs for removal from the regionally endangered Garry oak meadows that exist on campus, and provide detailed ecological data on the birds, mammals, plants and plant communities found there. Similar work is also now taking place in Mystic Vale. A partnership of students, unionized workers and faculty are working to stabilize the riparian area and reduce the stream sedimentation in the hope that fish might some day return.[19] The University is striving for zero pesticide use through the adoption of an Integrated Pest Management System.[20]

While site-specific practice is a crucial aspect of renewing a culture of stewardship and care for the commons, the true promise of ecological restoration doesn't stop at the University's borders. One of the region's major watersheds has its 20-acre (8.5-hectare) headwaters at UVic, occupying one fifth of the campus's forested area, and one tenth of its entire land base.[21] This is Councillor Gillespie's Bowker Creek where, from the heart of UVic, it once meandered in the open light for five miles (eight kilometers) through what became the three municipalities of Saanich, Victoria and Oak Bay. A perfect metaphor for the literal enclosure of the commons, Bowker Creek is now buried in pipes and culverts for most of this path, flowing unseen beneath the car tires and feet of local residents and passing the local shopping center, University Heights, which just a few decades ago was the site of greenhouses and old farm homesteads. The area was once known as the Cedar Plains where rainfall collected and flowed into the Bowker Creek tributary from the campus lands.

On its journey, open portions of the creek can still be glimpsed beside the occasional cluster of houses and through neighborhood parks, before it slips again into its lightless confines beneath the road. But a movement is growing to "daylight" the creek along its journey, and the Municipality of Saanich proposes to purchase several properties along one stretch of the creek to create a community greenway. The daylighting of urban creeks poses huge challenges to the built landscape. But what improvements it could yield for the quality of life in the world's cities, bringing a cool and natural lushness into the land of hot concrete and pavement and providing a new context for human-powered transportation. Instead, in Saanich, Bowker Creek continues its journey past and beneath another shopping center, Hillside Mall. With the passage of time, few are left who can remember when it flowed past vegetable gardens, through open fields and a tree nursery. Still fewer can recall an even earlier time when the creek was flanked by sword ferns and bathed in the scent of cedar groves. As it approaches its end at the sea, a few open sections catch the sun in lush city parks, just before it spills into Juan de Fuca Strait at Willows Beach. At that spot, an ancient midden of discarded clamshells, bones and artifacts attests to the extensive native use of that fresh water by the sea before these inhabitants were displaced by the nearby farm of the early European settlers, John Bowker and Mary Tod. The farm is long gone.

Concrete canoeing.
Ian Graeme of the Friends of Bowker Creek Society protests the burial of Bowker Creek under Cedar Hill X Road. Mt. Tolmie, which overlooks UVic, is in the distance.

Although daylighting a whole creek may be some years off, incremental steps are being taken in the name of sustainable land management. UVic is a member of the community steering committee in the Bowker Creek Urban Watershed Renewal Initiative. UVic also created an Integrated Stormwater Management Plan in 2004 and, as a result, has built a permeable-surfaced parking lot and

Photograph by Patricia Ty, 2001.

designed permeable walkways around some of its new buildings. A water recycling program treats wastewater discharged from UVic's Aquatic Facility and reuses it in the heating and cooling of a neighboring building and in the future irrigation of the surrounding grounds. The University also plans to use collected rainwater in the flush toilets of some newly constructed residence buildings on campus. Were the University and its surrounding neighborhoods really to embrace their ecological heritage, the sky would literally be the limit, from headwater springs to ocean shore.

As with green building, much is possible to lower the impact of development on the land. Cornell University advertises its Stormwater Management Wetlands Demonstration project along the East Ithaca Recreation Trail. The project is intended to protect the adjacent Cascadilla Creek and revitalize an existing wetland area, which retains and treats stormwater from the developed area nearby.[22] Similarly, the Duke

Daylighting urban creeks.

University Wetland Center project is reconstructing a degraded and overly eroded section of Sandy Creek as wetlands, helping to remove up to 70 percent of the creek's excess sediment and nutrient load.[23] The project includes an open lake, marshes, and hardwood stands and will eventually have a retention pond to accommodate stormwater runoff from the paved campus surfaces.[24]

The University of Wisconsin's Madison Arboretum encompasses 1,260 acres (510 hectares) of land on the southern half of Lake Wingra. The Arboretum features many distinct ecosystems, including different kinds of prairie lands, savannas, deciduous woodlands, boreal forest, marshes and gardens. The Arboretum has several horticultural collections, effigy mounds, historic artifacts, a Visitor Center and

20 miles (32 kilometers) of nature trails by which to tour the area.[25] The University of Michigan's Matthaei Botanical Gardens encompasses 350 acres (142 hectares) of native habitat that can be accessed by a network of walking trails. The Gardens contain a constructed wetland for water-quality improvement and are an educational resource — hosting classes, lectures and special events.[26]

Living and thinking at Lyle

Located on a picturesque 16-acre site adjacent to the Cal Poly Pomona campus, the Lyle Center functions as a living laboratory for education, research, demonstration and outreach. Spacious facilities allow faculty, staff, students and visiting scholars to work and live in an integrative community. The Center features passive solar designed buildings, renewable energy capture, water recycling, nutrient recycling, food growing systems, aquaculture and native habitat communities .... A key feature of the program is its integration of specialized disciplinary knowledge from a variety of university programs — agriculture, physical sciences, environmental design, business, engineering, social sciences and humanities — into a multidisciplinary research and practice-oriented core. The Center seeks to create knowledge that integrates scientific/technological understanding with contextual understanding of human culture.

— The John T. Lyle Center for Regenerative Studies, *About the Lyle Center* and *Masters of Science in Regenerative Studies*, Pomona, CA: The John T. Lyle Center for Regenerative Studies. Available at <http://www.csupomona.edu/~crs/index.html>.

Photograph by Christina Hughes, courtesy of the Lyle Center for Regenerative Studies, 2002.

Toward the bioregion

Underlying these actions is an implicit acknowledgement that a sustainable campus must exist within a healthy local and regional ecosystem and that healthy ecosystems matter to a living planet. If a place of buildings, lawns, parking lots and gardens is to support reinvigorated ecosystems, those who build and use these constructions must see themselves not just as individuals and consumers and car-drivers, but also as inhabitants of living ecosystems and as citizens responsible for the health of the green infrastructure around them. Infilling and densification and the adoption of *socio* ecosystem-based planning will allow universities to contribute to the habitat networks and greenbelts of their regional park systems. This is as much a social as it is an environmental exercise. As a recent report argued, in addition to taking an ecological "inventory," and developing modeling techniques of the "composition, structure and function" of the campus ecology, new techniques such as community mapping and participatory planning provide "valuable learning and community-building for those involved, which may increase the overall capacity to contribute to stewardship planning and practice. In the end, this participatory learning may be a key factor enabling societies to adapt and survive."[27]

In historical terms, the broader challenge is to revitalize participatory community-based institutions of collectively held knowledge and values.[28] To revitalize the connection of the land we occupy to its historical past is the first task. Restoration demands historical awareness; it is the ground in which we can embed the future. When one starts to think this way, one quickly sees just how little such collective awareness exists in the University, how little it acts as a brake on misadventure, let alone as a guide for future development. With a broader community (past, present and future), the process should be to invigorate a new *commons of care* that will, in turn, enhance social capital through evolving new skills and values in the citizenry. Such a commons will invite a shift in institutional power to a community that, though diverse, would be able to act more responsibly for communal benefits than has occurred in the past. For any campus in North America, becoming a state-of-the-art model of urban greenspace restoration and stewardship is still

Green infrastructure

Forests, waterways and watersheds, parks and other green spaces have often ended up as casualties of planning. As cities lose more trees and open space, community leaders are uniting around the idea of viewing green space as not only essential to replenishing the human spirit, but also as a form of essential infrastructure like roads, water lines or sewers. In fact, they have begun calling trees and other vegetation "green infrastructure" because they are so valuable to the economy and functioning of cities. Trees provide vital services in a globally warming world. They absorb carbon dioxide and give off oxygen. They prevent the "urban heat island effect," the phenomenon by which cities run higher temperatures because they are paved over with concrete and other surfaces that absorb rather than reflect the sun's heat. And trees absorb and clean stormwater that runs off streets. And green infrastructure often does the job better than anything human-built, for much less money!

— Francesca Lyman, "What Makes a Great Place? The New City Beautiful," *Yes! Magazine*, Summer, 2005. Available at <http://www.yesmagazine.org/default.asp?ID=149>.

a long way off; creating the necessary governance structures is even more remote. Despite the innovations on many campuses, the future of the natural areas remains at the discretion of an administration with more mainstream priorities. Creating a green building is a step, but an initial one in developing a sustainable city; so too, as universities poke and prod at pieces of ecosystem restoration, they are just beginning to touch the necessary task of creating healthier socio-ecosystems and sustainable/equitable regions.

Some, however, are experimenting at this larger level. The University of Stockholm is the world's only university located in the middle of the world's first national city park, the *Ekopark*, founded in 1995. A number of educational institutions are found within the Ekopark — the Royal Swedish Academy of Sciences, the Nobel Foundation and the Royal Institute of Technology. The motto of the Ekopark is "Protect — Preserve — Present." Achieved through long deliberations with a diverse group of stakeholders, decision making for the campus uses "planning for biodiversity" as its basis.[29] The over-riding goal is that the Ekopark's nature, culture and recreational outdoor facilities should not only be protected, preserved and presented, but also enriched and developed. To protect the region from abuse and damage in the future, the enabling legislation intends to create a "mental shield" around the park. Under the legislation, new installations or other measures may be created only if this can take place without encroaching on the park landscape or natural environment and without the natural and cultural values of the historical landscape being otherwise damaged.[30]

Cities everywhere have the potential to create their own Stockholm-type model. In Victoria, the province's capital, many natural areas could be included within North America's first urban Ecoregion. While such a region would ensure the protection and restoration of the region's green infrastructure, it could also phase in the adoption of global best practices in a range of industries, from transportation to building construction, from sewage treatment to agriculture. This would make the whole region a model of sustainability. Again the leadership potential for the planetary university is huge. By drawing on its internal expertise, its physical and financial resources, and its students, and by working cooperatively with local communities and governments, *the planetary university* could do what other institutions could not. Revitalizing ecosystem functioning at local and regional levels provides the critical foundation for this emerging pedagogy, but the impact of its actual practice — its social *praxis* — will be broader.

The historic erosion of physical ecosystem health has been accompanied by another loss, that of the social commons and the institutions that supported it. A hundred years ago, 22 percent of British Columbians were farmers. By 1991 that number had dwindled to a mere 1.5 percent.[31] The trend is everywhere the same, so that as everyone knows, small-scale farming is disappearing as a way of life. As corporate agriculture extends its dominance, urban regions increasingly rely on food that travels over vast distances, is produced on an industrial scale and arrives in a highly processed form. In the United States, food regularly travels between 1,500 and 2,400 miles (2,500 and 4,000 kilometers) before reaching the consumer.[32] While the globalization of the food industry enables consumers in rich countries to buy almost any product in just about any season, one type of food is now a rarity — that which is locally grown by local residents. One expert suggests that the "most pressing concern in relation to food security is the need to increase

Farm-to-college programs

Farm-to-college programs have been initiated all across the United States and even in a few places in Canada (like UBC) to connect colleges and universities with local producers in their area and provide locally grown food for campus meals. Through the organization of the Community Food Security Coalition, over 60 campuses across North America are linking local farmers with the purchasing departments and cafeterias of their institutions. Some programs are small and unofficial, providing for special dinners or other events, while others are larger and more comprehensive, incorporating many local products into daily food services. At Middlebury College, students have promoted local food by holding special dinners and inviting key community members. Middlebury now spends US$875,000 a year on locally farmed food. Yale University spends over US$1,500,000 on local food, regularly buying grass-fed beef, produce, poultry, milk, yoghurt and lamb, much of which is organically grown. Bastyr University in Kenmore, Washington, has an organic garden that produces food for its small student population, much like Oberlin, Middlebury, the University of British Columbia and many other schools that also have campus gardens. Students at Cornell University organize a harvest week each fall, presenting educational tents, tables and art promoting local food.

— Adapted from "Community Food Security Coalition: Farm-to-College Program," *Information about Individual Programs*, Venice, CA: Community Food Security Coalition. Available at <http://www.farmtocollege.org/list.php>.

the amount of food being grown within the region and on Vancouver Island. A considerable quantity of agricultural land is not under cultivation, and there are not enough trained and skilled farmers (particularly young farmers)."[33]

The shift to corporate provisioning corresponds directly with a shift in land use, as traditional farming areas have been subdivided and developed for residential housing or commercial strip malls. Despite a strong agricultural tradition, 61,776 acres (25,000 hectares) were taken out of Vancouver Island's Agricultural Land Reserve (ALR) between 1974 and 1999, with 4,942 acres (2,000 hectares) removed from the Capital Regional District (CRD), the region UVic sits in.[34] As this happens, the commons weakens, and with it the collective knowledge that is lost with each retiring farmer. Farming currently provides for only one percent of the regional labor force, and the average farmer spends 86 cents in operating costs for every Canadian dollar of income they earn.[35] Not surprisingly, farmers are no longer able to rely on farming as their sole income, forcing young people to turn away from choosing farming as a future career. At the same time, the popularity of local organic food is growing as people become more educated about the impacts of the global food trade and the health threats associated with industrial farming methods such as the mass production of poultry and beef.[36] As with the innovations needed to reduce oil use and automobile dependence, and the potential that exists to increase resource efficiency with green building, the university has another opportunity here to reinvent itself. In so doing, the university would nurture a whole new (old) level of equitable work and community.

In the age of peak oil, food supplies based on hydrocarbon-based fertilizers and long-distance transport are increasingly vulnerable. On Vancouver Island, as in most regions of North America, it is said that the local food supply would last but a few days were imports to be cut off. Yet, the local land base for farming is shrinking, while climate change makes large-scale agribusiness that is concentrated in warmer climates more and more risky. Meanwhile long-distance transport becomes more vulnerable to the growing scarcity and rising costs of oil. And everywhere the skills of local self-provision are disappearing. Were the University to respond to this situation, it would address something else, the University's own alienation — of its buildings from its land, of mental work from physical work, of the artificial from the natural sciences. A sustainable planet requires that this fragmentation be healed. To do so requires that we again locate the commons.

The place where we are

The sun shifts from behind a passing cloud, and the wind stirs up the dry green leaves in a gnarly little grove of aging pear and apple trees. "These orchard trees could be restored,"[37] says Geoff Johnson, watching the whirling wind carve its way through the long grasses and wildflowers of the slow meadowed landscape. Geoff Johnson is a local permaculture expert trained at Linnea Farm on Cortes Island, B.C., and in Australia and India. At the edge of the University grounds, 30.7 acres (12 hectares) of agricultural land lie fallow that include the old orchard, groves of Garry oak trees and large open fields. Known recently as the

"CJVI" lands after the radio station that sold the land to the University of Victoria for Can$195,000 in 1964,[38] this old farm is one of Gordon Head's last pieces of agriculture land, unused since the '60s. As a remnant of the Hudson's Bay Company's Uplands Farm from the 1850s, it is the oldest farmland on Vancouver Island. It is also one of UVic's key potential development reserves.

"Through a design that maintains the rural characteristics of the place, you could benefit the wider community and provide really progressive educational opportunities for a number of departments in the University," asserts Johnson. "As an extension of UVic, there would still have to be buildings on the site, but it could model permaculture and green building design ideas. It could be designed so that each element is taking advantage of what the other elements have to offer."

"I came to it from the perspective of wanting to develop skills around autonomy and self-reliance and the vision of a society made of smaller-scale, democratically organized communities where there is a large degree of self-reliance. Once I started doing it I realized how fulfilling and enjoyable it was and how it gave me a sense of peace." According to Johnson, UVic's CJVI land provides a perfect opportunity to revitalize

Learning from nature

Australian ecologist Bill Mollison has worked on perfecting a system whereby small-scale farmers would set up a low-maintenance garden, a woodland, and an animal and fish farm and then become self-sufficient — fed, clothed and powered by local resources that are literally right at hand. Designing *with* nature's wisdom is at the core of this farming philosophy, which is called permaculture, for permanent agriculture. In permaculture, you ask not what you can wring from the land, but what the land has to offer .... Wherever possible, permaculturists invite external forces such as wind or flooding to actually help do the work. They build windmills, for instance, or plant crops on floodplains where they can enjoy a yearly pulse of alluvial sediment .... Choosing synergistic planting arrangements — using "companion plants" to complement and bring out the best in one another .... The idea is to lay out crops so that those you visit most frequently are close by your dwelling (Mollison calls it edible landscaping), and those that require less vigilance are set out in concentric circles farther from the house .... The most laborious part of permaculture is designing the system to be self-maintaining.

— Janine Benyus, *Biomimicry: Innovation Inspired by Nature*, New York: Perennial (HarperCollins), 1997, pp. 37–38 the commons and combine theory with practice, thinking with doing, teaching with learning.

Johnson is not alone in his interest in the CJVI land. In 1997 a group of UVic students made a formal proposal to create the Camassia Learning Center for Sustainable Living on the CJVI farmlands. The proposal was well thought out, thorough and tailored to expand the capacities of the University. For example, it saw the remnant orchard as an ideal site for a "permaculture forest garden": "This type of garden mimics the structural features found in natural arboreal systems where a diverse, multi-layered plant community exists and in which beneficial relationships occur between species of plants, insects, and birds."[39] Its revitalization plan included a network of water catchment ponds and drip irrigation, community demonstration gardens, a native plant nursery, ethnobotanical gardens to draw attention to the area's natural and cultural history, allotment gardens, landscaping to enhance butterfly and bird populations, habitat restoration of the Garry oak stands, and building techniques that could showcase energy efficiency and green construction.

The University rejected the proposal, citing liability concerns and the project's reach beyond the established curriculum.[40] The University did not mention the economic value of the land, but its revised *Campus Plan* clearly leaves open the possibility for traditional suburban development. Indeed, in agreeing to study the future of the area, the *Plan* allows for developments that can offset the limitations imposed by protecting UVic's forested areas with a ten-year moratorium. The *Plan* states, "The CJVI Property has potential for temporary uses and permanent development, including academic expansion, faculty and student housing, sports and recreational facilities, parking and any special opportunity uses that may arise."[41] In the meantime, the land remains agriculturally derelict, kept out of sight, a reserve for development.

The potential of a Camassia-style project can be seen, however, in many other campuses, including the one across the water at the UBC farm. Founded in 2000, the UBC Farm was initiated at a time when UBC planned to develop its South Campus fields and forests. The Farm took root thanks to the presence of a far-sighted dean in the Faculty of Agricultural Sciences (now the Faculty of Land and

Food Systems). Working with student advocates, Dean Moura Quayle proposed an alternative vision to the University campus planning committee.

One of the farm's most visible successes has been the creation of a student-run organic market garden that turns cultivated field areas into an outdoor classroom for university students and visiting public schools. Research plots for investigating sustainable agricultural practices are built into the garden's crop rotation, as are community plots for poorer neighbourhoods (such as Vancouver's Downtown Eastside) as well as aboriginal, and immigrant groups. The market garden is intended to operate as a financially self-sufficient business.

The market garden produces over 250 varieties of fresh vegetables, berries, herbs, and flowers. The farm is also home to a free-range chicken flock, numerous beehives, an old vineyard, an arboretum, and a 1-km interpretive agroforesty and ecology trail through an 80-year old second growth forest. Most produce is sold through a weekend farmer's market on site, but the farm also supplies a Community Supported Agriculture box program, several well-known Vancouver restaurants, and even the University's Food services. Several teaching gardens exist on the site, including the "Land, Food, and Community Garden," that features school garden plots, a cob building, and a rainwater harvester. After five years of steady growth, supporters of the UBC Farm hope to

Fairview Gardens 1954

Fairview Gardens 1998

Michael Ableman, *On Good Land: The Autobiography of an Urban Farm* , San Francisco: Chronicle Books, 1998, pp. 10–13.

From rural to urban agriculture: Landscape change at Fairview Gardens.
In 1954 Fairview Gardens farm was set amidst the row crops and orchards of Goleta Valley, California. Forty-four years later, Fairview Gardens has become a 12¼-acre island surrounded by tract homes and shopping centers. It remains highly productive, however, producing more than 100 different fruits and vegetables, feeding 500 families and employing more than 20 people.

see it become an internationally significant Centre for Sustainable Food Systems, and thus be viewed by the academic and residential community as a vital campus asset. Instead, the University's official community plan, published in 1997, designates the UBC Farm lands as "Future Housing Reserve" that could be used for residential development after 2012.

THURSDAY, APRIL 7, 2005   THE PROVINCE | **NEWS | A11**

Farm's future provides food for thought

UBC: Research facility 'a treasure' but the land is slated for condos and townhouse

BY JOHN BERMINGHAM
VANCOUVER REPORTER

Mark Bomford, program co-ordinator at the UBC farm, is concerned that the university might turn the farm into condos. JASON PAYNE — THE PROVINCE

Vancouver's last working farm is earmarked for condos and townhouses.

The 36-hectare farm at the University of B.C. has been a farm for almost a century and is used for research in forestry and food production.

Last Friday, about 80 UBC academics discussed the future of the farm and how it could become a world leader in sustainable living instead of more condos.

Farm manager Mark Bomford said the farmland is protected for seven years but is reserved for housing. Within the next few years, condos will be built only 25 metres away.

"The farm can be a big contributor to the community," said Bomford. It currently supplies restaurants with fresh organic produce, puts on a summer market and conducts numerous tours for school children.

"The UBC farm would be a model for urban dwellers," said Bomford.

"It would let them see where food was growing, buy food that was locally produced and make the connections between what they buy and the impacts it has on society."

Over the next 15 years, UBC is to build a "University Town" for 28,000 people, earning $500 million for the university.

Moura Quayle, dean of the department of land and food systems, said the farm could share the land with an urban lifestyle.

"Urban agriculture has a place in the City of Vancouver," she said.

"We've got the opportunity to integrate . . . an agricultural landscape. It's just a question of connecting the different pieces of the fabric to make it all hang together."

Dennis Pavlich, UBC's vice-president of external affairs, said the farm is an integral part of the academic community.

While it's earmarked for housing, UBC would have to go through a long public process to develop it.

"It will be a big decision," said Pavlich. "None of that is going to happen before 2012. A decision may be made never to do it. There's nothing preordained."

The farm is currently used by 1,000 students.

Yona Sipos-Randor, 27, chose to study for her master's degree in forestry at UBC because of the farm.

"It has an incredible amount of educational value," she said. "It could be an interactive showcase, a demonstration site."

Tara McDonald, who runs the city's summer farmers' markets, which start May 14 at Trout Lake, said it would be tragic if the farm were paved over.

"We're losing our farmers," s said. "Losing this land within t city signals the complete decin tion of the whole tradition.

"This is a treasure. Once th farmland goes, it goes forever. Y can't get that back."

jbermingham@png.canwest.c

Photograph by Jason Payne, the *Province*, April 7, 2005, A11.

Long-distance food

Transporting food long distances is energy inefficient. We put in more energy (in the form of non-renewable fossil fuels) than we get out (in the form of food calories). For every calorie of iceberg lettuce flown in from Los Angeles, we use 127 calories of fuel.

— Andy Jones, *Eating Oil: Food Supply in a Changing Climate*, London, UK: Sustain: The Alliance for Better Food and Farming, 2001, p. 1. Available at <http://www.sustainweb.org/pdf/eatoil_summary.PDF>.

"We are resisting the cementification of the campus and are talking about the need for buildings that are ecologically sound. We are talking about rooftop gardens and the need for fruit trees on campus,"[42] says Alejandro Rojas, explaining that they are also talking about the need to defend UBC's organic farm from pressures to develop it as market housing. "So we are embattled, but the fronts of the battle are different. It's not the confrontational opening, marching, slogan-shouting style of the '60s. Now we are working in the classroom." Interest in having more such classrooms is growing at many universities — at UBC, UVic, the University of California, the University of Munich and around the world — to mitigate the negative impacts of the food industry. For food, like trees, cars and sprawled buildings, is all part of the quest to make universities working models of sustainability.

"We ask where the food comes from, and we find out that it comes from everywhere, but nowhere — because we don't know. This food has traveled excessive distance to get to UBC and it is associated with high food miles and negative environmental, social, and economic impacts," says Rojas. "Imagine what would happen in this province if UBC, UVic, SFU and all the colleges and all the schools moved 50 percent of their purchasing power to support local producers. That is what we are trying to do at UBC, and we are doing it in a very pragmatic way. We started by dreaming what the campus would look like if it were sustainable. Now we see shining eyes. The students are excited about the possibility of doing something that is tangible — something that is real."

Our commons future

Throughout the world, universities possess huge land assets that could, with imagination and leadership, revitalize the way we live in our cities. In transportation, urban design, architecture and building, ecosystem restoration and agricultural revitalization, the potential is vast, and the need is immediate. The educational potential exists in every discipline — in mechanical and civil engineering, town planning, land economics, agronomy, business, fine arts, even literature. Central to realizing this potential for most universities is their place in the land they occupy.

Were UVic, for example, committed to making its farmlands a model for the future, it would be difficult to restrain the collective imagination. New teaching and research centers would undertake the latest in biodynamic agricultural research, student interns managing two-acre intensive farms for the urban fringe and providing fresh local produce for the new urban village. Interspersed on this land and on other meadows at the University would be traditional plant harvests such as Bryce envisions for the local Songhees people. It is easy to imagine the vitality and youthful thrust that such uses would bring to an adventurous University. At the other end of the generational spectrum, the Center on Aging could undertake longitudinal studies on aging and gardening in a new seniors' home situated amidst these fields, an ideal experimental model for the developed world's aging population. Faculty and staff could even co-own the facility, the ownership structure and processes developed by the University's Institute for Cooperative Studies. To finance the facility, the business and law faculties could develop a voluntary program to allow employees to redirect a small portion of University pension funds from distant money markets to local reinvestment. The business faculty (and students)

Once a farm, soon to be a ...
Local residents pass through the CJVI lands on the edge of the University of Victoria's campus. To their right is an old orchard that still provides apples despite decades of neglect. The land is now used to dump soil dug up from construction on campus.

Photograph by Justine Starke, 2005.

could ensure a state-of-the-art building by designing a revolving green-capital building fund to pay off the capital costs quickly, through the reduced operating expenses associated with the green design and practices. Meanwhile students at the law school could develop global best practices in order to allow the land, owned by the University, to be managed as a commons by all the interests involved there.

What a model this place would then be![43] Accessed by a range of alternative transportation systems, linked to a developing urban village, the place could be a living testament of what can be achieved when a place uncovers its past — in liberated springs, revitalized native harvests, state-of-the-art farming — as a basis for future development. It would be an example of truly *conscious* planning. As student interns give tours of a picturesque and active new urban/rural landscape, they would be able to show the many visitors how, yes, ecosystem health and "green production" can coexist in a new communal vision.[44]

This is what is needed to create a new commons for the 21st century. Big changes will be required in our thinking, and in our public institutions, to take the real potential that exists at every university, but that still lies fallow, and let it grow. The opportunity that awaits a revitalized commons is still but a dream for those who would see a new power and ethic of care over the land. "We know that the dream may never be fulfilled," says Rojas wistfully, "but between the dream and current reality there is the realm of the potential, what could be, what eventually might happen if we dare to go there."

UVic's CJVI lands could be cultivated as an accessible community asset — the UVic-Farmlands.

Part III

THE GOVERNOR

CHAPTER 7

structured power

A S SOON AS SHE STARTS TALKING ABOUT HER WORK, whether it's recycled bikes, green buildings or campus botany, Sarah Webb's enthusiasm bubbles over. Webb is the sustainability coordinator at UVic, a position created several years ago but one she has held since 2003. "It's a great job," she says. "I love it."[1] With tangible excitement, she describes how last year she was able to divert 172 metric tons from the local landfill by composting wastes from university food services, a practice that "goes above and beyond complying with [regional] bylaws. How can you make this a model for the community?" Webb's entrepreneurial imagination brings forth a raft of technologically innovative ideas for energy use in campus buildings. One goal this year is to make dormitories more efficient: "Even though they have Energy Star appliances, let's go one step further — front-loader washers, front-loader dryers. You know, infrastructure. Things

Pride of place.
UVic Sustainability Coordinator Sarah Webb stands in a men's washroom to draw attention to the University's initiative to use recycled water in urinals and toilets.

Photograph by Darren Stone, *Times Colonist*, August 28, 2005, B1.

141

like energy efficient grills, and freezers and coolers and steamers." One technique for reducing energy use is education, with Webb planning a "dorm energy challenge where we are going to sub-meter the dorms and have a competition between them."

Webb also envisions a new partnership with a non-governmental group to "naturescape" the campus and make it more friendly to birds and butterflies, as well as an integrated stormwater program that increases natural groundwater recharge from surface waters and reduces the need for outflow piping. All of this "could have impacts into the broader community. You have architects taking this course on naturescaping and then walking out and seeing this very attractive piece of land." At the same time, Webb is less effusive about what she sees as the "biggest challenge — institutionalizing sustainability — so that it is not the off-side, or my department coming in to show you what to do. Rather, it becomes a part of the University …. I see a huge potential that we're not tapping into." It is not surprising that she finds this daunting. Webb's office has a staff of two.

On the other side of the continent, in a city noted for its revolutionary history, the sustainability revolution on campus is taking shape a bit more quickly. Leith Sharp is a sustainability coordinator at Harvard University in Cambridge, across the Charles River from Boston. A native Australian, Sharp started in the early days of campus sustainability as an undergraduate engineering student at the University of New South Wales where she helped to develop a sophisticated campus initiative that is now a decade old. After studying best practices in Europe and the United States, she took her expertise to Cambridge, Massachusetts, where she founded the Harvard Green Campus Initiative. Sharp's work, and Webb's, reflects a growing institutionalization of sustainability initiatives within the university.

Sharp sees two major impediments to making the university sustainable, one the flip side of the other. The first is "personal burnout" that campus leaders experience from a passion for change that is urgent but also, realistically, involves "a multi-decade journey."[2] Like Webb, she sees a potential that is so much greater than is being realized. The flip side of personal burnout is institutional inertia.

"The university is very hierarchical," she comments matter-of-factly, "and unless you somehow land in a position where you have a lot of power to begin with, it is very difficult to have the level of influence that you really do need ...."[3] Webb echoes this analysis: "It's the hierarchy of an institution. The reality is that we have a president and we have a board of governors. Is it looking at the way we can change those governance models to be more accommodating? But that is the governance model. How do we work within it?" Sharp's answer is that action has to be "strategic" to make the best use of the "small amount of power" one has. This situation applies at public universities like New South Wales and UVic or at a private one like Harvard where, in Sharp's phrase, the "fundamental organizational dynamics" are the same.

In fact, a lot more is at stake than physical changes. Writing about her early experiences at Harvard a few years ago, where only a handful of faculty were interested in her work, Sharp noted that universities promote a "myth of organizational rationality while facing the reality of organizational irrationality."[4] At the same time, like that of Webb, Sharp's long work has begun to pay off. She quickly rattles off Harvard's numerous achievements in 2004–2005: the sign-off by the University president on a set of sustainability principles, doubling the size of the Green Loan Fund to US$6 million, becoming the second-largest university purchaser of renewable energy in the United States with a dedicated fund to expand future renewable opportunities. Meanwhile, nine buildings are in the process of achieving environmental (LEED) certification. And, most importantly, Harvard is expanding core staff in the sustainability office to 13.[5]

Lagging behind Harvard, and playing catch-up, arch-competitor Yale University hired its first sustainability director in 2004, Julie Newman, a seven-year veteran of the Office of Sustainability at the University of New Hampshire. Yale has established campus-wide procedures for paper recycling and energy procurement, and the University is developing a strategy to reduce its greenhouse gas emissions in line with regional commitments. Newman's watchword too is "strategic" because "[we still] haven't got to the hard decisions yet." To reach Yale's potential, Newman's double challenge is to define "sustainability" broadly, yet build a substantive commitment to it. This entails the slow, plodding work of creating campuswide committees that can bring people together who will slowly alter the fabric of the University. So, "yes, there's support," she comments, but there's also a nervous hesitation evident in "a kind of risk analysis that's being done, that's unspoken."[6]

These three women (and sustainability coordinators are mostly women) represent the state-of-the-art at universities. Many of their innovations are path breaking. But is this situation — where one is always skirting the edge of burnout, pushing against an institutional bulwark with only a handful of helpers — the best that universities can aspire to? The story of university sustainability is certainly about getting more green buildings and teaching people about the benefits of demand management. But these are only the seeds of a revolution. For these seeds to take root and flower, we must address the character of the institutions in which these individuals work, structures of power-over-place that let certain things happen, but not others.

Nudging the iceberg

While Webb redirects compost and stormwater, more-visible activities continue to dominate the campus — high chain-link fences, bulldozers, construction trailers, cranes and building crews. Since the late 1990s, UVic has been experiencing a building boom, fuelled in one part by grants from the provincial government for the University to produce more doctors and engineers, and in another part by a near-doubling of tuition fees in recent years. One proposal would see UVic's first high-rise parkade. Meanwhile, at a behemoth such as the University of California system, over US$7 billion worth of new construction projects are in the pipeline.[7] High-profile environmental initiatives certainly provide good optics. But they could also, in Webb's words, remain in "the off-side" of the institution while a '50s ideology of growth without end persists — like a big-box retailer that imports clothing from sweat shops in Southeast Asia, but prominently adds windmills to power the lights in its parking lots and collects rainwater to flush its toilets.

Whether "greening the ivory tower"[8] is public relations or real progress will depend on who makes the decisions — and how. As the United Nations recently noted, issues of governance lie at the root of the world's environmental woes.[9] With university sustainability coordinators necessarily focused on the technical tasks at hand, and needing to be "strategic" every step of the way, a broader approach to governance is not yet on the agenda. Admittedly the challenge is a large one. Universities are big physical presences with hundreds

Building boom ...

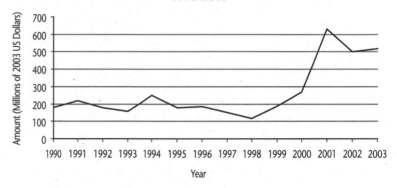

Harvard Annual Investments in Building Projects and Acquisitions: 1990-2003

Harvard University, adapted from the *Financial Report to the Board of Overseers of Harvard College*, Cambridge, MA: 2004, p. 21. Available at <http://vpf-web.harvard.edu/annualfinancial/pdfs/2003discussion.pdf>.

... but bigger benefits

The Harvard Green Campus Loan Fund lends interest-free dollars for campus projects that will serve to reduce greenhouse gas emissions. Projects currently have an average payback period of three years and an average return on investment of 33 percent. It is a win-win situation for everyone — the University saves money through lower operational costs, and the decrease in greenhouse gas emissions reduces Harvard's environmental impact. In addition, Harvard University President Summers has recently announced a new Green Building Loan Fund, which will be available to fund the cost difference between standard and high performance building design and technologies in building renovation and construction projects.

— Harvard Green Campus Initiative, New Green Building Loan Fund Announced by President Summers, *Harvard Green Campus Initiative Newsletter*, vol. 7, Spring 2005. Available at: <http://www.greencampus.harvard.edu/newsletter/>.

of buildings to maintain, thousands of classrooms to clean, hundreds of thousands of staff to pay, millions of students to register and billions of dollars in budgets to raise and balance. These places have to function. The goal, says Sharp, is "to hit that sweet spot of allowing for the organization to meet its daily functional requirements so that it can survive ... but also stretching its full capacity to innovate ...."[10] Or, as Webb sees it, you have to focus on "what makes good business sense" for the university, what can raise its profile and save money too.

Yet many university decisions that seem to be merely operational in nature are much more. For one thing, the economic calculus is not absolute — change the context, and what makes economic sense changes too. If the bus system works well, fewer people will need to own a car. And operational decisions have larger impacts that affect how all those who study, work or reside at the university live their lives. This shapes future values and behavior. What superficially may seem to be technical decisions begin to take on a *moral* character because they quietly condition all those affected by them. If parking is cheap and driving is made easy, while biking risks death on roads without bike lanes, and underfunded bus lines leave you stranded in the snow, four years of university "training" will encourage the new graduate-as-citizen to spend her first paycheck on a car, not a bus pass. And there is a subliminal civics lesson when these decisions are made somewhere else, by someone else, without any discussion about what's at stake. In this way, graduates can easily become inactive citizens and deferential consumers, products of a particular pedagogy of place.

Place + Space = Space + Place

What goes on in a place cannot be understood outside of the space relations that support that place anymore than the space relations can be understood independently of what goes on in particular places.

— David Harvey, "From Space to Place and Back Again: Reflections on the Condition of Postmodernity," *Mapping the Futures*, Jon Bird, Barry Curtis, Tim Putnam, George Robertson and Lisa Tickner, eds., London: Routledge, 1993, p. 15.

Clerics, engineers, bureaucrats

This is what the shadow curriculum teaches today. Every bit as much as Paris turned out good clerics, and Berlin good bridge builders, so Harvard and UVic turn out the 21st-century equivalent for the age of economism — well-trained producers and well-socialized consumers. This is Jacobs's concern about the Depression-inspired obsession with jobs that is still embedded in cultural memory, and that drives the university's self-definition as a credentializing institution.[11] At the same time, the galloping pace of economistic growth over the past 60 years has produced a scale and reach of organization that is all pervasive yet remote from personal influence. In the 1960s and 1970s, the university underwent a physical transformation from a stately, if elite, urban institution to a suburban, but mass, one. As it expanded in the 1980s, this institution outgrew its historic character as a self-regulating *collegium* to become a more fractured institution under the management of a swelling *administocracy* removed from collegial control.[12] In the 1990s it evolved even further into a fully-fledged higher education industry with an increasingly corporatist bent.

"Fort Book."

The University of Toronto's Robarts Library is an example of anti-social "brutalist" architecture. Replete with nicknames, including "The Turkey" and "The Bunker," it is one of the largest research libraries in North America and contains the bulk of the University's humanities and social sciences collection.

Photograph by Sascha Noyes, 2004.

The bureaucratic machine

Once it is fully established, bureaucracy is among those social structures that are the hardest to destroy. Bureaucracy is the means of carrying "community action" over into rationally ordered "societal action." Therefore, as an instrument for "societalizing" relations of power, bureaucracy has been and is a power instrument of the first order — for the one who controls the bureaucratic apparatus .... And where the bureaucratization of administration has been completely carried through, a form of power relation is established that is practically unshatterable .... More and more, the fate of the masses depends upon the steady and correct functioning of the increasingly bureaucratic organizations of private capitalism.

— Max Weber, in *From Max Weber: Essays in Sociology*, H.H. Gerth & C. Wright Mills, eds., London: Routledge & Kegan Paul, 1948, p. 228.

These changes speak to the centrist character of modern social organization rooted in hierarchical power and the long resource flows on which such hierarchy depends. An ever-present social tendency, centrist forces pervade all aspects of life and shape life in the process. The result is akin to what Foucault called "biopower," power that is so pervasive that it cannot be located anywhere but exists as a ubiquitous discipline internalized in our physical beings and identities. At the same time, centrism is embedded in numerous forms of organized political and economic activity across global space, from the corporate structure of General Motors and the professional monopoly of the American Medical Association, to the management of the local highway authority and the choices available at the neighborhood fast-food restaurant. It is manifest in the tiniest details of daily life, from the imported fish sticks in the cafeteria to the sea of parking spaces outside the office window. The momentum of centrist power fuels economic growth, social experience evolving as a side effect of this totalistic purpose. Taking control back from this structure of power, and redirecting the forces that underpin it, is what sustainability is all about.

Over recent centuries, centrist growth in the West has evolved complex systems that are managed by large, inaccessible organizations (whether they are of a public or private character) on which the whole of society depends. If the momentum of centrism is to be slowed, and even redirected, it will be essential to *open up these bureaucracies to more conscious, and collective, decisions.* The inherent inertia of these institutions explains why, as Sharp notes, change will be a multi-decade journey. Far from view, a complex administration determines who will supply the student cafeterias with colas and chips, who will design the spaces where people meet and discuss the day's headlines, who has access to what forms of transportation, how every shrub and pathway is chosen and laid and what will happen to the thousands of tons of waste and sewage that leave campus. It is into this sprawling structure that our sustainability coordinators have been catapulted, a structure that determines in precise detail the whole character of life of this place where generations of students learn to be citizens, or not.

To make this complex institution work, thousands of regulations (policies and procedures) exist to ensure that millions of administrative decisions occur daily in a smooth and efficient fashion. In such a complex bureaucratic system, the system's goals easily escape attention. So does its accountability, or lack thereof, for achieving them. This is the conundrum of Marcus Ford's economism. Even though it is beset by growing social and ecological crises, centrist growth is so pervasive that change is unthinkable. This is "how the world works"; one must be "realistic." To escape this conundrum, citizens must understand the character of this structured power just as much as they understand how transportation works, how buildings can be made more energy efficient or how we can rehabilitate degraded farmlands and farm knowledge.

By definition, bureaucratic institutions tend to be unaccountable, those who don't have power deferring to those who do, albeit with commentary through numerous "advisory committees." For example, despite the promising commitments of UVic's new *Campus Plan*, one neighbor complained at such an advisory meeting that it was all flutes and drums — high-sounding phrases about sustainability accompanied by the deep underlying beat of more development. There was a commitment to *consider* a "village core," but building sites that were actually proposed were still scattered everywhere. Automobile use

Public tension.

The University of Victoria's development plans provoke critical public response.

Times Colonist, Saanich News, and The Martlet.

should be limited, yet with no hard targets set for "transportation demand management," 2,300 more parking spaces were planned just in case. Sustainable building designs and green technologies were encouraged, but not mandated. A ten-year moratorium was placed on the development of several significant areas in the University's regionally significant forests and agricultural lands, during which time their future would be studied and today's protestors would graduate. Above all, the *Plan* explicitly stated that this was not a "regulatory" document.[13] These may be great ideas, but don't make them binding.

In this situation, the sustainability coordinator does the best she can. Meanwhile, faculty, staff and students are fragmented and act as individual consumers of bureaucratic power rather than as collective producers of community and place. Students work on student issues through their student associations, employees on staff issues through their unions and their collective agreements, and faculty concentrate on faculty interests through the faculty association. This institutional architecture — management from the top, fragmentation from below — is inherently conflictual and impedes the university's ability to work collectively. A decline in communal accountability accompanied the expansion of university administration in the 1980s and in the process increased the university's vulnerability to the infusion of

Hoping that greater size will lead to greater understanding.

Unfurling a huge banner in support of the preservation of a local woods, students highlight principles being demanded at Cornell but that would apply to every university that promotes its institutional commitment to sustainability.

Photograph by Garrett Meigs, 2005.

corporatist interests and values that followed. The weakness of communal values
is nowhere more apparent than with faculty members who as a collective entity
have enormous, but unused, power to motivate change. Instead, their work life is more
driven by external research funders, professional approbation and the allure of
conferences in exotic locations than by the
place of the university. Academics work as
part of a system of organizing, collecting
and disseminating knowledge that has no
physical domain.[14] This is particularly
acute with what we have called the *artificial sciences*. One finds there a dangerous
lack of interest in the social world in
which its practitioners move, or indeed
for the consequences of the knowledge
they generate.

Cold place.

With their local histories, traditions and communities, universities are places,
but in the contemporary world, they are non-places too. At the university, the
researcher delivers a lecture on the impacts of CO_2 emissions on the global climate, then drives to the airport for the flight to the conference on atmospheric
science. The school of health launches a study of teenager nutrition, while the
cafeteria downstairs fast-fries chicken wings (from a thousand miles away) en route
to a student's paper plate. At UVic the vending machines serve up bottled water
to consumers while "magic" springs lie dormant beneath the pavement outside.
The staff in Food Services are unconnected to the century-long agricultural richness that lies buried in the landscape beyond the loading dock. Universities pay
scant attention to the "ecology of everyday life,"[15] their mission being to process

students credentialed for the job but not educated about the world. As David Orr wrote many years ago, the product of a university degree is a population trained in hypocrisy.

> Students learn that it is sufficient only to learn about injustice and ecological deterioration without having to do much about them, which is to say, the lesson of hypocrisy. They hear that the vital signs of the planet are in decline without learning to question the de facto energy, food, materials and waste policies of the very institution that presumes to induct them into responsible adulthood. Four years of consciousness-raising proceeds without connection to those remedies close at hand.[16]

In fact, countless opportunities exist for the university to respond to these top-down spatial forces were it conscious of these opportunities and of their value. In responding, the university would dramatically expand its mission and its relevance. In the process, it would cease being an institutionalized barrier to collective place-making and become its champion. And it could do so on a world-changing scale.

Warm place.

To invigorate this collective potential, one must create a new political mission and a new rationality for this historic institution. Applying the ideas of the renowned French political theorist and education activist Pierre Bourdieu, one must consider how the university's own "field of power" might develop apart from an embeddedness in a "dominant field of power."[17] Which returns us to the

Enlightened rationality

For global sustainability on a finite planet, education should be oriented toward the life-sustaining values needed to create a society founded on mutual respect, spiritual fulfillment, a cultivated compassion for all others and a sense of participating consciousness with nature. Instead of a cold, hard, alienating enlightenment rationality, we need an enlightened rationality that both celebrates the full potential of human beings and acknowledges our full organic engagement with the natural world.

— William Rees, "Impeding Sustainability? The Ecological Footprint of Higher Education," *Planning for Higher Education*, vol. 31, no. 3, March–May, 2003, p. 95.

special character of the university and the crux of its opportunity for reinvigorating the "territorial" forms of organization discussed in earlier chapters. With the massive growth in the scale and reach of complex systems, from Exxon and the Internal Revenue Service, to Mexico City and the World Trade Organization, our diverse rationalities have become a single rationality, with a single goal of progress-as-growth. The modern university is enmeshed in this universalist thinking. As Michel Foucault explained, with the Age of Reason centuries ago, "We see the emergence of something like a sort of great uniform apparatus of knowledges." Within this apparatus, the university has been charged with selecting legitimate from "wild" knowledge and, with the assistance of government, to centralize such knowledge.[18] The pursuit of this one knowledge is now the cultural Holy Grail of

A reasonable course of re-action

Were we governed by reason, we would be on the barricades today, dragging the drivers of Range Rovers and Nissan Patrols out of their seats, occupying and shutting down the coal-burning power stations, bursting in upon the Blairs' retreat from reality in Barbados and demanding a reversal of economic life as dramatic as the one we bore when we went to war with Hitler. Instead, we whine about the heat and thumb through the brochures for holidays in Iceland. The future has been laid out before us, but the deep eye with which we place ourselves on Earth will not see it.

— George Monbiot, "With Eyes Wide Shut: Climate Change Threatens the Future of Humanity, But We Refuse to Respond Rationally," *The Guardian*, London: Guardian Newspapers, August 12, 2003. Available at <http://www.guardian.co.uk/>.

progress. Not even the university asks these questions about ultimate ends, instead pursuing more limited institutional ambitions. From the board of governors in the senate chambers, to the cost-calculating purchasing agent in the basement, a limited "organizational rationality" is the beginning and end of the conversation. As the momentum and the crises wash over us, democracy drifts in bureaucracy's wake.

The president and the groundskeeper

The underlying task of the sustainability coordinator is to address this lack of accountability by embedding new processes and procedures that will allow a new organizational rationality to take shape. In so doing, she confronts many bureaucratic tendencies to move in the opposite direction — of operational staff to do what is tried and true, of managers to "maintain flexibility" against imposed constraints in operational decision making, and of administrators to keep control over wild-eyed entrepreneurs and enthusiastic true believers. And within the dominant field of power, these compulsions are understandable. Facing complex challenges of budgets and growth, academic standards and institutional competition, and a diverse constituency of staff and students, faculty and funders, administrators want the freedom to manage these challenges in the best interests of the university. But where are the best interests of the 21st century university to be found? How is one to know? And who is to decide?

These questions cannot be answered in the abstract. At Harvard, Sharp points to an "institutional disconnect" between "the faculty who are engaged in the teaching and research mission of the institution, and the staff that keep the campuses running, who keep the lights working, and the wastes going away .... [T]here needs to be a new bridging between those constituencies."[19] Yet, again, why should there be? And how? Faculty are an established elite — well rewarded and with status, trained in an allegiance to a discipline, socialized into a department. And protected by the sinecures of academic freedom and tenure. These perks are an ancient inheritance with multiple benefits, especially for the free-thinking, even dissident, scholars whose activities challenge the university. But its benefits accrue most directly to the more numerous and well-rewarded artificial scientists who are not expected to question the new drugs and nanotech patents they produce. Their work is important in justifying the university's productivist value to state and corporate funders. Meanwhile, says Sharp, "The faculty will go all the way to China to trial a new combustion engine for buses; why don't you just try it in your own backyard?" Because the status and the interest and the rewards are elsewhere. To be invited to jet to China to do one's work means one *must* be important. Meanwhile the staff who keep the institution going are used but not seen, as invisible as the furniture in the common room. And the surrounding environment is but the space through which one travels from the office to the airport.

Despite the seeming power of the bureaucracy, individual staff members are largely voiceless in shaping the university's direction. The structure dominates. Yet staff are also the "experiential learners" who can bring innovation to daily life. Notes Sharp, "The physical campus is the hard-wired identity of the university [that] crystallizes the core habits of the institution [and] pretty much locks us into a set of habits around resource consumption and waste production ...." Yet operational managers are typically risk averse, subject to criticism if anything goes wrong and, therefore, resistant to change. Where a change agent is located is crucial. Although entrenched within facilities management, Newman's and Webb's goals are to maximize their abilities to connect across the campus. Again, as Sharp comments, if such agents are to be effective, "They have to have university-wide access to engage in open conversation with people, open idea development, and they have to not be overly constrained by hierarchy bearing down on them and requiring them to seek approval every time."[20] At the same time, this need for careful constituency-building within the bureaucracy demands caution in cooperating with the strongest agents of external change — students, critics, activists — whose idealistic demands from the outside can unsettle tentative support and retard the slow progress made on the inside. The result is an inherent incrementalism that acts as a constant brake on the potential for entrepreneurial initiative, an incrementalism built into the bureaucratic nature of the modern university.

health + well-being	community	knowledge	governance	economy + wealth
P33	P65	P113	P153	P177

"More than a table of contents"

The Concordia Campus Sustainability Assessment (2003) was completed by the student-led Sustainable Campus Project through a multi-stakeholder approach that used a framework adapted from one developed by a UVic graduate. This framework has been a popular focal point for student activists trying to educate their university communities about sustainable practices. The Concordia report was ranked secound of 1,200 entries in a survey of assessments compiled at Western Michigan University.

For full text, see http://sustainability.concordia.ca/ assessment/2006/php.

Another sustainability specialist is Matthew St. Clair, who works on energy and green buildings (and much else besides) at the University of California. As a graduate student at Berkeley, he worked with Greenpeace in an energy campaign that led to UC's standard-setting policies. Now working in the Office of the President in the University of California system, St. Clair uses Webb's terminology as his primary goal, to "institutionalize sustainability" on the campuses so that progress does not depend on internal personnel or external student activism.[21] His chosen route has been to build formalized advisory processes, "chancellor-level sustainability committees" on every campus. His realm is a vast one in a system with ten campuses, five medical centers and three national laboratories. To oversee this empire, the Office of the President maintains a staff of 1,800. To St. Clair, the potential benefits of moving this monolith are legion — inculcating a new culture in the University, sustaining a new social movement that had been so effective in mobilizing change in the past and (in his special area) actually having a substantive impact on the energy market. St. Clair is also seeing success. Green building, he says, is now "part of the thought process, the decision-making process for every new building. That's happened. There are 73 buildings that are being built as green buildings that would not have been otherwise ...."[22] And with their purchase of green energy, the UC and California State systems are now the eighth-largest institutional purchasers of such energy in the country.[23]

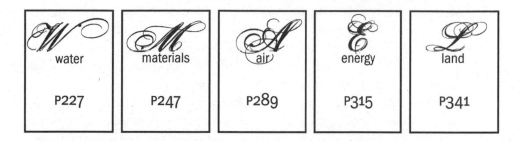

Braking for change?

These coast-to-coast achievements speak not just to what now exists or is likely, but even more to what is possible. While different campuses commit to specific initiatives to greater and lesser degrees, these changes still do not reflect either a *comprehensive vision* of sustainability or a *planning process* to make it happen. As one academic study noted in 2002, a conflict continues to exist "between the revolutionary changes called for by leaders in the sustainability in higher education movement and the incremental changes which typically occur in colleges and universities."[24] As we have seen, the core challenge is to redefine what is "rational" for these institutions at a time of historic crisis and opportunity. But to face this challenge we need structures that can allow the university to address big-picture collective ends. These are simply not on the agendas of decision makers whose focus remains on the specifics of raising more money, attracting the next research center and increasing the media profile. Somewhere some environmental values may find their way into operations to the extent that they make short-term economic sense and can be used to enhance the image.

And so the issue comes down to a new vision of the future — and of the institutional designs that might allow us to create that vision. By default, the chosen design is one of a lowly official in a small boat trying to nudge a big bureaucratic iceberg, all the while having to ease off the throttle for fear of overturning. At the university, the design sets Webb's "off-side" changes along an unaltered growth trajectory. As system theorists are wont to point out, system design determines system outcomes. To change the outcomes, one needs to alter system dynamics. And both require a new vision. There could be a different approach where one followed incremental changes — but toward a radically different outcome. This would be an explicit strategy of *incremental radicalism* where a university piles small changes on small changes, but explicitly geared to leveraging structural innovations toward systemic sustainability. To allow this to occur, system design must be reshaped dramatically. Put simply, sustainable systems will no longer function in the traditional bureaucratic mold, providing for the *linear* delivery of preordained outcomes in a system whose goals are beyond reconsideration. Instead, sustainable systems will enshrine *dialectical* processes that can continuously uncover, challenge and refashion outdated assumptions that lead to destructive goals and results, and that can then create new directions.

A dialectical approach requires a willingness to live with challenge and contradiction. In contrast, bureaucratic decision making discriminates between incremental means that are allowable and radical ends that are not. This is the old tension between those inside the tent and those on the outside, between the office workers and the tree-sitters, between the realists and dreamers. For bureaucratic managers, this tension is a source of discomfort to be minimized so as to get on with business. This tension is, however, irresolvable, inherent to social organization itself, to the ever-changing pulls between the seeming opposites of structured power and insurgent interests. An attention to the dialectic of centrist and territorial structures is informative by helping to reveal new practical mechanisms that might challenge the overwhelming dominance of centrism and redirect it through territorial innovations. Neither to be ignored nor overcome, the dialectic should be embraced as a fundamental principle of dynamic social organization. It is certainly the underlying principle of democracy. It is, in theory at least, also a principle of competitive markets. Its potential is, however, vastly neglected and should be embraced by all who are interested in ensuring that social power is, at whatever level and in whatever form, responsive to social needs.

Consider again the sustainability coordinator. She is inside the tent of power, but internally there are differences. For example, someone who is locked into a rigid bureaucratic ladder within a division of facilities management or operations is subject to vetoes from above by those who act as *innovation blockers*. Such blockages exist either because of the lack of exercise of greater authority from within the structure (e.g., lack of leadership from the president or other senior administrators) or because of the lack of interest or power by those outside the bureaucracy, say corporate funders or student protesters. To Newman, the goal is to "avoid blockages." But what a difference an innovative design can make. Unlike the top-down structure that exists at most universities (like UVic), Sharp's position at Harvard was intentionally established as a free-floater to allow her to be an *innovation enabler*. This was achieved by giving her an open mandate and making her accountable to both faculty and facilities management. The position effectively institutionalizes a constructive tension into the job. Says Sharp, "[The] reason why I took this job was because the governance structure itself was very informal and unevolved" — thus providing her with an "enormous amount of autonomy."[25] She was, in other words, free to "build new relationships" within the organization, to rebuild from within. To allow this to happen is, in turn, a sign of the confidence and sophistication of a university's leaders.

The nature of these internal relationships is now a hot topic in the broader higher education literature. On the one hand are those who address structural issues; on the other are those who are more concerned with relationships and communications.[26] As we can see, the two are mutually enforcing — interactive structures allow new relationships to evolve, linear

Dialogue from the treetops.
This banner was created by University of Victoria students during the tree-sit campaign to save Cunningham Woods. Playing on the University motto "Challenge Minds, Change Worlds," the students campaigned that spring for a new approach to both campus planning and University funding.

Photograph by Kelly Bannister, 2003.

Forces of reconstruction

The model of the hierarchical, exclusive ... university that flourished for several hundred years is in decline. While this model successfully resisted many past challenges and assaults, the present age of deconstructive and reconstructive forces flowing around and through it are historically unprecedented. These forces are undermining the "classical" university and will reshape it in unpredictable ways.

— R.A. Slaughter, "Universities as Institutions of Foresight," *Journal of Future Studies*, vol. 1, no. 3, November, 1998, p. 51.

ones do not. One thing is certain: the dynamics created by different system designs can become transformative and thus ratchet up the institution's creativity, or they can freeze it. Sharp's experience is again illustrative where, "at some point that incremental foundation building seems to situate you to then take great leaps forward." You need, she says, to set up the institution so that it "has the wherewithal to innovate in leaps and bounds." The greater one's power is within the system the greater also is one's ability to work with power-holders outside the system. In the process, one can build bridges to them, not to co-opt the other side but to work with the creative tension of the inside/outside dialectic.

But to liberate this creativity, we can do better.

active place

O N A CLEAR SPRING MORNING IN 2005, 200 delegates from around the world gathered in historic surroundings to launch the United Nations decade of "education for sustainable development." This designation had been proclaimed only a few months earlier, and enthusiasm was high for what might be accomplished in the years ahead. The venue was perfectly suited to the providential event: the Austrian city of Graz, a designated UNESCO World Heritage Site where the sidewalks are filled with pedestrians, the trams glide quietly along main streets and everywhere medieval buildings stand as testament to local care and pride. The delegates themselves gathered in the main building of the Karl Franzens University of Graz under the gilt murals and high, arched ceilings of the Aula conference room. For those committed to Leith Sharp's "multi-decade journey," this was an important occasion.

Central Graz.

Photograph by Leithen M'Gonigle, 2005.

161

Despite the old-world venue, it was to the United States that delegates turned for guidance. Introducing keynote speaker Julie Newman, one European representative noted that this foreigner held a position only yet dreamt of in their universities, that of sustainability coordinator. But Newman's message was a sanguine one. Prior to coming to Graz, she had conducted a review of campuses like Harvard, Tufts, Stanford, Carnegie Mellon and Brown that were known to be leaders in sustainability and were of a similar size to many European universities. Each of these institutions "has developed an institutionally specific 'sustainability strategy and vision,'" she informed the delegates, but "none of these universities has instituted a comprehensive sustainability strategy."[1] Newman's assessment confirmed the continuing inertia that was evident in an earlier study of sustainability programs at four other American universities. That review found that each university had focused on different objectives (some on operations, others on curricula) but all with indeterminate outcomes. Overall results were gradual, still "in their very early development states — too early, in fact, to determine if they have been successful .... "[2] At the start of the new decade, it was sobering that this was the example to which Europeans aspired.

Worldwide, universities face similar obstacles to sustainability, both in how universities are designed — the processes for making decisions — and in what they will do — their substantive visions of sustainability. Universities certainly need sustainability coordinators within their bureaucracies. But they need more, not just green buildings and more efficient transportation systems, but Newman's "comprehensive sustainability strategy" for their campuses, cities and regions. Universities everywhere lack both. This is the common need today — a broader mission for universities at a time of real planetary breakdown *and* strategies to break out of the bureaucratic cage that holds them back.

Despite the limited institutional progress within European universities, isolated initiatives are flourishing throughout the region and in locally responsive ways. In Ukraine, for example, a group of university professors founded the International Society of Doctors for the Environment with the explicit strategy of bringing academia into civil society to foster a permanent process of national medical-ecological education and recovery.[3] These "green doctors" work directly on the consequences of the long-term chemical and nuclear contamination left from the Soviet period. Thousands of radiation victims remain from the Chernobyl accident. In Venice a different approach is being taken by the Ca' Foscari University through its Fondazione Eni Enrico Matteri (FEEM), a non-profit research institution to promote new management and governance systems for the Mediterranean.[4] In Hamburg a huge technology transfer agency, TuTech Innovation, opened in January 2005 to bring sustainability initiatives from the universities into the broader world.[5] One such initiative, URBAL, aims to redress structural imbalances in urban-rural (urbal) relations. Meanwhile, a new student group, the Swiss-based oikos International, works with business schools in Europe to bring sustainability into a more entrepreneurial curriculum. Oikos cosponsored the Graz gathering.

The optimism that beckons with these specific projects competes with a broader worry, that of the increasing bureaucratic control being exerted over Europe's universities. Reflective of the nation-building stage explained in Ford's book, *Beyond the Modern University*, a technocratic tradition has long shaped continental European universities as direct conduits to the state managerial elite. Emanating partly from the Continent's growing economic integration, many national governments have begun to assert a more direct role in university management. For example, a number of countries — Austria, Britain, the Netherlands and some Scandinavian countries — have instituted "performance agreements" with individual universities that tie future state funding to the university's meeting agreed-upon production targets, often accompanied by state-appointed control of the university's board of governors. Insofar as national governments remain committed to a paradigm of unsustainable growth — whether it's Boeing or Airbus, Ford or Daimler-Benz — these externally imposed agreements are problematic. Some students at Graz complained that these performance agreements have already reduced dialogue and debate with the university administration and marginalized activist sustainability initiatives. Meanwhile, in keeping with a continuing economism, Volkswagen in Germany has started its own private university.[6]

At the same time, many speakers in Graz praised European Union initiatives for their success in coordinating universities to advance Continental sustainability. At the ministerial level, the European commitment dates back to the so-called Bologna Process inaugurated in 1997 and, even earlier, to the Copernicus Charter (1993) that launched a virtual European-wide Copernicus "Campus." The Campus now boasts an organizational membership of over 330 universities in 38 countries.[7] Undoubtedly, discussion of sustainability — however defined — has achieved higher political prominence in Europe than it has in North America. But what the discussion implies for basic changes is unclear given Europe and North America's shared economistic goals.

To motivate change directly, from the bottom up, the incipient campus sustainability movement faces a two-sided challenge — to redirect decision making through new institutional arrangements at the university, and to create a new vision for those institutions. No roadmap exists that can tell us how to shift the "system dynamics" at universities to enable big changes that can evolve incrementally, yet quickly. The challenge of the planetary university comes down to this: creating realistic reforms that produce transformative, but evolutionary, change. For proposals to be meaningful, they must not be add-ons but *integral* to the university in its institutional processes and its substantive actions. Changes that step back from taking an integral approach are so marginal as to be almost irrelevant to the institutional needs. This

21ˢᵗ century governance

It is simply unrealistic to expect that the governance mechanisms developed decades or even centuries ago can serve well either the contemporary university or our society more broadly. It seems clear that the university of the 21ˢᵗ century will require new models of governance and leadership capable of responding to the changing needs and emerging challenges of our society and its educational institutions.

— James J. Duderstat, "Governance and Leadership," *A University for the 21ˢᵗ Century*, Ann Arbor: University of Michigan Press, 2000, p. 257.

is especially so because the reasons for hesitation are themselves at the core of unsustainability.

A modest proposal: Process

Where, when and how such an imaginative transformation will take hold is an open question. It already exists in varying degrees, but nowhere at a comprehensive level. However, in looking back at UVic's tree-sit and the popular mobilization that led to the University's new *Campus Plan*, it is now clear that the University was presented with an opportunity, the global significance of which was not appreciated at the time. In 2003, in response to the activist demand for a more cooperative approach to campus planning, the University struck a high-level task force to review its planning structure. UVic already had a sustainability coordinator, and in looking beyond that position, the University was moving to the forefront of the global movement.

The commission was chaired by Marsha Hanen, a philosopher and former president of the University of Winnipeg. At the time, Hanen was president of a non-profit foundation dedicated to ethics in leadership. A year after her report had been submitted, Hanen recalled that at the time she "had a naïve view about what the opportunity might be. I didn't have a sense of the depth of what one might look at."[8] Hanen was excited about the potential for the University to move beyond the weak efforts of other universities to achieve interdisciplinarity. Faculty will tell you, says Hanen, that what happens out there in the campus "doesn't matter for what I want to do. I'm in my lab, and what I want to do is my research." Instead of disciplinary integration, Hanen sees ever-greater fragmentation in these large bureaucracies, reflecting the "relatively new" situation where universities have developed "this huge infrastructure. There was a point when Harvard had three presidents in a hundred years."

After eight months of consultations, Hanen's committee recommended a wholesale revision of UVic's planning structure and process, one that reached far beyond the sustainability coordinator that is still the state of the art in North America and the ideal for Europeans. One proposal was to create an overarching "office of integrated planning and sustainability" that could bring the academic curriculum together with groundskeeping, the physicist with the philosopher, and imaginative planning with operational practicality. Another was to create more elected positions in more-inclusive and transparent planning bodies, a process that could bring public dialogue into private discussions. By elevating consensus over conflict, it might even simplify bureaucratic management in the process. At the same time, Hanen notes that there's "not a single model of governance that's the best one."

To enhance the university's civic mission, Hanen believes that new structures must overcome the fractured, adversarial nature of the university. She points especially to the separation of the administration from other segments of the university, including faculty and the neighboring community. With its unionized staff, for example, "there's no worse time in a university than when contract talks are going on .... But it's a big mistake to see things as adversarial." Given these established structures, and the pressures of funding, this is difficult. Says Hanen, "Almost everything pushes you in the other direction." How, one might ask, can one create structures that allow collaborative relations that can elicit the "common good"?

One place where a community responsibility has begun to reshape the structure of the university is at Yale. As we have seen, the University is the largest employer in New Haven — its payroll was over US$900 million in 2004,[9] and it is the city's largest property taxpayer. Out of a concern to make the University more of an active social participant in the economic development of that rather depressed city, Yale created a new Office for New Haven and State Affairs, represented in the administration by its own Vice-President. Michael Morand, a former city councilor in New Haven, now occupies this position. His staff of 16 addresses four elements in the community: economic development, neighborhoods (including property management and with important focus on the public school system), the downtown and communications. Morand is particularly enthusiastic about the University's "community investment program" that embodies his belief that to have a "thriving university, you need a healthy community."[10] Through his office, for example, the University has assisted 676 employees to become homeowners in New Haven, over half of whom come from minority communities.[11]

Morand emphasizes the importance of having this office at the vice-presidential level, where he is one of five such officials: "[It] makes a huge difference, as no decision is taken at the University without having that impact assessed by my office …. And everyone gets it; everyone understands the importance of this office." Indeed, a wide range of faculty is involved in carrying out the work, from the Law School's community clinics to the involvement of the School of Architecture in neighborhood projects, to Nursing and Medicine in community health, with similar projects in other professional schools.

Yale's initiative could be adapted to move beyond the Hanen proposal with, for example, a Vice President for Planning, Innovation and Sustainability. A designated VP seems like a marginal proposal, but if properly structured, it could elevate sustainability within the University in a systemic fashion. It would certainly overcome the situation that prevails at most campuses, such as at Marcus Ford's Northern Arizona State. Ford laughingly proclaims that on its new sustainability committee, "No one has read my book," while for the senior

Portal to possibilities.

To implement sustainability planning, an authoritative planning body (left side of diagram) would set direction for the internal operations of the Vice President's office, including a full Sustainability Office. This Office would, in turn, infuse sustainability initiatives throughout all components of the university (right side of diagram). An independent secretariat would make state-of-the-art information from across the globe available to all members of the university.

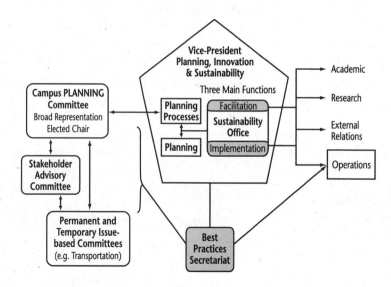

POLIS Project on Ecological Governance, *Planning for a Change: Innovation and Sustainability for the 21ˢᵗ Century at the University of Victoria*, Victoria: University of Victoria, October 2003, p. 22.

administrator, "It is just another committee; we schedule it around her schedule which is terribly full, and even still she misses about half the sessions."[12] Or as Julie Newman explains, if her position were at the level of the VP for New Haven and State Affairs, she would be more able to set the agenda, to be part of an "integrated commitment like it is to New Haven. That's the difference between our levels."[13]

However much this proposal would advance beyond the status quo in North America and the dreams in Europe, it would be transformative only if the VP were made accountable to a broadly participatory planning body. Were this body given real decision-making authority to direct the vice-president's actions, a seemingly modest change would convert the position from that of a top-down conduit of authority to that of an institutional facilitator of bottom-up power. Where the decisions of the planning body/VP were also subject to the override of the university president, the safeguard would exist in a mutual veto. The result would be transformative because such an office would infuse a strong territorial voice into the heart of university decision making, allowing a creative external/internal tension to challenge the linear power structure that currently dominates university planning. Such a procedural reorientation (in some such "strong" form) provides an essential criterion of legitimacy for the planetary university.

This type of proposal is simple and doable even though it is far from where we are today and still far from where we ultimately have to go. But its impact would be more than incremental because it is a first step to creating the new dynamics for systemic change. Such proposals should be at the top of the agenda of every university, a necessary first step in creating a planetary university.

More than a modest proposal: Vision

For a university to contemplate such a procedural change, it must be motivated by a larger substantive vision. Today sustainability coordinators make operations more efficient, marginally constraining damage to the environment and perhaps saving money in the process. This provides a modicum of incentive for university administrators, augmented by the good PR that such work brings to the institution.

Something far grander motivates the campus sustainability movement, however. This grander vision must be brought into the university mainstream.

The university, writes geographer Susan Roberts, is "one of the strangest institutions"[14] around, a unique hybrid with diverse assets unequalled by any other Western institution. A corporation run by a board with a president as its chief executive officer, it is also a bureaucracy modeled on late 19th-century principles of public administration. It houses a vast diversity of considered expertise in its departments, faculties and research centers (in business lingo, a unique "cluster"), as well as the world's most abundant store of youthful expectation and energy in its students. It has a large land base, often the largest in the city or region. It has huge financial assets and a broad base of income. It is at the center of a city and region's cultural and economic life. It is a huge industry in its own right. It trains all the other major industries of modernity. It is administered internally, but not by professional managers. It is still relatively independent, with an open political culture. As geographer Keith Bassett describes it, it is a "proto-public sphere."[15] Its products are diverse — from research patents to skilled workers to educated citizens — and their value is impossible to quantify. It is explicitly oriented to creating social value. Its buildings and campuses are not just real estate. It embodies all this in just one local *place*. But it also embodies this in hundreds, no thousands, of places across the planet.

Yale's 6-step program

1. Create an institutional strategy and vision
2. Continue to engage the ongoing grassroots efforts of students, staff and faculty
3. Develop a governance/decision-making structure that engages a broad-based coalition
4. Develop a management structure that outlines a clear system of policy development
5. Institutionalize results, (i.e., Ad hoc committees/Director projects/ACEM grants)
6. Establish a sustainability metrics to measure progress

— Julie Newman, "The Onset of Creating a Model Sustainable Institution: A Case Study Analysis of Yale University, *Proceedings: Committing Universities to Sustainable Development*, Graz, Austria: Conference organized by Graz University as part of the UN Decade of Education for Sustainable Development, April 20–23, 2005, p. 27.

Like other modern institutions, the contemporary university grew out of human society's greatest ever wealth-generating era. However, if the processes that created this wealth cannot be sustained in the future, this situation presents the campus sustainability movement with its own unique opportunity. Government policies and corporate activities have not been successful in challenging or redirecting unsustainable process at the macro level at which they operate; quite the contrary, across whole industries and societies, they keep making things worse. Given the gridlock that exists at that level, the challenge is for the university sustainability movement to develop new strategies that allow universities to lead change at a micro level without waiting for some big government or some mega-corporation. Unlike the single-interest pursuits of the corporation or the fragmented, but large-scale, political responsibilities of governments, a specific university could be broad in its vision, yet less constrained in its actions because of its local nature. It could foster a new course of social evolution that is directed specifically at micro-level transformations, but with macro-level implications. To achieve this, we propose a new strategy of what we call *comprehensive local innovation*. It happens where the university draws a porous boundary around itself and, within that area, *does everything differently*.

The scope: Comprehensive

Doing "everything" is, of course, not practical — at least not yet. But it is possible to adopt a comprehensive mandate, to be all-inclusive in one's quest for sustainability — addressing what is taught in engineering and medicine, in physics and economics as well as what is done in the shadow curriculum of institutional operations. As environmental sustainability also entails social sustainability, the range of topics is almost limitless — from energy efficiency to community development, from food security to holistic health. So too is the university's daily fare of practices — from recycling waste to pension fund investment, from staff relations to student internships. Such innovation is motivated by growing human and social awareness — by social "science." It will also inspire and draw on practical solutions emanating from the natural and applied sciences and from the professions. And it will be active.

To be this comprehensive would draw on the university in ways no other modern institution could match. Although it would not mean an enforced conformity to a new ideology, a comprehensive approach entails a new willingness to discuss and debate the possibilities for the university at this historical juncture — its mission and structures, the roles of the disciplines, the nature of the curriculum and the new possibilities for research and practice in every field. To challenge, and perhaps to reinvent, the 21st century university and all who pass through it would open to examination the destructive disciplinary fragmentation left from the modernist era that the 20th century university has internalized and still promotes. It would as well prize the *active theory* of those self-critically engaged in making social change, consciously moving the academy beyond its overarching allegiance to the *passive theory* of the disinterested academic absorbed in the printed text.

Take, for example, law, the professional faculty in which the authors' research center is situated. A student today can graduate with a law degree and go into practice without ever considering the law's social role in this age of economism, let alone engaging in changing it. Focused on wills and real estate, property and securities, the role of *law* itself escapes attention. Yet law has long helped constitute the centrist institutions that define modernity: the historic "enclosure of the commons" that began throughout Europe in the 1400s; the global displacement of indigenous peoples since the 1500s and the accompanying colonization of resource-rich continents; the creation of the state system with its continual accretion of authority to a legally constituted and exclusive sovereign power; the development of the private corporation in the 1800s and the rise of public bureaucracies over the past century; and the recent assertion of global trade rules as a de facto global "constitution."[16] Legal regulation is central to the growth of a "geography of consumption"[17] including suburbs, shopping malls, TV and an entire landscape shaped by what one political economist calls "consumer spending as state project."[18] What might a more comprehensive view of law look like today, and what might it portend for a more sustainable and equitable trajectory for the future?

Sustainability requires changes that are both fundamental (because the sustainability crisis is a historic crisis of modernity) and realistic (because solutions must actually happen). In the law school, specific legal innovations await development in every area considered in this book, from new tax structures that discourage resource use to municipal bylaws that encourage densification and green building.[19] Systemic legal reforms could also address commons-based forms of ownership that emanate from local needs, such as the sustainable lumber co-operative that Middlebury College helped create in Vermont to supply wood products for its new construction. At UVic, new commons regimes await creation for the development of diverse use (usufructuary) rights over potentially productive university and municipal lands. The list goes on — from more facilitative laws for community reinvestment to less-restrictive accreditation of health practitioners to new models of worker participation in large institutions. These initiatives should lead to new forms of community self-regulation that were less dependent on formal bureaucratic processes or remote centers of power. Indigenous peoples are attempting just such self-regulation worldwide, as is the broad movement for community-based alternatives. Building on the importance of local sustainability as a basis for planetary development, constitutional lawyers might even address models that could take modernity past the central state and the megacorporation with the creation of legal networks of city-states and bioregions.

Law is but one discipline with so much to gain by seeing beyond the modernist assumptions of locked-in institutional unsustainability. Over its long history, the university has changed dramatically with radical shifts in perspective — from religious to secular, from statist to corporatist. As the university's social context changes — better still, where the university changes that context — its *truth* will change. To engage explicitly at this level would certainly be educational; it would also be liberating. Reminiscent of the demands of the students in Paris in 1968, the first new building of the 21st century university should perhaps be a designated dialogue center to talk about these things! Such dialogue could begin to resituate the natural in the philosophical sciences and reintegrate applied knowledges with theoretical enquiries. Through enhanced dialogue, the university would better bridge popular with academic cultures, insurgent (or complementary) knowledges with the dominant (professional) discourses. The last place that should be afraid of such dialogue and experimentation is the university. Or what's it for?

Let us be very clear here. *Only* through such reconsiderations will we begin to address the deeper roots of unsustainability. Today those natural and applied sciences that are so useful to power — from engineering to chemistry, genetics to medicine — are shaped in certain directions, well rewarded if they stay on

Creating demand

Middlebury College championed the establishment and rapid growth of a certified wood industry in Vermont. Over the past five years, Middlebury has created demand by using nearly 200,000 board feet (bf) of green certified wood (both from the College's own land as well as family-owned forests in the state) in campus construction projects.

— Campus Consortium for Environmental Excellence, "Construction: Using Green Certified Wood, Middlebury," *Best Management Practices for Colleges and Universities*, New England, MA: United States Environmental Protection Agency, April 2003, p. 1. Available at: <www.epa.gov/ne/assistance/univ/pdfs/bmps/ MiddleburyCertifiedWood.pdf>.

The Great Hall in Middlebury College's Bicentennial Hall. The Great Hall in a new state-of-the-art research facility at Middlebury College was paneled with red oak that was supplied through Middlebury's partnership with Vermont Family Forests.

Photograph © Jeff Goldberg/Esto, design by Payette Associates.

track, and protected so long as they do reconsider their foundations. By reassessing our inherited knowledges as part of a project of collective survival, we will be able to address the existential divide that presently enshrines certain ways of knowing in our social being while suppressing those others that Foucault called "subjugated knowledges." In the process of a deepened enquiry, new frontiers will open up that will be more physically sustainable, and intellectually more fulfilling as well. Above all, a broadened social practice will lay the groundwork for a new ethic of global sustainability, one that can advance our intellectual allegiance beyond *rationality* to *consciousness*, our personal allegiance beyond consumption to awareness, and our social world beyond the autonomous self to the relational being.[20]

The place: Local

Second is the commitment to the *local*. This is perhaps the most difficult and important aspect of the comprehensive local innovation (CLI) strategy because it demands a paradigmatic understanding of the value of place beyond its function as a space in which to learn.[21] In responding to ecological crisis, people have long been told to "think globally, act locally." But to be taken seriously, strategies for political and economic reform have had a macro focus, making change dependent on remote state and federal institutions, multinational corporations or international treaties. Meanwhile, local action means individual consumers turning down the thermostat or underfunded municipalities struggling to keep the buses running. At the university, to be local is to be insignificant, producing a self-fulfilling loop of local inaction. A historical perspective of the University's local place is nonexistent in UVic's collective consciousness. But only when we stop long enough to *look down* might the place itself achieve a presence, an importance, that could justify some investment in it. To counter this "dis-placement," the future of a planetary university will be realized only in conjunction with that university's reconnection with its placed past.

Since the higher education boom of the 1960s, academic knowledge has been increasingly fragmented, symbolized in the thousands of specialized journals read by only handfuls of experts and specialists. This produces diverse knowledges but not a collective conversation to draw on these knowledges for social needs. A place-based strategy would redress this situation by actively drawing on this knowledge to establish precedents or models at the local level that might seem to be of only micro significance but, by their nature, would effectively spread outward globally. One interesting and unique effect would be to bring home the expertise now sequestered away in the library and put it into the service of a collective consideration as to what can be done right there and, by extension, elsewhere. And doing it, this would represent a historic reversal with written forms of expertise now being translated back into oral ones. In the process, abstract disciplinary barriers would give way to new languages and discussions, and new cooperative values and actions. Thus might Jacobs's looming Dark Age be headed off with the revitalization of territorial memory and intelligence, and collective place-making.

One of the effects of the widespread incorporation of sustainability coordinators within American universities is that "college administrators are vying to outdo each other," reports the *Washington Post*. "It's almost like an episode of 'Can You Top This?' says a Princeton official."[22] Here again, the university is unique as an institution that is local and particular, yet also networked and comprehensive. This is part of the exceptional potential of the higher education industry — it is not concentrated in one or two large manufacturing centers but can be found in almost every city of any size in the industrialized world. And in these cities, they are not just large economic forces, but ones with special characteristics that allow them to reshape their regions. For example, every college and university is a magnet that draws resources into the local economy from afar, "major sources of external funds that help drive local economies."[23] Of Columbia's total budget, 74 percent comes from outside New York City, but 68 percent of it is spent inside the City.[24] Eight out of nine US dollars that Brown University spends in Rhode Island comes from outside the state. In 1999 Harvard spent one billion US dollars more in Boston than it raised in tuition and fees locally.[25]

In these local economies, the purchasing power is huge: "US universities alone purchase more than all but 20 countries in the world."[26] One study almost a decade ago estimated the annual expenditures for goods and services from 1,900 urban-core universities in the US at US$136 billion, "nine times greater than federal direct spending on urban business and job development in the same year."[27] These same institutions owned more than US$100 billion in land and buildings, spending many billions every year on capital improvements.[28] As these expenditures ripple out across the region, conscious changes in priorities would have wide effects. A single institution has huge local potential. When the University of Pennsylvania implemented a Buy West Philadelphia program, it increased local spending from US$1 million in 1986 to US$57 million in 2000.[29] By 2005 almost 60 campuses in 27 states had student-run farms, and some 200 campuses had signed up with farm-to-college programs that match up local farmers with area universities.[30] The University of Montana in Missoula now allocates over US$400,000 to local farm products, about 17 percent of the school's overall food budget.[31] One can only imagine the impact of these initiatives were they moved from the fringes to the heart of university planning.[32]

Local actions can provide simpler alternatives to complex global systems. The planetary university takes seriously both its boundedness by place and its global relations. The local question

Centre for Dialogue

Through the use of full concentric circles, the Asia Pacific Hall at Simon Fraser University's Wosk Centre for Dialogue is designed to include a large number of participants in an effective format for collective deliberation. Among the many discussions hosted by the Centre was the Citizen's Assembly on Electoral Reform that was created by the Province of British Columbia. The Assembly called for the implementation of a system of proportional representation to make representation in the Legislature more reflective of the wishes of citizens. The Centre has proven very popular and effective for many such small deliberations.

Photograph courtesy of the Wosk Centre for Dialogue, Simon Fraser University.

is a global question: How does my institution and my place use local (and non-local) resources? Like the cities they helped create, universities depend on external inputs of energy and resources (throughput), their "ecological footprint"[33] vastly exceeding any surplus generated by their regions. At the same time, were universities to direct their sizable inflows of external capital toward practices that reduced their region's ecological imports, they would start building new low-impact infrastructure in the cities, reorienting what products get traded and how capital moves. In so doing, they would meet the territorial challenge by redirecting a region's dependence on linear flows from anonymous spaces elsewhere (flows of oil, tropical lettuce and abstract capital) into the construction of circular processes of more efficient places where people are (retrofitted houses, biodynamic local agriculture, community reinvestment).

Defining the eco-city: contracts still available

British engineers will this week sign a multi-billion contract with the Chinese authorities to design and build a string of "eco-cities" — self-sustaining urban centers the size of a large Western capital ....

The eco-cities are regarded both as a prototype for urban living in over-populated and polluted environments and as a magnet for investment funds into the rapidly growing Chinese economy ....

[Peter Head, the director in charge of the first eco-city] said: "It is part of a new awareness of the environment by the Chinese government. They realise that with their growing population and economy they have to overcome the problems of environmental pollution and resource depletion" ....

The eco-cities are intended to be self-sufficient in energy, water and most food products, with the aim of zero emissions of greenhouse gases in transport systems ....

Head said: "This is no gimmick. It is being led at the highest levels of the Chinese government. They are very committed to developing a new paradigm of economic development."

— Frank Kane. "British to Help China Build 'Eco-cities,'" *The Observer*, London: Guardian Newspapers, November 6, 2005, Available at <http://www.guardian.co.uk/china/story/0,1635246,00.html>.

This is the larger promise of local — invigorating a new model of economy and culture that could break the macro gridlock. This goal has always been the basic thinking behind the community economic development movement that was

Networks and local action

[Seattle] Mayor Greg Nickels joined a select group of municipal leaders from around the world [at the Montreal Conference on Climate (COP 11) on December 8, 2005] in an effort to put cities at the forefront of the battle against global warming .... To date, 192 [US] mayors representing more than 40 million people have joined the mayor's Climate Protection Agreement.

"The US leads the world in greenhouse gas pollution when we should be leading it toward a solution," Nickels said. "That is why it is so important for cities like Seattle to step up and provide the leadership that is lacking in Washington, DC."

— Seattle.gov,
<http://www.seattle.gov/News/detail.asp?ID=5725&Dept=40>,
accessed December 13, 2005.

born in the 1960s, but that is still peripheral in those few departments of economics and schools of business where it is even taught. This model of development underpins the proposals envisioned in earlier chapters. It entails a shift in emphasis from economic wealth generation based on non-local exchange (the input-output model) to one that takes far better advantage of the multiplier effects that result from the more dynamic recirculation of capital and resources locally. This strategy also builds on the growing recognition today of the importance of "clusters" (such as exist at the university) in regional economies.[34] With the goal of sustaining healthy socio-ecosystems as a central criterion of economic research and action, economic development would be more diverse and would foster a place-based pluralism. To achieve it would require new forms of education — in agriculture and resource conservation, in the cultural industries and cooperative businesses — that would provide not just skills for a placeless job, but experiences for community citizenship. New forms of knowledge would emerge to bring intellectual expertise together with experiential learning, and new technologies and forms of best practices that could be networked from the bottom-up. Small-scale innovations would then drive large-scale change — in the words of the cluster theorists, the "local buzz" of innovation traveling along the "global pipelines" of business information.[35]

In the process of these developments, new political and economic structures would follow naturally as placeless individual rights begin to intersect with place-based collective responsibilities. Instead, today's postmodern politics (and its justifiable suspicion of a single truth) defers to the multiple truths of a "pluralism" of self-defining groups floating detached in a global "cosmopolis." An ecological pluralism would also grant a critical role to something that cosmopolitan pluralists ignore at their peril — the diverse and healthy socio-ecosystems that can sustain these plural interests! Centrist power would, in turn, be legitimate according to how well it served territorial equity. This is the strategy of CLI if it could redirect this field of power *by grounding each institution in the complex stewardship of its own place*. This strategy confronts the momentum of centralist power while it invigorates the local foundations of global sustainability.

The mission: Innovation

All of this is possible because of the university's comparatively "fluid" power structure (to use Leith Sharp's term). As Pocklington and Tupper note, "[The] idea that universities should be run as democracies makes them profoundly different from other large North American workplaces."[36] Building on this democracy is central to the third element of CLI, *innovation*. Here the key is not specific knowledges or technologies or products. These are too numerous and diverse to catalogue, as a conversation with sustainability coordinators like Sarah Webb demonstrates. Instead, specific innovations will come about automatically with new institutional designs that can instill a dialectical tension within

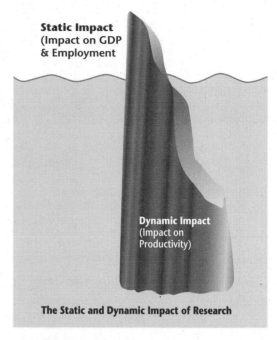

Static Impact
(Impact on GDP & Employment)

Dynamic Impact
(Impact on Productivity)

The Static and Dynamic Impact of Research

Fernand Martin & Marc Trudeau, "The Economic Impact of University Research," *Research File*, vol. 2, no. 3, March 1998, p. 2.

Just the tip of the iceberg ...

The dynamic impact of university research expenditures is far higher than the traditional models of static impact suggest because such research produces technological improvements and graduates trained in sectors beyond the university itself. The benefits of developing sustainability at universities would thus be magnified across other sectors of the economy, as well as through space and over time.

university decision making. Here the substance of what gets created comes full circle back to the process of how it gets created.

The expertise for systemic innovation already exists within the university. Take, for example, the lecture circuit industry on corporate innovation where management gurus like Henry Mintzberg and Michael Porter have become almost household names. Many of these gurus are academics (these two being at McGill and Harvard respectively). And their messages for (corporate) success are revealing:

- to create an "environment that's flexible and empowering and that welcomes ideas, tolerates risk, celebrates success, fosters respect and encourages fun;"[37]
- to embrace "change management" that incorporates dissent and alternative viewpoints into decision making;[38]
- to foster employee empowerment, bottom-up innovation and flattening of organizational structures;[39]
- to create "matrix" models of horizontal as well as vertical relationships in corporate organization.[40]

Ironically, innovations in the corporate world that follow from this university-generated literature are applied everywhere except the institution in which they originate. In the terms of another management guru, Peter Senge, the university is not itself a "learning organization," that is, an organization "[where] people continually expand their capacity to create the results they truly desire, where new and expansive patterns of thinking are nurtured, where collective aspiration is set free, and where people are continually learning how to learn together."[41] A central theme of this corporate literature is that reorienting internal power relations reaps enormous benefits. Given the limited objectives of the corporation (production, profit and growth), this is an admittedly easier task, but the lessons apply more broadly. Richard Daft's proposal for innovation through "ambidextrous management" thus describes the tension needed in campus planning, where the "using department" would exist in dynamic relations with the "creative department," the former mechanical and linear, and the latter experimental and interactive.[42]

Across the campus from the business school, the schools of planning and public administration similarly debate techniques of *integrated planning and participatory process* as central to organizational innovation. The adjectives here are familiar — transparent, accountable, holistic, comprehensive and strategic. The relevance to the university is evident. That is, the thrust of integrated planning is to move beyond the fragmented focus by operational managers on physical or utilitarian attributes to embrace the *whole* university, from the groundskeepers to the top researchers, the presiding president to the incoming student. Many members of the academy will, of course, protest the application of complex planning, let alone corporate, models to the university. But learning from such models would revitalize the collegial system of governance that, ironically, may be the university's best chance to turn back the flowing tide of corporatism.

In the process, the university will directly address the need for system innovation in complex organizations for the 21ˢᵗ century. And this is ultimately the promise of comprehensive local innovation — *to develop new structures and processes of local/global production and distribution.* This is a huge goal — an Earth-changing goal. As discussed in earlier chapters, the foundation for a sustainable economics must be the maintenance of healthy socio-ecosystems, the very systems being eroded and consumed by placeless centrism. However, to develop a new place-sensitive economics will require new forms of land management, such as the commons regimes that can layer diverse, cooperative community management systems onto existing ownership rights and jurisdictions. Similarly it will need to develop a new approach to economic organization that is also rooted in community. Critical management theorist Martin Parker calls this merger an "orgunity."[43] Despite the awkward name, the concept is important. As Parker explains, in community-based entrepreneurial organizations, behaviors should be:

Comprehensive capacities.
The chart below depicts one
strategic perspective of the
many roles that the university
can play in shaping its
environment. Other capacities
would include, for example,
citizen development and
mobilization.

guided by a sense of identity — what might be called a virtue ethic ....
[This entails] an Aristotelian approach to the corporation [because it] stresses that there are places where people find meaning ... where self-interest and group-interest are potentially identical, and where no one is an island. So action within a communitarian organization would not be the result of individual calculation but are somehow constitutive of my understanding of self."[44]

Active learning

Comprehensive local innovation is a one place/every place approach that seeks to create directly a comprehensive working precedent. It draws voluntarily on the university's diverse human expertise and energy and the global reach of its inhabitants. To create such precedents would complement existing roles for the university. It invests local actions with global scholarly significance, helping to shift personal allegiances to the value of developing globally relevant, *local* experiences. The university's institutional design is of central importance, whether it be a new vice-president or a new office of integrated planning or other changes that are grander still. Whatever designs are developed, the university's capacity for greater or lesser achievement exists not just at the level of individual researchers and departments, but at the level of its existence as a whole place. As Webb puts it, the university needs to find that "spark."

Herein lies the potential of the university as a whole learning organization that is also a learning

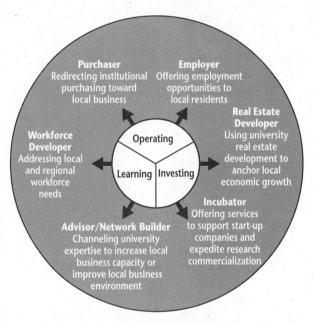

Initiative for a Competitive Inner City, *Leveraging Colleges and Universities for Urban Economic Revitalization: An Action Agenda*, CEOs for Cities, Spring 2002, p. 12. Available at <http://ceosforcities.org/research/2002/leveraging_colleges/colleges_1.pdf>.

community. As involved employees are to the innovative corporation, so might involved faculty, staff, students and the surrounding community be to the innovative university. Then we would have created a truly active place of learning.

Local agents

If we take seriously the relational construction of space and place, if we take seriously the locally grounded nature even of the global, and take seriously indeed that oft-repeated mantra that the local and the global are mutually constituted, then there is another way of approaching this issue. For in this imagination "places" are criss-crossings in the wider power-geometries which constitute both themselves and "the global." In this view local places are not simply always the victims of the global; nor are they always politically defensible redoubts *against* the global. For places are also the moments through which the global is constituted, invented, coordinated, produced. They are "agents" *in* globalisation .... [T]his fact of the inevitably local production of the global means that there is potentially some purchase through "local" politics on wider global mechanisms. Not merely defending the local against the global, but seeking to alter the very mechanisms of the global itself. A local politics with a wider reach; a local politics *on* the global — and we do need to address global politics too. This, then, is a further, different, basis for the recognition of the potential agency of the local.

— Doreen Massey, "Geographies of Responsibility," *Geografisa Annaler,* vol. 86B, 2004, p. 11.

CHAPTER 9

social movement

ALMOST A YEAR TO THE DAY, THE PLACARDS WERE BACK. The tree-sit had come down the previous spring, the new *Campus Plan* had been ratified, a blue-ribbon panel had issued its report on the reform of planning, and still the protestors weren't satisfied. This time their target was a May meeting of UVic's board of governors. As the board members — lawyers, business leaders, senior University administrators, faculty and student reps — filed into their tidily arranged tables, a motley crew of students, faculty and community members greeted them with boldly printed signs: *Wanted: Open Planning* and *Participatory Democracy; We Support Open Process;* and *Top-down Decisions, Do We Really Want This?*

Neither side had seen it coming. To the protestors, the Hanen Report, *Planning Possibilities,* had been released just six months earlier and had recommended the right stuff — a broadly participatory planning body, open elections for many of its members, open meetings, a commitment to fully consultative practices, and a new office of integrated planning above Operations that would guide its activities. And the University president had publicly accepted its recommendations.[1] In practice, however, the University administration changed little, altering the name of the main committee from "development" to "planning" but leaving control over decision making firmly within the operational department. No elections, no new planning office, no possibility for real deliberative dialogue. The

185

University still didn't get it. The culture hadn't changed. After so many years of struggle, the protestors felt duped and betrayed.

The administration, however, was prepared, and one by one, the board members went round the assembly and applauded the University's actions, decrying the demands of the protestors. The University *was* implementing the report, they said, as if reading from a prepared text. In a unanimous vote, the board ratified two changes.[2] The principles of the Hanen Report that the protestors wanted to see were not being implemented, but what could they do? Launch another tree-sit? Occupy an office? No, it was too late for that. The momentum was gone; it was summer after all, and most students had headed home. And so, after years of conflict, just as the University had come to the edge of taking a momentous step forward, the administration had pulled back, retrenched and politely engineered its own failure. Knowledge had succumbed to power.

Yet why should there be any surprise? After all, this had been the experience all along where only outside agitation had forced change — student organizing, faculty petitions, media releases, public workshops, banners and placards, the ring around the clearcut, the folks in the trees. It is well known that change comes from the periphery, not the center, of power. Everywhere sustainability coordinators must learn to step ever so lightly around this power — little changes, technical ones, built slowly. Big changes are still out of view, perhaps waiting over the horizon. But, excited at the potential of a reformed campus and, taking the University at its word, the protestors had let down their guard, and implementation had been turned over to the very operational department that was to be reformed. Quickly it was back to business as usual.

Thus the internal reforms proposed in the previous chapter are only a part of the story of creating the new planetary university. Whatever the ideals, students do need an infrastructure that functions to schedule classes and process their U-Pass. But for an administration to get beyond the status quo demands a willingness to cross boundaries — between the functions of the past and the needs of the future, between those on the inside with power and those on the outside without, between the university and the city that surrounds it, between actions at local level and needs at the global level. Difference and dialogue and even conflict are all part of crossing old boundaries, so that change on one side can be continuously motivated by challenge from the other. But how to do this? Is there not a contradiction here?

To the board of governors, there was no contradiction. The demonstration was but a small annoyance, a delay in getting to the business at hand. But as the protestors filed out, they knew what the University had lost — principles of good planning, promises extracted over long years of struggle and prospects of a more creative future. This conflict in a back room of the University Club was not just a small matter to them. It was a micro example of a macro problem where an institution cannot act, and therefore turns an opportunity for change into an exercise in public relations.

Though few would have noticed the connection, the significance was underscored in the following weeks with the release of a new book. Jared Diamond's *Collapse: How Societies Choose to Fail or Succeed*[3] headed straight to the top of the *New York Times* bestseller list and to the front pages of the local newspaper. It examined some two dozen societies over thousands of years, many of which had collapsed — from prehistoric Polynesian culture on Easter Island to the once thriving Native American civilizations of the Maya and Anasazi, to medieval Greenland and the Viking colony that once ruled it. Diamond's goal was to distill from these histories lessons for today's global society in order that it might survive its many current perils. One of his central conclusions was that sustainable structures of power must be able to absorb,

Creeping normalcy

Politicians use the term "creeping normalcy" to refer to such slow trends concealed within noisy fluctuations. If the economy, schools, traffic congestion or anything else is deteriorating only slowly, it's difficult to recognize that each successive year is on the average slightly worse than the year before, so one's baseline standard for what constitutes "normalcy" shifts gradually and imperceptibly. It may take a few decades of a long sequence of such slight year-to-year changes before people realize, with a jolt, that conditions used to be much better several decades ago, and that what is accepted as normalcy has crept downwards.

— Jared Diamond, *Collapse: How Societies Choose to Fail or Succeed*, New York: Viking Books, 2005, p. 425.

and respond to, negative feedback. Linear systems of power that ignore or suppress critical signals are, he concluded, prone to collapse. Interactive systems that listen to, indeed seek out, such challenges are able to adapt. Between the kafuffle at the University Club and Diamond's bestseller, this (essentially dialectical) understanding has been gathering momentum. Though the issues are now discussed in the classroom, they are not yet practiced in the buildings around the academic quadrangle.

Boundaries of dialogue

The about-face on Canada's West Coast is not uncommon. One year later, the situation was eerily replayed at Cornell University in the eastern United States. The so-called Redbud controversy had simmered at the University and in the town of Ithaca, New York. Cornell is a powerful presence in Ithaca, the area's third-largest economic force.[4] Despite its past sustainability initiatives, and its approval of the favorable publicity generated by these initiatives, the administration planned a 176-stall parking lot for construction in the Redbud Woods of the old Cornell family estate. Students were adamantly against it and, in their opposition, cited the University's own public statements. Cornell President Jeffrey Lehman had recently proclaimed that "great universities must continue to promote the spiritually satisfying coexistence of people with one another and with our planet."[5] In 2004 he designated sustainability as one of the University's three primary goals.[6] As with other universities, however, no comprehensive commitment or master plan existed for the University. Discretionary authority remained with the senior administration.

A century ago, the estate on which the Redbud Woods were located (where Ezra Cornell had also lived) had been bequeathed to Cornell by a distinguished local conservationist Robert Treman. Treman had helped establish the American parks system in the 19th century and had been instrumental in helping the Ithaca region preserve its scenic gorges. According to Treman's instructions, the woods had been left "to nature as the best gardener."[7] Ithaca residents and Cornell students looked forward to the arrival each spring of the purple glow of the Redbud's blossoms. When Cornell sought to clearcut the area, the City of Ithaca denied it permission. But the University administration was committed to its parking lot, and through two court cases, Cornell argued successfully that the area was not a "historic site" that had to be protected.[8]

As the crews cranked up their chainsaws, students moved in and took up positions in the woods, erecting tent platforms high in the trees, sinking lockdown mechanisms in the ground and effectively halting operations. One group of students occupied the president's office while another surrounded the administration building to keep the police from arresting those who had chained themselves to the desks inside. Eventually the faculty took notice. Elizabeth Sanders, a professor of government who teaches courses on institutions, power and social movements, quickly became one of the administration's fiercest critics arguing that "sustainability to the administration means doing scientific studies about the rainforest, or engineering a green building, But if they find a need for more parking here, they just cut down the woods. It just doesn't compute. There's just no linkage to the lofty rhetoric about sustainability."[9]

At the same time, some of Cornell's leading scientists, including nationally renowned entomologist Thomas Eisner and restoration ecologist Thomas Whitlow, proposed what are by now familiar alternatives to more parking lots — minibus services, a ban on freshman parking, free bus passes, better facilities for bicycles.[10] The faculty also proposed a moratorium to allow an independent review to resolve the situation. But to the dismay of Cornell's long-time supporters, the administration would not budge in its commitment to the parking lot. "We love this University," says Sanders. "We love what it could be. We love our fellow faculty. We love the old land grant tradition. There's just such positive energy. And students so need this victory. For most of them it's the first time they have been in the social movement. It would just be so devastating for them."

In response to the continued opposition and the proposals for compromise, the president called a meeting of all parties. Even as they assembled, however, work crews moved in and began constructing a perimeter fence to seal off the contested area. In response, some dozen students took up their positions in the trees and lockdowns. With a dangerous confrontation looming, the Redbud Woods faculty working group released a statement stressing that the protestors faced the "evident intent on the part of Cornell University to use overwhelming coercive force."[11] In exchange for ending of the main protest, the administration offered a deal promising to provide two years of free transit passes for incoming students, to renew a one-year contract for a sustainability intern, and to create a public forum on democracy and sustainability.[12] With an offer of an amnesty from the administration, the students acquiesced.

But it was still not over. As the students vacated the forest and the University began cutting, a new group of young Ithaca residents reoccupied the woods. In its drive to get the job done, reports Sanders, the University administration "denied them food, medicine and sleep (with floodlights all night) and even a safety rope for one of the young girls until her parents' desperate pleas convinced a nice policewoman to send one up."[13] Despite an earlier promise to preserve some of the larger, rarer trees, they were cut. One such tree was a rare 200-year-old yellow oak. The second group of protestors "thought they had a pledge not to cut that huge old tree, older than Cornell University itself, if the protestors came down voluntarily," reports Sanders. "And they finally did, completely exhausted. But it was cut and chopped up right before their tired eyes." Everything was cut, says Sanders. And some 90 protestors were charged with trespass and arraigned in city court. Despite national publicity, no larger campus movement mobilized to bring support to the protesters from outside the area.

As the City of Ithaca and Cornell University battled it out in court and on the ground, the City of Berkeley and the University of California (Berkeley) were also heading to court over the University's 15-year development plan. It included 2,300 new parking spaces and 2.2 million square feet of new construction, new offices that Mayor Tom Bates termed the "equivalent of a new Empire State Building right in the heart of Berkeley."[14] UC Berkeley is another behemoth — the San Francisco Bay area's fifth-largest employer, with 13,500 permanent employees,

Place lost

We deplore the administration's obdurate determination to destroy this rich urban woodland in order to build a 176-space parking lot. It reached its decision in tortuous ways and maintained it for years despite widespread public opposition and well-informed, often expert, objections by students, faculty, community officials, scientists, urban planners and the public. Most recently, Cornell has deflected (and at times undermined) attempts by campus and community groups to reach compromise solutions and mediated agreements. That saddens us immensely.

Photograph by Simon Wheeler, courtesy of the *Ithaca Journal*, 2005.

We salute the activists who have stuck to their principles and, time and time again, turned standoffs on the ground or at the negotiating table into victories both strategic and moral. Among them are some of the University's finest students and most principled young leaders. Through reasoned discourse and nonviolent action, the group [members] have held their ground, literally and figuratively, for weeks and then months. Their physical courage and intellectual integrity have astounded us. In years to come they will take great pride in their conduct in this conflict, today and in the last months.

— Redbud Woods Faculty Working Group. Excerpt from statement made the day the demonstrators signed an agreement with Cornell administration in the face of forcible removal of the protestors and the imminent destruction of the woods. Signed by 33 Cornell University faculty members, July 18, 2005. Available at <http://www.redbudwoods.org/former/Faculty-Statement.html>.

Hanging on.
Ithaca and Cornell University Police dig Jean-Pierre Verdijoat's metal-clad arm out of the ground to clear the way for cutting the University's Redbud Woods and the construction of a parking lot. Verdijoat locked down in a last-ditch attempt to reverse the administration's decision to pave the woods after months of unsuccessful public opposition from students, faculty, neighbors and the City of Ithaca.

Yellow oak resistance

There were four of us up in the 200-year-old yellow oak that we had our tree-sit in …. we were up there for two full nights and part of a third night …. the Cornell police were there on the ground telling us that they would not bring us food or harnesses but they made it clear to us that it was coming from the top down …. all I know is that the police told us that the orders were coming from the top.

The second night they brought in much brighter lights and a second generator which was stationed very close to us, and they had a very large police presence on the ground …. our supporters attempted to bring us in food … but they were unable to because of the massive police presence on the ground ….

People in the trees.

This platform was erected in a black walnut tree rising above the canopy of Redbud Woods to impede the razing of the woodland.

Wednesday was bad. Wednesday they cut down half of the forest around us. And basically all of the trees to one side of our tree. That was very hard to watch …. We had the opportunity to have conversations with a lot of the officers while we were up in the tree …. a lot of them were quite sympathetic to us. They were just doing their job. Whenever you come up against an institution with that much power and that much money they generally get what they want ….

We're going to do our best to use our trials to really put Cornell's sustainability practices on trial. It's not so much about whether we are found guilty or not guilty; it's more a question of what we were fighting for.

— Briana Binkerd-Dale, Redbud Woods activist, *Interview*, August 11, 2005.

Photograph by Barbara Deutsch Lynch, 2005.

9,980 student employees, occupying over 1,200 acres (500 hectares) in, and adjacent to, Berkeley (and 3,000 acres in outlying areas).[15] A huge generator of traffic, the University also provides economic spin-offs, as well as cultural and intellectual vitality to the city. Bates is enthusiastic about the diverse academic expertise that has translated directly into cooperative work with the city in areas such as health care, public education, city planning and business. The University is, says Bates, a "fabulous resource."

Unlike Cornell, UC Berkeley decided to work out an accommodation with the City. The results are exemplary. The City agreed to implement a new rapid bus system by 2010, while the University committed to increase its support for urban services and infrastructure, increase local purchasing and encourage spin-off businesses and reduce its future construction of parking lots. The City and University also created a new cooperative planning process that would include a diversity of participants and a staged process for resolving conflicts.[16]

Despite opposite outcomes, the conflicts at both Cornell and Berkeley speak to the need to create transformative change inside institutions the daily operations of which construct the very systems that need to change. When the power to make innovative change is controlled from inside and from the top, and outside advocates are marginalized and delegitimized, a meeting across the divide is difficult. As discussed in the previous chapter, a realignment of internal power relationships is necessary. But so too are the relations between those on the inside and those on the outside. And that, of course, is the rub — how best to bring the ideas of those outside the institution inside. Simple innovations do exist that can cross this boundary. This is the promise, for example, of a best-practices secretariat that informs the full university community of state-of-the-art developments around the globe. For such measures to have a real impact, however, the university needs a novel approach to decision making that is *integrated* but also *insurgent*. This commitment would recognize that place-based decisions are situated not just in institutions, but in a whole social ecology of local networks and relationships. To implement such a process also requires an institutional willingness to accept

*Berkeley
Settlement
Agreement.*

2020 LRDP LITIGATION SETTLEMENT AGREEMENT

C. WHEREAS, UC Berkeley is an urban campus located partly within the geographical boundaries of the City of Berkeley; and

D. WHEREAS, the City Environs are as much a part of the Berkeley experience as the campus itself, and the quality of the city life is a large part of what makes UC Berkeley a unique and desirable place to learn, work, and live; and

E. WHEREAS, the City of Berkeley and UC Berkeley seek to respect the unique social and cultural character of the Downtown, create an appealing, safe and pedestrian-oriented Downtown environment and revitalize the Downtown economy; and,

J. WHEREAS, the University wishes to plan future investments not merely to meet the program needs of the University, but also to enhance the image, experiential quality, and economic and cultural vitality of downtown Berkeley, by joining with the city of Berkeley in preparing a Berkeley Downtown Area Plan; and

K. WHEREAS, the City of Berkeley and UC Berkeley share a vision for a cooperatively planned Downtown Berkeley that includes the following elements:

Sustainability: promoting a sustainable downtown that serves as a model of urban stewardship and the wise use of resources, and relieves development pressures on residential neighborhoods;

Livability: enhancing the image and experience of the downtown, preserving its unique cultural and social character and its comfortable pedestrian orientation; and

Vitality: strengthening the downtown as a vital city center offering employment, housing, cultural and recreational opportunities for Berkeley residents.

2020 Long Range Development Plan (LRDP) Litigation Settlement Agreement, between the University of California, Berkeley, the Regents of the University of California and the City of Berkeley, May 25, 2005.

enabling constraints, that is, constraints that can *force* innovation. This is what Cornell spurned, and UC Berkeley embraced.

Democracy inside and out

Democracy has historically assumed a constrained role within the formal world of electoral politics. The public speaks through the ballot box. In recent years, the public participation movement has expanded citizen involvement, arguing that governmental decision-making rests ultimately on democratic legitimacy — and that democracy produces better decisions. Yet the legitimacy of university actions does not rest on such foundations. This exemption for the university is a historic artifact, and an artifical one. And it lacks justification. As a result, the activities of the undemocratic university implicitly teach not the importance of democracy, but its marginality.

The recent corporatization of the university has led to even less democracy. Ironically, the literature on corporate performance offers lessons for the university. For example, it is widely accepted that even a limited democratization of corporate decision making offers benefits by creating new vertical lines of internal communication and movement. Corporate democratization is justified in functional terms because it liberates entrepreneurs, visionaries and leaders from the confines of the top-down corporate structure. Some of the changes proposed in previous chapters reflect similar concerns for functional innovation at the university, innovations that are impossible without greater democracy.

In the public sphere, advocates of institutional reform trumpet the potential of deliberative democracy to foster "ideal speech situations" where decisions can be made openly, with the

Insulated elites

A conflict of interest involving rational behavior arises when the interests of the decision-making elite in power clash with the interests of the rest of society. Especially if the elite can insulate themselves from the consequences of their actions, they are likely to do things that profit themselves, regardless of whether those actions hurt everybody else.

— Jared Diamond, *Collapse: How Societies Choose to Fail or Succeed*, New York: Viking Books, 2005, p. 430.

involvement of those affected, in reasoned dialogue, and with ongoing accountability.[17] Such situations will, in Hannahs Arendt's phrase, elicit an "enlarged mentality" through the engagement of "a multiple, anonymous, heterogeneous network of many publics and public conversations."[18] A value of deliberative democracy is to subject dominating power to liberating debate, as well as to expand the sphere of democracy beyond the formal politics of occasional voting. Such an expansion would embrace the everyday worlds of government agencies, private businesses and civil society. The broad interest in deliberative democracy translates especially well to the "college," a term that describes the university (collegium) as well as a general way of working as a community (collegial). George Fallis argues that the university has a "core commitment for social citizenship" but also that its "democratic role goes much beyond ... [as it is] an education in political citizenship."[19]

One of North America's leading democratic theorists, Iris Marion Young, claims that "communicative democracy" generates "truth value."[20] At the same time, she and other writers recognize that power can never be displaced, that open deliberations will always exist in tension with people in authority and that newcomers will advance new issues that challenge established processes. Large institutions inherently tend to enclose themselves, and to become unresponsive to outsiders and new social forces. As Marcus Ford explains about his own experience at the university, "There are huge opportunities here to do something truly novel, and the payoff both locally and globally could also be huge. Yet instead they worry about transfer credits from students from the community college."[21]

A social commitment to democracy means that no final design, no end point, exists. The shape and range of democratic institutions must necessarily remain open to "political contestation." As the renowned political theorist Chantal Mouffe argues, democracy should be, if not antagonistic between enemies, at least "agonistic" between "friendly enemies."[22] This prescription for continuous dialogue, challenge and reform certainly makes theoretical sense. In practice, however, to extol continuous conflict is challenging even for democrats whose stock in trade is argument and debate. For officials working in an operational department (with its culture of management and control), such conflict is antithetical. Yet as Julie Newman puts it, the "success of my job as the sustainability coordinator inside the University depends on the continued activism of sustainability advocates outside."[23]

Given their real world efficacy, these democratic insights have begun to make broader inroads. For example, planning scholars also point to the dangers of creating tidy, perfectly sealed processes. As UBC's professor of planning Leonie Sandercock notes, the historical paradigm of expert planning produces lifeless cities that embody the planner's "presumed ability to control the future through action guided by rationality, and protected by the authority of the central state. Their rational urban plan would treat the city as a machine ... breaking it down into its essential functions (housing, work, recreation and traffic) ... and reassembling them (in the Master Plan) as a totality."[24] Instead, Sandercock wants to reinvent the discipline itself into what she sees as "insurgent planning."[25] By reframing planning politically, new sources of power and legitimacy emerge that can alter the force field of the city.

Similar insights also exist at the boundaries of the scholarship of business organization. British theorist Martin Parker argues that the concept of "management" itself imposes 19th-century rigidities on 21st-century organizations. Challenging the managerial assumptions of top-down control and authority, Parker favors a more fluid, dynamic and interactive approach to corporate decision making, suggesting that we "treat organization as a verb rather than a noun, an ongoing institution within which assumptions about both means and ends are continually being renegotiated ... help[ing] prevent the organization not to become too stratified, and hence work against the possibility that any one group might become dominant."[26]

In light of these insights, one might ask why there are so many accredited business schools but so few (and nonprofessional) centers for cooperative studies. Or why there are so many medical schools but so few schools of complementary medicine. Is this a result of the individual disciplines *or their shared structure of governance*? What precludes engineering schools from leading the challenge to the automobile, or agricultural faculties from championing the cause of biodynamic farming? In every case, entrenched organizational power trumps responsive collective reason. If so, institutional redesign is critical. But there is also a contradiction here — that of asking power to reform the basis of its power. This is especially problematic where it must do so to achieve goals different from those on which it has been founded. The challenge is that of a transformative rationality, where expert decision-making evolves into empowered dialogue, and high-level planning gives way to collective negotiation. In this vein, Parker articulates a post-management corporation where "management becomes simply another term for coordination."[27]

To reach beyond the philosophical and organizational certainties of the past requires a strategy of *incremental radicalism*. Change takes place step by step — but toward a very different future. Such a strategy may even offer the basis for a revitalized political liberalism that can escape the economistic status quo, but can do so incrementally. Here, too, new thinking (this time from legal scholars) points to the potential for a "democratic

Insurgency planning

1. Means-ends rationality may still be a useful concept — especially for building bridges and dams — but we also need greater and more explicit reliance on **practical wisdom**.
2. Planning is no longer exclusively concerned with comprehensive, integrated and coordinated action ... but more with negotiated, political, and focused planning.
3. There are different kinds of appropriate knowledge in planning. "Art or science" is the wrong way to phrase the question. Which knowledges, in what situations, is more to the point. Local communities have experiential, grounded, contextual, intuitive knowledges .... Planners have to learn to access these **other ways of knowing**.
4. From our modernist reliance on state-directed futures and top-down processes, we have to move to community-based planning, from the ground up, geared to **community empowerment**.
5. We have to deconstruct both "the public interest" and "community," recognizing that each tends to exclude difference. We must acknowledge that there are **multiple publics** and that planning in this new multicultural arena requires a new kind of **multicultural literacy**".

— Leonie Sandercock, *Towards Cosmopolis: Planning for Multicultural Cities*, London: John Wiley and Sons, 1998, p. 30.

experimentalism" in both public and private realms. Recognizing that the boundaries around democracy are arbitrary, this field advances the use of democratic strategies to reform complex systems that are too big, too centralized, too inflexible and that do not empower collective innovation at the levels where people actually live and work.[28] If no one would countenance city governments like Ithaca or Berkeley being run without a democratic base, why should bigger and more influential universities that tower over these communities be able to avoid democratic accountability? If Simon Fraser University's "UniverCity" embraces a new urbanism in physical design, then why should it not also embrace the city in its institutional design — with councillors, elections and democratic deliberations?

The call for enhanced democracy at the university is particularly justified where, as is common today, student tuition can account for half a college's operating budget — yet without proportionate representation. Meanwhile low-paid sessional instructors may teach half the load — without any status at all. At stake is the university's social legitimacy. It is time for the university to negotiate a new social contract.

> ## A social contract
>
> The social contract with universities is formulated over time and shaped by history .... The social contract requires continuous reflection and dialogue among the university and society, as each era renews the social contract according to its needs .... The university must permit public scrutiny of its affairs, be transparent in how choices are made to achieve its academic mission and be accountable to government and to the public about how public funds have been spent .... In order to maintain its autonomy, the university must make a commitment to dialogue — about these tasks and the role of university in society. The social contract implies an obligation on the university to reflect upon these tasks, to think and to write about them publicly, to articulate their value in society, to defend them when they are threatened but also to reconsider them in light of criticism and evolving social needs.
>
> — George Fallis, "The Mission of the University," submission to the Rae Commission, in Government of Ontario, *Postsecondary Review: Higher Expectations for Higher Education*, Toronto: York University, October 2004, p. 35.

Locating planet U

Jared Diamond demonstrates that unreflective societies are unsustainable.[29] They resist critical feedback, he argues, doing what they have done before, providing

Post postmodern U

Deterministic logic, critical reasoning, individualism, humanistic ideals, a search for universal truths, overarching theories about knowledge, and belief in progress are hallmarks of modernism. The university was a central organization for modernism and the professorate were key figures in advancing modernist premises ....

Researchers have found that the premises of a single discipline are no longer sufficient for investigating different aspects of postmodern life. Similarly, the university no longer is a site that seeks to develop a unified theory, but rather it is a conduit for diverse conversations about the nature of a particular phenomenon. The university becomes more a facilitator for dialogue than a repository of truth ....

The postmodern challenge is to decide which approach to knowing is appropriate to specific interests and needs. Such a suggestion assumes that organizational forms will differ. Governmental regulations and calls for accountability need to allow for a variety of types and frames, rather than impose universal definitions of standardized curricula and the like ....

The changes that are upon society are taking place with such rapidity and are of such a magnitude that to assume that universities will be able to survive without considering those changes will doom academia to becoming organizational anachronisms ....

— William G. Tierney, "The Autonomy of Knowledge and the Decline of the Subject: Postmodernism and the Reformulation of the University," *Higher Education*, vol. 41, 2001, pp. 353–72, with permission of Springer Publishers.

well for those at the top but ignoring the consequences of their actions down the ladder. Diamond's critique invites us to reconsider what we, by definition, do not consider, those things that we take for granted, especially entrenched patterns of social behavior. His is an apt characterization for the historic patterns of growth and scale that now so abstract the modern world from its context, and blind it from its alienating impact. In contrast, a postmodern understanding is (in theory at least) situated in relations that are interactive, knowledges that are contextual and truths that celebrate difference and diversity. This new understanding is well established in departments of philosophy and political science, in the sciences of ecology and physics. Even if it is difficult to project that understanding to the larger world, no realistic choice exists.

This crisis of structure and thought opens up possibilities specific to the university. In a postmodern world, "We don't have to give up reason," says Ford. "I kind of like reason.

But what we call reason is often a kind of unreflective dogmatism. When they say it is only rational to be self-interested, I don't think that is rational. What we need is a deeper kind of reason." Similarly, democratic theorist John Dryzek calls for a new kind of reason based on the recovery of interactive political *and* ecological relationships, what he terms "ecological rationality."[30] Meanwhile, Pocklington and Tupper call for a new commitment to "reflective enquiry" as the basis for the university to regain its educative role.[31] Still others talk about a new "scholarship of engagement" where communal interests are acted on and the university assumes an active cultural, not just instrumental, value.[32] In this new world, the university would have a practical role, that of building social capital. This can be attained by educating individuals with the "practical reason" necessary for full citizenship. As Elizabeth Sanders remarks of her experience of Redbud conflict, "The students who are doing this are the most committed students, the best students I have ever met."

The deeper kind of reason that Ford calls for is not linear but dialectical. Where modernism pursues a linear progress extending ever further into a future somewhere *out there,* Ford's constructive postmodernism invigorates a transformative insurgency for a present *right here*. This entails a limited rationality in the service of a fuller consciousness and an isolated self in the quest for a relational being. Evolution is possible. To return again to Jane Jacobs:

> If the hazard is rot from within a dominant culture, or its failure to adapt, obviously the pressing immediate task is for society to be sufficiently self-aware to recognize the threat of accumulating cultural weaknesses and try to correct them …. Vicious spirals have their opposites: beneficent spirals, processes in which each improvement and strengthening leads to other improvements and strengthenings …. Beneficent spirals, operating by benign feedback, mean that everything needful is not required at once: each individual improvement is beneficial for the whole.[33]

To become a model that is beneficial for the whole, the planetary university must cross a divide of the political imagination. There one will also find Planet U, that is, the movement itself. Its mission is to usher in a fourth stage in the university's evolution. Its strength will be found in each planetary university that informs, and is informed by, all the others. Linked in networks of territorial diversity and shared planetary commitment, the Planet U movement embodies the new shape of global sustainability, where the *networked local* replaces the placeless center. Indeed, by demanding that *your* university become a *planetary* university, a transformation will occur in local dialogue, in what represents an acceptable level of local innovation.

A wormhole strategy

The planetary university is a place-based actor that also exists across space. Situated locally, the university possesses the planet's most diverse set of network linkages. One would be hard pressed to imagine another institution where messages fly daily to and fro on topics as diverse as medical imaging technology and food security, postmodern rationality and green buildings. Such networks can be quickly harnessed for institutional change, allowing for feedback between the geographically diverse universities, while also working to benefit each local place. A network structure can translate local experience into new levels of collective conversation and, in so doing, create new and richer forms of social intelligence. By developing a movement that can then draw the global back to the local, global diversity enhances local sustainability. And then back again.

Innovation is possible: Participatory budgeting

This is a system that lets local populations in each neighborhood of Porto Alegre decide, in assemblies that are open to the entire population, the priorities for the public budget allocated to their locality. In other words, it is the population itself that determines, in an original demonstration of direct democracy, if the budget's funds should be used to build a road, a school, or a medical center. Subsequent assemblies let the population monitor the implementation of the chosen projects, while a City Council of the Participatory Budget, made up of delegates elected by the assemblies, manages the distribution of the budget to the different neighborhoods, following criteria decided on in common.

— Michael Lowy, "A 'Red' Government in the South of Brazil," *Monthly Review*, vol. 52, no. 6, November, 2000, p. 1.

Networking between different university movements is critical. Some such networks already exist. In Canada, for example, the Sierra Youth Coalition works on dozens of university campuses to both advocate change and disseminate information. In the United States, Second Nature, University Leaders for a Sustainable Future (ULSF), and the Portland-based Association for the Advancement of Sustainability in Higher Education (AASHE), facilitate interchange between

Another world is possible.

A crowd from the World Social Forum (WSF) is cheered on as it makes its way through the streets of Porto Alegre, Brazil, in 2003. The ongoing WSF allows individuals and organizations opposed to globalization to share visions of an alternative future and to compare strategies and tactics to make that vision a reality. In 2001 the city of Porto Alegre hosted the first WSF that drew around 12,000 participants. For the 2005 WSF, more than 150,000 participants traveled from all over the world to Porto Alegre under the unifying motto that "Another World is Possible."

Photograph by Simone Bruno, 2003.

engineering students and facility managers, university presidents and non-governmental activists, professors of microbiology and researchers in developing countries. In Europe one finds several formal university networks, such as the COPERNICUS-CAMPUS and the Regional Centers of Expertise (RCEs) for Learning for Sustainable Development.[34] As the movement for Planet U takes form, it will link with the many other social movements that intersect with the concerns of every planetary university.

Interest in this movement is growing. For example, Matt St. Clair, the UC sustainability specialist, found that from the first meeting of UC sustainability employees in 2004 to its next meeting in 2005, the number of attendees doubled from 250 to 500:

> It definitely is a movement right now at the universities. I see evidence of it everywhere across the country, not just here in California. When I see conferences of professional associations, I see the whole agenda is full of sustainability topics. It's amazing. When the physical plant administrators get together. When the educational buyers get together. When the campus planners get together. And there are all these sustainability coordinator positions popping up everywhere. All this momentum![35]

One of most important movement strategies is to bridge the boundaries between the generations. On the one hand is the postwar generation that grew up with the suburban university. Schooled in the pursuit of economism, it is today its prime beneficiary. And it is seeing its failure. What this huge and powerful demographic force does in the coming decades — across disciplines, job categories, social classes, genders, races, and geographies — is critical to planetary survival. On the other hand is today's generation of students being schooled in a period of deepening unsustainablity. And their future is at stake. To bring these generations together will be the catalyst for Planet U.

The emergence of the movement for Planet U is as important for tomorrow's world as was the creation of the environmental movement in the decades of yesterday.

Its unique capability is to foster macro change from micro precedents. This entails a kind of "wormhole" strategy like the physicist who argues that to cover great cosmic distances one cannot go the way one can see. Instead, one must "jump levels" in a fashion presently unknown — global change through the local back door. The real upside of the spiral of change is to be found not by reaching for the top, but by going down. It is time to re-discover that institution that, in our own backyards, we have for so long taken for granted. In the process, we might just sustain the world by reinventing the university.

Democratic mission

If tormenting worry had to be summarized in a single sentence it would be: In the post-industrial society of the 21st century, the economic mission of the university will flourish and the democratic mission will wither. We must not allow this to happen.

— George Fallis, "The Mission of the University," submission to the Rae Commission, in Government of Ontario, *Postsecondary Review: Higher Expectations for Higher Education*, Toronto: York University, October 2004, p. 53.

THE VISIONARY

re-enchantment

T HE MOOD AT THE REUNION WAS UPBEAT, the gathering itself one of many that had become popular by the end of the UN decade in 2015. As the participants convened, they acknowledged a growing list of collective achievements. This meeting at UVic was particularly special because it was combined with an anniversary of the tree-sit from, by now, almost two decades earlier. By now even the University administration recalled those days with affection, amusement and appreciation.

The site was the University's recently constructed Circle House for Dialogue where delegates excitedly exchanged news of ongoing projects and emerging visions. Despite their diverse backgrounds, they shared a basic consensus: centrist waste and instability were out, and territorial revitalization and sustainability were in. Circle House was itself a University project designed to give physical form to a related consensus: the global imperative of active, local democracy. Indeed, the University had recently taken an even bolder step by creating a regular "place parliament." The local parliament hosted the reunion, and it packed Circle House with citizens from throughout the region and beyond. As Todd Litman had predicted, opening multiple channels of discourse had stimulated a "cascade effect."

Across the planet, incessant trade conflicts, skyrocketing energy costs and devastating environmental disruptions had also contributed to the cascade. Basic changes were happening in economic thinking. Finally, real economic initiatives were underway. Brittle systems once taken for granted had cracked, and so talk of "demand management," "smart growth" and "food security" now made sense. A broader social understanding — that a sustainable planet depends on the health of place — had begun to take root. At the world's now numerous planetary universities, opportunity was indeed the flip side of dialogue. For these places offered what had long been absent from the struggle for global social change — a locus for action.

With the university a mobilizing force, everywhere there was rebuilding. Automobile production was fast becoming a sunset industry, and people had turned their attention to recovering, not destroying, their place. They had become less enchanted with so much moving around. For local travel, they used their free U-Pass to ride the many buses and trams. With fewer cars, neighbourhoods were becoming active again. Bike businesses boomed. Projects for suburban "vitalization" were rendering rush hours obsolete. Meanwhile, small farms and organic cooperatives were springing up everywhere supported by a global justice movement that actively fostered "low-impact living." Landscapes were being restored. With its commitment to revitalizing the "commons" through local First Nations and neighborhood associations, UVic now hosted the country's first "edible campus."

From economics to engineering and education, whole faculties had embraced new models and technologies of ecodevelopment. What began as a North American, then European, movement was adapting to diverse needs in different countries throughout the world. As jobs had dwindled in the old economy, business schools promoted techniques for community re-investment and values-based enterprises. Universities pioneered strategies to reduce the world's historic dependence on resource and capital throughputs, freeing their regions of the massive waste generated by the old growth economy. In response, these regions were able to focus on what worked: local restoration, resource efficiency and economic equity.

At the planetary university, students trained for global citizenship. With community service in the core curriculum, students reveled in breaking the disciplinary boundaries entrenched in ivory-tower abstraction. Passive theory in the library jousted with the active theory being developed on the urban farms, in the neighborhood and at new community health and nutrition centers. With its roots giving strength to the socio-ecosystems of home, and its branches reaching into countless networks abroad, the planetary university found itself at the forefront of global change. Networked localism emerged as an important component of sustainable global governance. Best practices whirled around the gathering at Circle House as fast as they were now whirling around the globe.

Between discussions, delegates at the place parliament wandered throughout the University grounds inspecting the camas harvest under the Garry oaks and the urban-intensive plots on the old Uplands Farm. They debated their decisions in the plaza of the urban village, wandered by the healing springs and daylit creeks and studied the retention ponds being planted for regional bird and butterfly habitat. In this re-enchanted landscape, scents of the soil filled the air.

At the place parliament, it was clear that people's energies could bear fruit. Restoring planetary health, one university at a time, one place at a time, had become a common goal, propelled by a new global movement. One could experience it first hand. Planet U was here.

A path through Mystic Vale.

Photograph by Justine Starke, 2005.

NOTES

Preface

1. For a summary of the meeting and its outcomes, see *Earth Negotiations Bulletin*, December 12, 2005, vol. 12, no. 291. Published by the International Institute for Sustainable Development, it is available online at <www.iisd.ca/climate/cop11/>.
2. For a more academic analysis of the argument of this book, see Michael M'Gonigle & Justine Starke, "Minding Place: Towards a (rational) political ecology of the sustainable university," *Journal of Environment and Planning D: Society and Space*, vol. 24, no. 3, 2006 (forthcoming).

Chapter 1: tree-sit

1. Ingmar Lee, *Interview*, July 22, 2004. Note to reader: After the initial citation of an interview, subsequent uses in the chapter of that interview will not be referenced.
2. Maurita Prato, *Interview*, January 25, 2005.
3. Alejandro Rojas, *Interview*, August 23, 2004.
4. Philip G. Altbach, "India and the World University Crisis," in *The Student Revolution*, edited by Philip G. Altbach, Bombay: Popular Press, 1970.
5. Hugh Johnston, *Radical Campus: Making Simon Fraser University*, Vancouver: Douglas & McIntyre, 2005.
6. "The Struggle Site," *Paris '68*, [online], [Cited July 25, 2005], 2005, <http://struggle.ws/pdfs/paris68.pdf>.
7. Johnston, Ibid, p. 128.
8. Ibid, and James Harding, "The New Left in BC," in *The New Left in Canada*, Dimitrios J. Roussopoulos, ed., Montréal: Black Rose Books, 1970.

9. Peter L. Smith, *A Multitude of the Wise: UVic Remembered*, Victoria: The Alumni Association of the University of Victoria, 1993, pp. 162–163; "Taylor Refuses Last Student Plea," *The Martlet*, Victoria: University of Victoria Students' Society, April 7, 1967, 1.

10. University of British Columbia, *Facts and Figures*, [online], [Cited October 19, 2005], <www.pair.ubc.ca/studies/index.htm> and <www.publicaffairs.ubc.ca/ubcfacts/>.

11. James Lovelock. *The Revenge of Gaia: Why the Earth Is Fighting Back — and How We Can Still Save Humanity*, London: Allen Lane, 2006.

12. Jane Jacobs, *The Death and Life of Great American Cities*, New York: Random House, 1961.

13. Jane Jacobs, *Dark Age Ahead*, New York: Random House, 2004.

14. Ibid., p. 20.

15. Ibid., pp. 24–25.

16. Ibid., pp. 60-61.

17. Ibid., p. 175.

Chapter 2: genealogy of an ancient edifice

1. Peter L. Smith, *A Multitude of the Wise: UVic Remembered*, Victoria: The Alumni Association of the University of Victoria, 1993, p. 134.

2. Iain Hunter, "Frozen Precut Sod Turned to Start Varsity Buildup," *Daily Times*, January 22, 1962, p. 11.

3. Brad Morrison, *The Life, Family and Accomplishments of Richard Biggerstaff Wilson 1904–1991*, Victoria, private manuscript in possession of the author, 1996, pp. 87–88.

4. Marcus Ford, *Interview*, June 17, 2005.

5. Marcus Ford, *Beyond the Modern University: Towards a Constructive Post-Modern University*, Westport: Praeger, 2002, p. 15.

6. Ibid., p. 10.

7. Nathan Scharner, *The Medieval University*, New York: A.S. Barnes, 1962, p. 56; in Marcus Ford, 2002, p. 22.

8. John Ralston Saul. *Voltaire's Bastards: The Dictatorship of Reason in the West*, Toronto: Penguin, 1992, p. 41.

9. Ford, 2002, p. 27.

10. George Fallis, "The Mission of the University," in *Postsecondary Review: Higher Expectations for Higher Education*, Toronto: Government of Ontario, 2004.

11. Arthur Herman, *How the Scots Invented the Modern World: The True Story of How Western Europe's Poorest Nation Created our World and Everything in It*, New York: Crown Publishers, 2001.

12. Fallis, op. cit., p. 12.

13. Ford, 2002, p. 29.

14. Fallis, op. cit., p. 12.

15. Tom Pocklington & Allan Tupper, *No Place to Learn: Why Universities Aren't Working*, Vancouver: UBC Press, 2002, p. 23.

16. Thomas D. Snyder, ed., "120 Years of American Education: A Statistical Portrait" [online], [Cited August 31, 2005], Washington: National Center for Education Statistics, 1993. <http://nces.ed.gov/pubs93/93442.pdf>.

17. Saul, op. cit., p. 6.

18. Ford, 2002, p. 39.

19. Bruno Latour, *We Have Never Been Modern*, Cambridge: Harvard University Press, 1993.

20. Ford, 2002, p. 40.

21. Latour, op. cit.

22. Ford, 2002, p. 31.

23. Ford, 2005.

24. Clark Kerr, *The Uses of the University*, 3rd ed., Cambridge: Harvard University Press, 1982.

25. Association of Universities and Colleges of Canada, "Trends in Higher Education, 2002: Summary of Findings" [online], [Cited July 26, 2005], Ottawa, November 18, 2004. <http://www.aucc.ca/publications/auccpubs/research/trends/summary_e.html>.

26. Association of Universities and Colleges of Canada, "Quick Facts" [online], [Cited July 26, 2005], Ottawa: Association of Universities and Colleges of Canada, February 17, 2005. <http://www.aucc.ca/publications/research/quick_facts_e.html>.

27. Association of Universities and Colleges of Canada, "A Strong Foundation for Innovation" [online], *Background papers on universities and Canada's Innovation Strategy*, [Cited July 5, 2005], Ottawa: Association of Universities and Colleges of Canada 2002, p. 2. <http://www.aucc.ca/_pdf/english/reports/2002/innovation/inno_backgr_e.pdf>.

28. Statistics Canada, "Postsecondary Graduates: Proportion of Population Aged 25 to 54, Canada, 1996, Table 109-0005" [online], [Cited July 25, 2005], Ottawa: Statistics Canada, 1996. <http://estat.statcan.ca>.

29. U.S. Department of Education, "Postsecondary Educational Institutions and Programs Accredited by Accrediting Agencies and State Approval Agencies Recognized by the U.S. Secretary of Education" [online], [Cited July 25, 2005], Office of Postsecondary Education, 2005. <http://ope.ed.gov/accreditation/>.

30. National Center for Education Statistics, "NCES Fast Facts: 'Postsecondary Enrollment 2001'" [online], [Cited July 25, 2005], Washington, 2005. <http://nces.ed.gov/fastfacts>.

31. National Center for Education Statistics, "Chapter 3: Postsecondary Education: Faculty, Staff and Salaries" [online], *Digest of Education Statistics, 2003*, [Cited August 1, 2005], Washington, 2003. <http://nces.ed.gov/programs/digest/d03/ch_3.asp#2>.

32. Australian Bureau of Statistics, "3101.0 Australian Demographic Statistics" [online], [Cited July 25, 2005], Australian Government, 2004. <http://www.abs.gov.au/>.

33. National Center for Education Statistics, "Expenditures of Title IV Degree Granting Institutions: United States, Fiscal Year 2001" [online], [Cited July 25, 2005], Washington, 2001. <http://nces.ed.gov/>.

34. Martin Irvine, "Emerging e-Education Landscape" [online], *CIO Series: A Blackboard Strategic Whitepaper*, [Cited July 10, 2005], 2002. <http://www.blackboard.com/docs/wp/CIOSeriesWhitePaper.pdf>.

35. Louis G. Tornatzky, Paul G. Waugaman & Denis O. Gray, "Innovation U: New University Roles in a Knowledge Economy" [online], [Cited July 25, 2005], Southern Growth Policies Board, 2002. <http://ip.research.sc.edu/PDF/InnovationUniversityBook.pdf>.

36. Kenneth D. Campbell, "University Patents Support 246,000 Jobs, Contribute Billions to Economy" [online], [Cited July 25, 2005], Boston: MIT News Office, 1999. <http://web.mit.edu/newsoffice/1999/patents-0113.html>.

37. National Association of State Universities and Land Grant Colleges, "Value Added: The Economic Impact of Public Universities" [online], [Cited July 25, 2005], Washington: Office of Public Affairs, 1997. <http://www.nasulgc.org/publications/Value_Added.pdf>.

38. Eric Bloch, "Testimony to Congress," National Science Foundation, 1988, in James J. Duderstadt, "Future of Higher Education in the Knowledge-Driven, Global Economy of the 21st Century" [online], *175th Anniversary Symposium, October 31, 2002*, [Cited August 1, 2005], Toronto, University of Toronto, 2002, p. 3. <http://milproj.ummu.umich.edu/publications/toronto/download/Toronto_103102.pdf>.

39. Pocklington & Tupper, op. cit.

40. Derek Bok, *Universities in the Marketplace: The Commericalization of Higher Education*, Princeton: Princeton University Press, 2003; See also, Ronald G. Ehrenberg, ed., *Governing Academia: Who Is in Charge at the Modern University?* Ithaca: Cornell University Press, 2004.

41. Noel Castree & Matthew Sparke, "Introduction: Professional Geography and the Corporatization of the University: Experiences, Evaluations and Engagements," *Antipode*, vol. 32, no. 3, 2000, pp. 222–29.

42. Fallis, op. cit., p. 24.

43. Michel Foucault, *Power/Knowledge: Selected Interviews and Other Writings 1972–1977*, Colin Gordon, ed., New York: Pantheon Books, 1980, p. 54.

44. Saul, 1992, p. 16.

45. Jacques Derrida, "White Mythology," in *Margins of Philosophy*, Alan Bass, trans., Chicago: Chicago University Press, 1982, p. 213.

46. Michel Foucault, *Society Must Be Defended: Lectures at the Collège de France, 1975–76*, edited by Mauro Bertani and Alessandro Fontana; translated by David Macey. New York: Picador, 2003, p. 183.

47. Ford, 2005.

Chapter 3: archaelogy of a buried landscape

1. Cheryl Bryce, *Interview*, October 26, 2006.
2. Al Mackie, *Personal communication* (with Jessie Cowperthwaite), October 21, 2005. Mackie is a senior archaelogist with the British Columbia provincial government.
3. William G. Tierney, "The Autonomy of Knowledge and the Decline of the Subject: Postmodernism and the Reformulation of the University," *Higher Education*, vol. 41, 2001, p. 356.
4. David Harvey, *The Condition of Postmodernity*, Oxford: Basil Blackwell, 1989.
5. Sheila Potter, "Camas Comeback," *Saanich News*, July 1, 2005, C1.
6. Wilson Duff, "The Fort Victoria Treaties," *BC Studies*, no. 3, Fall 1969, p. 4.
7. Grant Keddie, *Notes: Archaeological Sites in the Cadboro Area, a Very Brief Overview*, [Document in possession of the author], Victoria: Royal BC Museum, 1990.
8. Duff, op. cit., p. 43. Trutch wrote this description in 1869.
9. James Douglas, in Duff, op. cit., p. 36.
10. Arthur J. Ray, *I Have Lived Here Since the World Began: An Illustrated History of Canada's Native People*, Toronto: Key Porter, 2005, p. 186.
11. Paul Tennant, *Aboriginal Peoples and Politics: The Indian Land Question in British Columbia, 1849–1989*, Vancouver: UBC Press, 1990, p. 242.
12. Ray, op. cit.
13. Ibid., p. 187.
14. Cole Harris, *Making Native Space: Colonialism, Resistance, and Reserves in British Columbia*, Vancouver: UBC Press, 2002, pp. 19, 21.
15. Duff, op. cit., p. 52.
16. Richard Wolfenden (Government Printer), "Che-ko-nein Tribe: Point Gonzales to Cedar Hill," *Papers Connected with the Indian Land Question 1850-1875, 1877*, Victoria: Government Printing Office, 1987 (orig. ed. 1875), p. 8.
17. Dave Elliott Sr. (Janet Poth, ed.), *Saltwater People*, Victoria: Saanich School District 63, 1983, pp. 69–70.
18. Don Mitchell, formerly a professor of archaeology, University of Victoria, *Personal communication*, October, 4, 2005.
19. Ursula Jupp, *From Cordwood to Campus in Gordon Head 1852–1959*, Victoria: Ursula Jupp, 1975, p. 7.
20. Grant Keddie, *Songhees Pictorial: A History of the Songhees People as Seen by Outsiders, 1790–1912*, Victoria: Royal BC Museum, 2003, p. 107.
21. Jupp, op. cit., p. 152.
22. Ibid., p. 153.
23. D.W. Higgins, *The Mystic Spring: And Other Tales of Western Life*, Toronto: William Briggs, 1904, p. 21.

24. Sheila Potter, "Gillespie's Trail," *Saanich News*, December 15, 2004, B1.

25. Robert Gillespie, *Interview*, January 10, 2005.

26. Jupp, op. cit., pp. 172–174.

27. Bill Nicholson, *Interview*, April 01, 2004.

28. Ursula Jupp, "Gordon Head, Since 1959," *The Islander*, November 16, 1980, 8.

29. Jane Turner & Don Lovell, *The Changing Face of University of Victoria Campus Lands*, Victoria: University of Victoria Archives, 1999.

30. Dennis Minaker, *The Gorge of Summers Gone: A History of Victoria's Inland Waterway*, Victoria: Dennis Minaker, 1998, p. 84.

31. Planning Department of Saanich, "A Plan for the University Area," Victoria: Corporation of the District of Saanich, 1965, p. 7.

32. Ibid., pp. 11–12.

33. Municipality of Saanich Archives, "Collection of Statistics on Estimated Population and Area in Saanich," Victoria, n.d.

34. Emily MacNair, "A Baseline Assessment of Food Security in British Columbia's Capital Region," Victoria: Capital Region Food and Agriculture Initiatives Round Table, 2004.

35. Ibid.

36. Statistics Canada, "The Loss of Dependable Agriculture Land in Canada," *Statistics Canada Rural and Small Town Canada Analysis Bulletin*, vol. 6, no. 1, January 2005. Ottawa: Statistics Canada.

37. Capital Regional Planning Board of B.C., "University Study Area: A Report on Land Use and Major Roads in the Vicinity of Gordon Head University Campus," Victoria, June 1962, p. 2.

38. Ibid.

39. G. Murdoch, "A History of the Municipality of Oak Bay," Victoria, [Unpublished document] 1968; Aman Paul Gill, *Staying the Course: Resisting Change in a Planned Middle Class Neighborhood*, Master's thesis, University of Victoria, 2005.

40. M. Wisenthal, "Table W 1-9, Total Full-time Enrollment 1950–1974" [online], *Historical Statistics of Canada, Section W (Education)*, F.H. Leacy, ed. [Cited July 26, 2005], Ottawa: Statistics Canada, n.d. <http://www.statcan.ca/english/freepub/11-516-XIE/sectionw/sectionw.htm>.

41. Ibid.

42. Thomas D. Snyder, ed., "120 Years of American Education: A Statistical Portrait" [online], [Cited August 31, 2005], Washington: National Center for Education Statistics, 1993. <http://nces.ed.gov/pubs93/93442.pdf>.

43. Ibid.

44. Dwight Young, "Alternatives to Sprawl" [online], [Cited July 26, 2005], Cambridge: Lincoln Institute of Land Policy, 1995. <http://www.lincolninst.edu/pubs/dl/864_Alt%20to%20Sprawl.pdf>.

45. Worldwatch Institute, "Curbing Sprawl to Fight Climate Change" [online], [Cited July 26, 2005], Washington: Worldwatch Institute, 2002. <http://www.worldwatch.org/press/news/2002/06/28/>.
46. Ibid.
47. James Howard Kunstler, *Geography of Nowhere: The Rise and Decline of America's Man-made Landscape*, New York: Simon & Schuster, 1993.
48. G. Benko, "Introduction: Modernity, Postmodernity, and the Social Sciences," in *Space and Social Theory: Interpreting Modernity and Postmodernity*, G. Benko & U. Strohmayer, eds., Oxford: Blackwell, 1997, p. 23.
49. Timothy W. Luke, "Global Cities vs. 'global cities': Rethinking Contemporary Urbanism as Political Ecology," *Studies in Political Economy*, no. 70, 2003, p. 26.
50. David Orr, *Ecological Literacy: Education and the Transition to a Postmodern World*, Albany: State University of New York Press, 1992.
51. David A. Gruenewald, "The Best of Both Worlds: A Critical Pedagogy of Place," *Educational Researcher*, vol. 32, no. 4, 2003, pp. 3–12.
52. A. Merrifield, "Place and Space: A Lefebvrian Reconciliation," *Transactions of the British Institute of Geographers*, vol. 18, 1993, pp. 521–25.

Chapter 4: leaving carbon city

1. Richard Heinberg, *The Party's Over: Oil, War and the Fate of Industrial Societies*, Gabriola Island: New Society, 2003; PFC Energy, "PFC Energy's Global Crude Oil and Natural Gas Liquids Supply Forecast" [online], [Cited August 2, 2005], 2005, http://www.csis.org/energy/040908_presentation.pdf; Kjell Aleklett, "Peak and Decline of World Production of Oil," presented at the International Workshop on Oil Depletion: Uppsala University, May 2002; Michael C. Ruppert, *Peak Oil and the Big Picture* [onlinc], Speech, August 31, 2004, [Cited July 28, 2005], YubaNet, November 30, 2004. <http://www.yubanet.com/cgi-bin/artman/exec/view.cgi/13/15732>.
2. Peter M. Jackson & Robert W. Esser, "Worldwide Liquids Capacity Outlook to 2010: Tight Supply or Excess of Riches," Cambridge: Cambridge Energy Research Associates, 2005.
3. *World Energy Outlook 2005: Middle East and North Africa Insights, Executive Summary* [online], [Cited November 29, 2005], Paris: International Energy Agency, 2005, p. 43. <www.worldenergyoutlook.org/>.
4. William Toor & Spense Havlick, *Transportation and Sustainable Campus Communities: Issues, Examples, and Solutions*, Portland: Island Press, 2004, p. 1.
5. Ruppert, op. cit.
6. Ibid.
7. Worldwatch Institute, *Vital Signs 2005*, New York: W.W. Norton, 2005, p. 30.

8. Ibid.

9. Ruppert, op. cit.

10. "The 2005 Global 500," *Fortune Magazine*, New York, July 25, 2005, vol. 151, no. 15; "Fortune Global 500," *Fortune Magazine*, New York, May 3, 1982, vol. 105, no. 9.

11. Richard Hill, "Portland Trims Carbon Dioxide to 15-Year Low" [online], *The Oregonian*, [Cited August 31, 2005], June 9, 2005. http://www.oregonlive.com/news/oregonian/index.ssf?/base/front_page/1118311291318380.xml&coll=7>.

12. Clive Ponting, *A Green History of the World*, New York: Penguin, 1991, p. 338.

13. Ibid., p. 330.

14. Henry Ewert, *Victoria's Streetcar Era*, Victoria: Sono Nis Press, 1992, p. 91.

15. Ken Rouche, "Streetcars and Fairfield," *Fairfield Observer*, Victoria: Fairfield Community Association Newsletter, March 2001, pp. 1–2.

16. Scott Ingbritson, *A Brief History of Transit in Victoria and the Lower Mainland*, [online], [Cited October 21, 2005], Victoria: BC Transit. <http://www.transitworkers.novatone.net/PUBLIC/a_brief_history_of_transit.htm>.

17. Henry Ewert, op. cit., p. 127.

18. Geoffrey Castle, ed., *Saanich: An Illustrated History*, Victoria: The Corporation of the District of Saanich, 1989, p. 49.

19. Al Mankoff, "Revisiting the American Streetcar Scandal," *In Transition Magazine*, Newark, Summer 1999, vol. 4, quoted in Jane Jacobs, *Dark Age Ahead*, New York: Random House, 2004, p. 186.

20. Ibid., p. 58.

21. Geoffrey Skelsey, *The ALRV and CLRV Turn at the Canadian National Exhibition Terminus, in the Shadow of the Gardener Expressway, September 2000* [online], [Cited October 20, 2005], Tramway Resources, 2000. <http://www.tramwayresources.com/trams/ttc10.html>.

22. Toronto Transit Commission, *Operating Statistics: Key Facts* [online], [Cited October 5, 2005], Toronto, 2004. <http://www.toronto.ca/ttc/pdf/operatingstatistics2004.pdf>.

23. San Francisco Municipal Railway, *On the Move Over 90 Years: 1919–2002*, San Francisco: State of Muni, 2002.

24. Jay Walljasper, "Enlightened Cities Around the World: 7 Urban Wonders," *UTNE Reader*, Nov–Dec 2001, p. 82.

25. Rex Burkholder, *Interview*, January 20 & February 24, 2004.

26. Todd Litman, *Interview*, January 8, 2004.

27. Bunt & Associates Engineering Ltd., *UVic Traffic Audit 2004*, Victoria, 2004. In addition to the cars entering UVic directly are those that pass through it along Sinclair Road.

28. Carlos J.L. Balsas, "Sustainable Transportation Planning on College Campuses," *Transport Policy*, vol. 10, 2003, pp. 35–49.

29. William Toor & Spense Havlick, *Transportation and Sustainable Campus Communities: Issues, Examples, and Solutions*, Portland: Island Press, 2004, p. 6.

30. Urban Systems, "U-Pass Review: Final Report," [online], [Cited August 20, 2005], Vancouver: University of British Columbia Transportation Planning Department — TREK: "Trip Reduction, Research, Education, and Knowledge," May 4, 2005. <http://www.trek.ubc.ca/research/pdf/U-Pass%20Review%20Final%20Report.pdf>.

31. "Campus Traffic Patterns Changing, Audit Shows." *The Ring*, Victoria: University of Victoria, January 2005, vol. 31, no. 1, p. 1.

32. Corinne Dibert, "The Parking Issue: Does UVic Need More Parking Lots?" Research paper, in possession of authors, Victoria: University of Victoria, 2003.

33. Toor & Havlick, op. cit., p. 190.

34. Ibid., p. 80.

35. Ibid., p. 123.

36. Jeffrey Brown, Daniel Baldwin Hess & Donald Shoup, "Unlimited Access," *Transportation*, vol. 28, 2001, p. 243.

37. Toor & Havlick, op. cit., p. 4.

38. William Toor, "Sustainable Transportation for Campus Communities," paper presented at EFS West's North American Conference on Sustainability and Higher Education, University of Portland, October 21–23, 2004.

39. Balsas, op. cit., p. 38.

40. Environmental Center, University of Colorado at Boulder, "Growing Without Increasing Traffic," in *Blueprint for a Sustainable Campus* [online], [Cited August 31, 2005], 2000. <http://ecenter.colorado.edu/greening_cu/2002/page3.html >.

41. Cornell Chronicle, "CU Designated by Government as a 'Best Workplace for Commuters,'"[online], [Cited October 27, 2005], Ithaca: Cornell University, August 26, 2004. <http://www.news.cornell.edu/Chronicle/04/8.26.04/commuter_workplace.html>.

42. Environmental Protection Agency, "Transportation Management: If You Build It They Will Come," [online], [Cited August 31, 2005], New England: Environmental Protection Agency, April 2003, p. 1. <http://www.epa.gov/ne/assistance/univ/pdfs/bmps/CornellTransportation.pdf>.

43. Litman, op. cit..

44. Julian Hunt, ed., *London's Environment: Prospects for a Sustainable World City*, London: Imperial College Press, 2005.

45. William Dietrich, "A Tale of Three Cities," *Seattle Times*, February 2, 2003, 1.

46. Ron Collins, "Wind-generated Electricity to Power Calgary's C Train" [online], [Cited October 18, 2005], Washington: American Public Transport Association, 2005. <http://www.apta.com/services/intnatl/intfocus/windelec.cfm>.

47. Walljasper, op. cit., p. 82.

48. Friedrich Schmidt-Bleek, "Chapter 1: Making Sustainability Accountable: Putting Resource Productivity into Praxis," in *A Report by the Factor 10 Club* [online], [Cited October 19, 2005], 1999. <http://www.factor10-institute.org/pdf/F10REPORT.pdf>.

Chapter 5: taking the high street

1. Paul Merrick, *Interview*, November 5, 2004 and July 14, 2005.

2. Robert Campbell, *Universities Are the New City Planners* [online], [Cited September 1, 2005], Boston: *Boston Globe*, March 20, 2005. <http://www.boston.com/ae/theater_arts/articles/2005/03/20/universities_are_the_new_city_planners/>.

3. University of Victoria, "Facts and Figures" [online], [Cited July 27, 2005], Victoria, 2005, July 18, 2005. <http://www.uvic.ca/about/factsfigures/>.

4. City of Victoria, "Employment" [online], [Cited October 14, 2005], Victoria: City of Victoria, 2004. <http://www.city.victoria.bc.ca/common/pdfs/profiles_city_emplym.pdf>.

5. University of Victoria, op. cit.

6. UBC Public Affairs, "Facts and Figures: 2004/2005" [online], [Cited August 28, 2005], Vancouver: University of British Columbia, 2005, May 30, 2005. <http://www.publicaffairs.ubc.ca/ubcfacts/index.html>.

7. Susan Bloch-Nevitte, "University Bolsters GTA Economy with $4.7 Billion Impact" [online], *University of Toronto News*, [Cited August 16, 2005], Toronto, December 9, 2003, updated January 12, 2004. <http://www.news.utoronto.ca/bin5/031219a.asp>.

8. Office of New Haven and State Affairs, *Yale and New Haven* [online], [Cited August 1, 2005], New Haven: Yale University, 2005. <http://www.yale.edu/onhsa/facts.htm>.

9. Ira Harkavy & Harmon Zuckerman, "Eds and Meds: Cities' Hidden Assets" [online], *Survey Series*, [Cited August 29, 2005], Washington: The Brookings Institution, Center on Urban & Metropolitan Policy, 1999, p. 1. <http://www.brookings.edu/es/urban/eds&meds.pdf>.

10. Ibid., p. 2.

11. Ibid., p. 3.

12. Peter Marcuse & Cuz Potter, "Columbia University's Heights," in *The University as Urban Developer*, David C. Perry and Wim Weiwel, eds., Armont: M.E. Sharpe, 2005, p. 45.

13. Carol K. Strayhorn, "The Impact of the State Higher Education System on the Texas Economy" [online], [Cited July 28, 2005], Austin: Window on State Government, Texas Comptroller of Public Accounts, 2005. <http://www.window.state.tx.us/specialrpt/highered05/>.

14. IFC Consulting, "California's Future: It Starts Here — UC's Contributions to Economic Growth, Health, and Culture,": prepared for the University of California, Oakland, 2003.

15. Richard M. Rosan, *The Key Role of Universities in Our Nation's Economic Growth and Urban Revitalization* [online], [Cited July 28 2005], Cambridge: Lincoln Institute of Land Policy, 2002. <http://www.uli.org/AM/Template.cfm?Section=Search&template=/ CM/HTMLDisplay.cfm&ContentID=5524>.

16. BankBoston Economics Department, "MIT: The Impact of Innovation, a Special Report of the BankBoston Economics Department," Cambridge: MIT Press, 1997.

17. Barbara Sherry, "Universities as Developers: An International Conversation," in *Land Lines Newsletter*, Cambridge: Lincoln Institute of Land Policy, 2005.

18. David C. Perry & Wim Weiwel, *The University as Urban Developer*, Armont: M.E. Sharpe and Lincoln Institute of Land Policy, 2005, pp. xiii-xiv.

19. Jan Gehl & Lars Gemzøe, *New City Spaces*, Copenhagen: Danish Architectural Press, 2000.

20. Ibid.

21. Rex Burkholder, *Interview*, January 20 & February 24, 2004.

22. Christopher Alexander, Sara Ishikawa & Murray Silverstein, *A Pattern Language: Towns, Buildings, Construction*, New York: Oxford University Press, 1977, p. 223.

23. Cheeying Ho, *Interview*, February 20, 2004.

24. Patrick Condon, *Interview*, February 20, 2004.

25. Emily MacNair & Shannon McDonald, *A Path Less Taken: Planning for Smart Growth at the University of Victoria*, Victoria: POLIS Project on Ecological Governance, 2001.

26. Doug Ward, "Mountaintop Fourth Avenue: There Will Be Nothing of the Suburban Mall Look to SFU's New UniverCity Community" [online], [Cited August 29, 2005], Vancouver, *Vancouver Sun*, April 27, 2004. <http://www.univercity.ca/bmcp/vancouversunapril27-04.html>.

27. Joel Kotkin, *The New Suburbanism: A Realist's Guide to the American Future* [online], [Cited November 20, 2005], Costa Mesa: The Planning Center, November 2005. <www.planningcenter.com/resources/index.html>.

28. Michael Geller, *Interview*, Feb 16, 2004.

29. Michael Geller, in Ward, op. cit., p. 1.

30. Joe van Belleghem, *Speech*, Dockside Proposal, Victoria, December 7, 2004.

31. Dockside Submission to Council, Victoria, December 8, 2004, "The Emergence of Ecological Modernization: Integrating the Environment and the Economy?"

32. Van Belleghem, op. cit.

33. Paul Hawken, Amory Lovins & L. Hunter Lovins, *Natural Capitalism*, Boston: Little, Brown, 1999.

34. Stephen C. Young, ed., *The Emergence of Ecological Modernization: Integrating the Environment and the Economy?* London, Routledge, 2000.

35. Facilities Management, *Sustainability* [online], [Cited July 27, 2005], Victoria: University of Victoria, 2005, updated June 29, 2005. <http://web.uvic.ca/fmgt/sustain.html>.

36. Freda Pagani, "UBC: Canada's Unexpected Leader in Campus Sustainability," paper presented at the North American Conference on Sustainability and Higher Education, October 21–23, 2004, Portland, Oregon: Education for Sustainability Western Network, 2004.

37. Second Nature, *The University Modeling Sustainability as an Institution* [online], [Cited September 23, 2005], Boston, 2001. <http://www.secondnature.org/pdf/snwritings/factsheets/UnivModelSust.pdf>.

38. Northeast Energy Services Company Inc. (NORESCO), "Columbia University," [online], *Higher Education*, [Cited August 2, 2005], Westborough, 2000. <http://www.noresco.com/site/content/CaseStudy_174.asp>.

39. Pagani, op. cit.

40. Matthew St. Clair, "The University of California Goes Solar: How Students Convinced One of the Largest University Systems in the United States to Adopt an Ambitious Sustainability Policy," *Sustainable Development Education: Holistic and Integrative Educational and Management Approaches for Ensuring Sustainable Societies (A Global Conference for Educators and Educational Policy Makers)*, ed. Campus Monterrey Tecnológico de Monterrey. Monterrey, Mexico: Environmental Management for Sustainable Universities, June 2004.

41. Robert C. Dynes, President, *University of California Policy on Green Building Design and Clean Energy Standards*, Oakland: University of California, Office of the President, June 16, 2004, pp. 1, 3, 4.

42. Middlebury College Trustees, *Designing the Future Guiding Principles of Middlebury College* [online], [Cited September 23, 2005], Middlebury College, 1999. <http://community.middlebury.edu/~enviroc/gbprinciples.html>.

43. Second Nature, op. cit.

44. Duke University, *Duke Green Power Challenge* [online], [Cited August 19, 2005], Durham: Duke University, August 5, 2005. <http://www.duke.edu/sustainability/green_power_challenge.html>.

45. Second Nature, op. cit.

46. Centre for Interactive Research on Sustainability, *Accelerating Sustainability* [online], [Cited August 19, 2005], Burnaby: Simon Fraser University, 2005. <http://www.sfu.ca/~clayman/CIRSPPT.pdf>.

47. Peter Calamai, "Sustaining Biosphere's Legacy: Facility in London to Feature Sealed Environments; Federal Money for This and Project in Vancouver," *Toronto Star*, March 13, 2004, F5.

48. David Orr, *Ecological Literacy: Education and the Transition to a Postmodern World*, Albany: State University of New York Press, 1992.

49. David Orr, *Interview*, February 27, 2005.

50. Malcolm Curtis, "Radical Dockside Plan Wins Plaudits," *Times Colonist*, December 8, 2004, A1.

51. Walter Prescott Webb, *The Great Frontier*, Austin: University of Texas Press, 1951, p. 14.

52. John I. Gilderbloom & R. L. Mullins, *Promise and Betrayal: Universities and the Battle for Sustainable Urban Neighborhoods*, Albany: State University of New York Press, 2005.

53. Herman E. Daly, *Steady-State Economics*, 2nd ed., Washington: Island Press, 1991.

Chapter 6: locating the commons

1. Dennis Normile, "Conservation Takes a Front Seat as University Builds New Campus," *Science*, vol. 305, no. 5682, 2004, pp. 329–31.

2. Ibid., p. 329.

3. Ibid., p. 330.

4. Ibid.

5. Ibid.

6. Tetsukazu Yahara, in Normile, op. cit., p. 330.

7. Briony Penn, *Interview*, April 18, 2004.

8. Graham Watt-Gremm, "Towards Ecological Stewardship and Planning at the University of Victoria, British Columbia," Unpublished document, Victoria, 2003.

9. James MacKinnon, "Unique UVic Habitat Disappearing," *The Martlet*, Victoria: University of Victoria Students' Society, October 29, 1992, 1.

10. W.G. Hoskins & L. Dudley Stamp, *The Common Lands of England and Wales*, London: Collins, 1963.

11. Jan DeVries, *The Economy of Europe in an Age of Crisis, 1600- 1750*, Cambridge: Cambridge University Press, 1976.

12. Karl Polanyi, *The Great Transformation: The Political and Economic Origins of Our Time*, Boston: Beacon Press, 1944.

13. Chet Bowers, "The Relevance of Eco-justice and the Revitalization of the Commons Issues to Thinking About Greening the University Curriculum" [online], [Cited July 31, 2005], unpublished document, Eugene, 2004, updated June 21, 2005. <http://www.c-a-bowers.com/>.

14. Mark A. Benedict & Edward T. McMahon, "Green Infrastructure: Smart Conservation for the 21st Century" [online], *Sprawlwatch Clearinghouse Monograph Series*, [Cited August 29, 2005], Arlington: The Conservation Fund, 2003. <http://www.sprawlwatch.org/greeninfrastructure.pdf>.

15. Shawn Hall, "UVic Saves Vale," *The Martlet*, Victoria: University of Victoria Students' Society, September 16, 1993, 4.

16. Alisa Smith, "UVic Ignores Claim to Mystic Vale," *The Martlet*, Victoria: University of Victoria Students' Society, January 21,1993, 1.

17. Hall, op. cit.

18. D.V. Gayton, "Ground Work: Basic Concepts of Ecological Restoration in British Columbia," Kamloops, BC: Southern Interior Forest Extension and Research Partnership, 2001.

19. Thomas Winterhoff, "Hobbs Creek Is at Risk," *Saanich News*, February 7, 2001, 10.

20. Facilities Management, *Annual Sustainability Report 2003* [online], [Cited August 29, 2005], Victoria: University of Victoria, 2003.
    <http://web.uvic.ca/fmgt/assets/pdfs/FACI%20Sustain%20report.pdf>.

21. This discussion is based on: Adam Mjolsness, *Bowker Creek History: A Mini-Ethnography*, special research report, in the possession of the authors, Victoria: University of Victoria, April 2003; and, Capital Regional District Environmental Services, *Bowker Creek Watershed Management Plan* [online], [Cited November 3, 2005], Victoria: Bowker Creek Urban Watershed Renewal Initiative, January 2003.
    <http://www.crd.bc.ca/es/environmental_programs/stormwater/bowker_creek.htm>.

22. Environmental Compliance Office, *Stormwater Management Wetland Demonstration Project* [online], [Cited October 27, 2005], Cornell University, Sustainable Campus, 2005.
    <http://www.sustainablecampus.cornell.edu/natural-areas-freds.htm>.

23. Tim Lucas, *Construction Begins on DUWC Wetland Restoration Project* [online], [Cited August 18, 2005], Durham: Duke University Wetland Center News, 2004.
    <http://www.env.duke.edu/wetland/newsitems804.htm>.

24. Duke University Wetland Restoration Project, *Wetland Restoration* [online], [Cited August 19, 2005], Durham: Duke University, updated August 5, 2005.
    <http://www.duke.edu/sustainability/wetland_restoration.html>.

25. University of Wisconsin Arboretum, *About the Arboretum* [online], [Cited July 31, 2005], Madison: University of Wisconsin, 2005. <http://uwarboretum.org/about/>.

26. Matthaei Botanical Gardens and Nichols Arboretum, *Home* [online], [Cited July 31, 2005], Ann Arbor: University of Michigan, 2005. <http://sitemaker.umich.edu/mbgna>.

27. Watt-Gremm, op. cit., p. 11.

28. Bowers, op. cit.

29. Boverket, The National Board of Housing, Building and Planning, *Participatory Planning Processes: The National City Park* [online], [Cited August 15, 2005], Stockholm, 2004, p. 1.
    <http://www.boverket.se/novo/filelib/arkiv10/progress/participatoryplanningprocess.pdf>.

30. Ibid.

31. Emily MacNair, "A Baseline Assessment of Food Security in British Columbia's Capital Region," Victoria: Capital Region Food and Agriculture Initiatives Round Table, 2004, p. 10.

32. Brian Halwell, *Home Grown: The Case for Local Food in a Global Market, Worldwatch Paper 163*, Thomas Prugh, ed., Danvers: Worldwatch Institute, 2002, p. 6.

33. MacNair, op. cit., p. 14.

34. Ibid., p. 8.

35. Ibid., p. 7.

36. Ibid., p. 12.

37. Geoff Johnson, *Interview*, March 2, 2004.

38. University of Victoria Archives, University Secretary's Fonds. Accession No. 94-088, Box 1, File 31. "Mortgage Agreement 1964." Victoria: University of Victoria, 1964.

39. Camassia Learning Centre for Sustainable Living Society, "Camassia Learning Centre for Sustainable Living: Request for the Use of the Mystic Vale Farmlands," unpublished document, Victoria, 1997, p. 11.

40. G.A. Robson, University of Victoria Facilities Management, "Re: CJVI Property Proposal for Use as the Camassia Learning Centre for Sustainable Living," letter to Sol Kinnis, Camassia Learning Centre for Sustainable Living Society, Victoria, November 13, 1997.

41. University of Victoria, *Campus Plan 2003* [online], [Cited August 29, 2005], Victoria: University of Victoria, Vice-President Finance and Operations, 2003, 31. <http://web.uvic.ca/vpfin/campusplan/>.

42. Alejandro Rojas, *Interview*, August 23, 2004.

43. Jason Found & Michael M'Gonigle, *UnCommon Ground: Creating Complete Community at the University of Victoria*, Victoria: POLIS Project on Ecological Governance, March 2005.

44. Enrique Leff, *Green Production: Toward an Environmental Rationality*, Margaret Villanueva, trans., New York: Guilford Publications, 1995.

Chapter 7: structured power

1. Sarah Webb, *Interview*, July 11, 2005.

2. Leith Sharp, *Interview*, June 23, 2005.

3. Sharp, ibid.

4. Leith Sharp, "Green Campuses: The Road from Little Victories to Systemic Transformation," *International Journal of Sustainability in Higher Education*, vol. 3, no. 2, 2002, p. 136.

5. Sharp, op. cit.

6. Julie Newman, *Interview*, June 20, 2005.

7. Matthew St. Clair, *Interview*, June 27, 2005.

8. Sarah Hammond Creighton, *Greening the Ivory Tower: Improving the Track Record of Universities, Colleges, and Other Institutions*, Cambridge: MIT Press, 1998.

9. Institute of Advanced Studies, "International Sustainable Development Governance — The Question of Reform: Key Issues and Proposals" [online], [Cited September 1, 2005], Tokyo: United Nations University, 2002, p. 8. <http://www.ias.unu.edu/binaries/ISDGFinalReport.pdf>.

10. Sharp, op. cit.

11. Jane Jacobs, *Dark Age Ahead*, New York: Random House, 2004.

12. Susan M. Roberts, "Realizing Critical Geographies of the University," *Antipode*, vol. 32, no. 3, 2000, p. 231.

13. University of Victoria, *Campus Plan 2003* [online], [Cited August 29, 2005], Victoria: University of Victoria, Vice-President Finance and Operations, 2003, p. 8. <http://web.uvic.ca/vpfin/campusplan/>.

14. Michael R. Curry, "The Fragmented Individual and the Academic Realms," in *Textures of Place: Exploring Humanist Geographies*, P. Adams, et al., eds., Minneapolis: University of Minnesota Press, 2001, pp. 207–20.

15. Chaia Heller, *The Ecology of Everyday Life: Rethinking the Desire for Nature*, Montréal: Black Rose Books, 1999.

16. David Orr, *Ecological Literacy: Education and the Transition to a Postmodern World*, Albany: State University of New York Press, 1992, p. 104.

17. Pierre Bourdieu, *Homo Academicus*, Stanford: Stanford University Press, 1988.

18. Michel Foucault, *Society Must Be Defended: Lectures at the Collège de France, 1975–76*, (January 7, 1976)," edited by Mauro Bertani and Alessandro Fontana; translated by David Macey. New York: Picador, 2003, p. 183.

19. Sharp, op. cit..

20. Ibid.

21. St. Clair, op. cit..

22. Ibid.

23. Ibid.

24. Michael P. Shriberg, "Sustainability in U.S. Higher Education: Organizational Factors Influencing Campus Environmental Performance and Leadership," PhD thesis, University of Michigan, Ann Arbour, 2002, p. 2.

25. Sharp, op. cit.

26. Adrianna Kezar & Peter D. Eckel, "The Effect of Institutional Culture on Change Strategies in Higher Education: Universal Principles of Culturally Responsive Concepts?" *Journal of Higher Education*, vol. 73, no. 4, 2002, pp. 435–60; Adrianna Kezar, "What Is More Important to Effective Governance: Relationships, Trust, and Leadership, or Structures and Formal Processes?" *New Directions For Higher Education*, no. 127, 2004, pp. 35–46; William G. Tierney & James T.

Minor, "A Cultural Perspective on Communication and Governance," *New Directions For Higher Education*, no. 127, 2004, pp. 85–94.

Chapter 8: active place

1. Julie Newman, "The Onset of Creating a Model Sustainable Institution: A Case Study Analysis of Yale University," in *Proceedings: Committing Universities to Sustainable Development*, Graz, Austria: Graz University, 2005, p. 23.
2. M. Starik, T.N. Schaeffer, P. Berman & A. Hazelwood, "Initial Environmental Project Characterizations of Four US Universities," *International Journal for Sustainability in Higher Education*, vol. 3, no. 4, 2002, p. 344.
3. Lew Gerbilsky (International Society of Doctors for the Environment), "Education for Sustainable Development: A Look from the Ukraine," in *Proceedings: Committing Universities to Sustainable Development*, Graz, Austria: Graz University, 2005, pp. 175–80.
4. Gabriele Zanetto, "Ca'Foscari University of Venice from Local to International Cooperation," in *Proceedings: Committing Universities to Sustainable Development*, Graz, Austria: Graz University, 2005, pp. 210–18.
5. Walter Leal Filho, "European Reference Point for Technology Transfer for Sustainable Development: Mission and Projects," in *Proceedings: Committing Universities to Sustainable Development*, Graz, Austria: Graz University, 2005, pp. 71–80.
6. Volkswagen AutoUni, Wolfsburg, Germany, Website [online], [Cited October 27, 2005]. <http://www.autouni.de/autouni_publish/master/en/communications/contact.html>.
7. Friedrich M. Zimmermann, "The Role of Management in Sustainable Universities," in *Proceedings: Committing Universities to Sustainable Development*, Graz, Austria: Graz University, 2005, p. 11.
8. Dr. Marsha Hanen, *Interview*, July 8, 2005.
9. Office of New Haven and State Affairs, *Yale and New Haven* [online], [Cited August 1, 2005], New Haven: Yale University, 2005. <http://www.yale.edu/onhsa/facts.htm>.
10. Michael Morand, Vice-President of New Haven and State Affairs, *Interview*, July 15, 2005.
11. Office of New Haven and State Affairs, *Strong Neighborhoods: Homeownership* [online], [Cited August 30, 2005], New Haven: Yale University, 2004. <http://www.yale.edu/onhsa/homeowner.htm>.
12. Marcus Ford, *Interview*, June 17, 2005.
13. Julie Newman, *Interview*, June 20, 2005.
14. Susan M. Roberts, "Realizing Critical Geographies of the University," *Antipode*, vol. 32, no. 3, 2000, p. 230.
15. Keith Bassett, "Postmodernism and the Crisis of the Intellectual: Reflections on Reflexivity, Universities, and the Scientific Field," *Environment and Planning D: Society and Space*, vol. 14, 1996, pp. 507–27.

16. Michael M'Gonigle, "Between Globalism and Territoriality: The Emergence of an International Constitution and the Challenge of Ecological Legitimacy" *The Canadian Journal of Law and Jurisprudence*, vol. XV, no. 2, July 2002, pp. 159–174.

17. P. Jackson & N. Thrift, "Geographies of Consumption," in *Acknowledging Consumption: A Review of New Studies*, D. Miller, ed., London & New York: Routledge, 1995.

18. George Lipsitz, "Consumer Spending as State Project," in *Getting and Spending: European and American Consumer Societies in the Twentieth Century*, Charles McGovern, Matthias Judt & Susan Strasser, eds., Cambridge: Cambridge University Press, 1999, pp. 127–147.

19. See, for example, James A. Kushner, *The Post-automobile City: Legal Mechanisms to Establish the Pedestrian-friendly City*, Durham: Carolina Academic Press, 2004.

20. R. Michael M'Gonigle, "A New Naturalism: Is There a (Radical) 'Truth' Beyond the (Postmodern Abyss)?" *Ecotheology*, vol. 8, January 2000, pp. 8–39.

21. David Orr, *Ecological Literacy: Education and the Transition to a Postmodern World*, Albany: State University of New York Press, 1992.

22. Juliet Eilperin, "Colleges Compete to Shrink Their Mark on the Environment," *Washington Post*, June 26, 2005, A01.

23. Greg Licamele, "Gauging GW's Impact on the Local Economy," [online], *By George!*, [Cited August 2, 2005], Washington: George Washington University, 2002. <http://www.gwu.edu/~bygeorge/juneByG!/impact.html>.

24. Neal Pierce, *Wake-up Call for Academia* [online], [Cited August 2, 2005], Washington Post Writers Group, May 29, 2002. <http://www.ceosforcities.org/press/>.

25. CEOs for Cities and the Initiative for a Competitive Inner City, *Leveraging Colleges and Universities for Urban Economic Revitalization: An Urban Action Agenda* [online], [Cited August 2, 2005], Chicago, 2002, 7. <http://ceosforcities.org/research/2002/leveraging_colleges/colleges_1.pdf>.

26. Nan Jenks-Jay & Anthony Cortese, in "Conference Proceedings Summary," Institutions, Climate Change and Civil Society: Acting Now to Protect Our Future, Medford: Tufts University, Tufts Institute of the Environment & Tufts Climate Initiative, April 24, 1999, p. 10.

27. CEOs for Cities and the Initiative for a Competitive Inner City, op. cit., p. 7.

28. Ibid., p. 2.

29. Ibid., p. 3.

30. Julia Silverman, "Students Flock to Campus Organic Farms" [online], *SFGate.com*, [Cited August 2, 2005], San Francisco: *San Francisco Chronicle* (Associated Press), July 22, 2005. <http://www.sfgate.com/cgi-bin/article.cgi?file=/news/archive/2005/07/21/national/a121337D32.DTL>.

31. Ibid.

32. See, for example, John I. Gilderbloom & R.L. Mullins, *Promise and Betrayal: Universities and the Battle for Sustainable Urban Neighborhoods*, Albany: State University of New York, 2005.

33. William Rees, "Impeding Sustainability? The Ecological Footprint of Higher Education," *Planning for Higher Education*, vol. 31, no. 3, March–May 2003, pp. 88–98.

34. See Meric S. Gertler, *Manufacturing Culture: The Institutional Geography of Industrial Practice*, Oxford: Oxford University Press, 2004. And see, D.A. Wolfe and M. Lucas, eds., *Global Networks and Local Linkages: The Paradox of Clusters in an Open Economy*, Montreal and Kingston: McGill-Queens University Press, 2005.

35. D.A. Wolfe and M. Lucas, eds., ibid., Introduction, p. 19.

36. Tom Pocklington & Allan Tupper, *No Place to Learn: Why Universities Aren't Working*, Vancouver: UBC Press, 2002, p. 6.

37. Ruth Anne Hattori & Joyce Wycoff, "Innovation DNA" [online], [Cited August 30, 2005], Louisville: Innovation Network, January 2002, p. 28. <http://www.thinksmart.com/articles/new_world.pdf>.

38. Russel L. Ackoff, *Re-creating the Corporation: A Design of Organizations for the 21ˢᵗ Century*, New York: Oxford University Press, 1999; Royston Greenwood & C.R. Hinnings, "Understanding Radical Organizational Change," in *Organization and Governance in Higher Education*, ASHE Reader Series, M. Christopher Brown II, ed., Boston: Pearson Custom Publishing, 2000, p. 314; Charles Ransom Schwenk, *Identity, Learning and Decision Making in Changing Organizations*, Westport: Quorum Books, 2002.

39. Loraine Powell, "Shedding a Tier: Flattening Organisational Structures and Employee Empowerment," *International Journal of Educational Management*, vol. 16, no. 1, 2002, pp. 54–59.

40. Henry Mintzberg, *Structure in Fives: Designing Effective Organizations*, Englewood Cliffs: Prentice Hall, 1993.

41. Peter M. Senge, *The Fifth Discipline: The Art and Practice of the Learning Organization*, 1ˢᵗ ed., New York: Doubleday/Currency, 1990, p. 3.

42. Richard L. Daft, *Organization Theory and Design*, 7ᵗʰ ed., Mason: South-Western Educational Publishing, 2001.

43. Martin Parker, *Against Management: Organization in the Age of Managerialism*, Cambridge: Polity Press, 2002, p. 81.

44. Ibid., p. 77.

Chapter 9: social movement

1. Board Approves Campus Planning Report," *The Ring*, Victoria: University of Victoria, March 4, 2004.

2. University of Victoria, Board of Governors, Open Session Minutes, Victoria: University of Victoria, Office of the Secretary, May 12, 2003.

3. Jared Diamond, *Collapse: How Societies Choose to Fail or Succeed*, New York: Viking Books, 2005.

4. George E. Pataki & Linda Angello, *Employment in New York State* [online], [Cited August 30, 2005], Albany: State of New York Department of Labour, Division of Research and Statistics, March 2003. http://www.labor.state.ny.us/workforceindustrydata/PDFs/enys0303.pdf; James Fogler & Bruce Estes, *The Ithaca Journal* [online], [Cited August 30, 2005], Ithaca: Gannett, 2005. <http://www.gannett.com/map/ataglance/ithaca.htm >.
5. Jeffrey Lehman, President, "Presidential Inauguration Speech," Ithaca: Cornell University, 2003.
6. Jeffrey Lehman, President, "State of the University Address" [online], [Cited October 26, 2005], Ithaca: Cornell University, October 2004.
    <http://www.sustainablecampus.cornell.edu/org-policy-Lehman10-29-04-4thOrder.htm>.
7. Michelle York, "Protests Slow Cornell's Effort to Build a Parking Lot," *New York Times*, June 7, 2005, B5.
8. Jill Raygor, "Paving Paradise," *Ithaca Times*, June 16, 2004, [online], [Cited December 12, 2005], <www.ithacatimes.com>, http://www.zwire.com/site/news.cfm?newsid=11976664&BRD= 1395&PAG=461&dept_id=216620&rfi=8; New York State Supreme Court, Appellate Division, Third Judicial Department, case number 96595, March 17, 2005.
9. Elizabeth Sanders, *Interview*, Victoria: July 12, 2005.
10. Ibid.
11. Redbud Woods Faculty Working Group, "Statement Read on Behalf of the Redbud Woods Faculty Working Group" [online], [Cited August 2, 2005, 2005], Ithaca: redbudwoods.org, July 18, 2005. <http://www.redbudwoods.org/Faculty-Statement.html>
12. Julian Dautremont-Smith, *Education for Sustainability Western Network Announcements*, [online], [Cited October 26, 2005], Portland, July 20, 2005.
    <http://www.efswest.org/contact/contact.html>.
13. Elizabeth Sanders, personal communication with Michael M'Gonigle, August 1, 2005.
14. Tom Bates, Mayor of Berkeley, *Interview*, Victoria, July 15, 2005.
15. University of California at Berkeley, "UC Berkeley's Economic Impact: Generating Jobs on Campus and Beyond" [online], [Cited August 2, 2005], Berkeley, 2005.
    <http://www.berkeley.edu/econimpact/jobs.html>.
16. University of California, Berkeley, the Regents of the University of California, and the City of Berkeley, *2020 Long Range Development Plan (LRDP) Litigation Settlement Agreement*, Berkeley: University of California, May 25, 2005.
17. J. Habermas, *The Theory of Communicative Action I: Reason and the Rationalization of Society*, Boston: Beacon, 1984.
18. Seyla Benhabib, "Toward a Deliberative Model of Democratic Legitimacy," in *Democracy and Difference*, Seyla Benhabib, ed., Princeton: Princeton University Press, 1996, p.87.
19. George Fallis, "The Mission of the University" [online], *Postsecondary Review: Higher Expectations*

for Higher Education, [Cited July 28, 2005], Toronto: Government of Ontario, 2004, 42. <http://www.cou.on.ca/content/objects/The%20Mission%20V3.pdf>.

20. Iris Young, *Inclusion and Democracy*, New York: Oxford University Press, 2002, 31.

21. Marcus Ford, *Interview*, Victoria, June 17, 2005.

22. Chantal Mouffe, *The Democratic Paradox*, New York: Verso, 2000.

23. Julie Newman, *Interview*, Victoria, June 20, 2005.

24. Leonie Sandercock, *Towards Cosmopolis: Planning for Multicultural Cities*, London: John Wiley and Sons, 1998, p. 23.

25. Ibid., p. 34.

26. Martin Parker, *Against Management: Organization in the Age of Managerialism*, Cambridge: Polity Press, 2002, p. 208.

27. Ibid., p. 209.

28. Michael C. Dorf & Charles F. Sabel, "A Constitution of Democratic Experimentalism," *Columbia Law Review*, vol. 98, no. 2, 1998, pp. 267–473. Archon Fung and Erik Olin Wright, (eds). *Deepening Democracy: Institutional Innovations in Empowered Participatory Governance*. London: Verso, 2003.

29. Diamond, op. cit., p. 425.

30. John S. Dryzek, *Rational Ecology: Environment and Political Economy*, New York: Blackwell, 1987.

31. Tom Pocklington & Allan Tupper, *No Place to Learn: Why Universities Aren't Working*, Vancouver: UBC Press, 2002.

32. Sam Marullo & Bob Edwards, "From Charity to Justice: The Potential of University–Community Collaboration for Social Change," *American Behavioral Scientist*, vol. 43, no. 5, 2000, pp. 895–912.

33. Jane Jacobs, *Dark Age Ahead*, New York: Random House, 2004, pp. 174–75.

34. M.C.E. van Dam-Mieras, "RCE-Europe: Regional Centres of Expertise in the Context of the UN Decade Education for Sustainable Development," in *Proceedings: Committing Universities to Sustainable Development*.

BIBLIOGRAPHY

Ableman, Michael. *On Good Land: The Autobiography of an Urban Farm*. San Francisco: Chronicle Books, 1998.

Ackoff, Russel L. *Re-creating the Corporation: A Design of Organizations for the 21ˢᵗ Century*. New York: Oxford University Press, 1999.

Aleklett, Kjell. "Peak and Decline of World Production of Oil." Paper presented at the International Workshop on Oil Depletion, Uppsala University, May 2002.

Alexander, Christopher, Sara Ishikawa and Murray Silverstein. *A Pattern Language: Towns, Buildings, Construction*. New York: Oxford University Press, 1977.

Altbach, Philip G. "India and the World University Crisis." In *The Student Revolution*, edited by Philip G. Altbach. Bombay: Popular Press, 1970.

Arbess, Bobby. "High Density Destruction." *The Martlet*. Victoria: University of Victoria Students' Society, 1993, 7.

Association of Universities and Colleges of Canada. *Quick Facts* [online]. [Cited July 26, 2005]. Ottawa: Association of Universities and Colleges of Canada, February 17, 2005. <http://www.aucc.ca/publications/research/quick_facts_e.html>.

Association of Universities and Colleges of Canada. *A Strong Foundation for Innovation* [online]. [Cited July 5, 2005]. Background papers on universities and Canada's Innovation Strategy, Ottawa: Association of Universities and Colleges of Canada, 2002. <http://www.aucc.ca/_pdf/english/reports/2002/innovation/inno_backgr_e.pdf>.

Association of Universities and Colleges of Canada. *Trends in Higher Education, 2002: Summary of Findings* [online]. [Cited July 26, 2005]. Ottawa, November 18, 2004. <http://www.aucc.ca/publications/auccpubs/research/trends/summary_e.html>.

Australian Bureau of Statistics. *3101.0 Australian Demographic Statistics* [online]. [Cited July 25, 2005]. Australian Government, 2004. <http://www.abs.gov.au/>.

Balsas, Carlos J.L. "Sustainable Transportation Planning on College Campuses." *Transport Policy*. Vol. 10, 2003, pp. 35–49.

BankBoston Economics Department. "MIT: The Impact of Innovation, a Special Report of the BankBoston Economics Department." Cambridge: MIT Press, 1997.

Barnet, Richard J. *The Lean Years: Politics in the Age of Scarcity*. New York: Simon & Schuster, 1980.

Bassett, Keith. "Postmodernism and the Crisis of the Intellectual: Reflections on Reflexivity, Universities, and the Scientific Field." *Environment and Planning D: Society and Space*. Vol. 14, 1996, pp. 507–27.

Bates, Tom. Mayor of Berkeley. *Interview* July 15, 2005.

Bein, Magnus and Jolene Clarke. "Ecological Stewardship: From Fragments to Fusion." Victoria: University of Victoria, 2003.

Benedict, Mark A. and Edward T. McMahon. "Green Infrastructure: Smart Conservation for the 21st Century" [online]. [Cited August 29, 2005]. *Sprawlwatch Clearinghouse Monograph Series*. Arlington: The Conservation Fund, 2003. <http://www.sprawlwatch.org/greeninfrastructure.pdf>.

Benhabib, Seyla. "Toward a Deliberative Model of Democratic Legitimacy." In *Democracy and Difference*, edited by Seyla Benhabib, pp. 67–94. Princeton: Princeton University Press, 1996.

Benko, G. "Introduction: Modernity, Postmodernity, and the Social Sciences." In *Space and Social Theory: Interpreting Modernity and Postmodernity*, edited by G. Benko and U. Strohmayer. Oxford: Blackwell, 1997.

Benyus, Janine. *Biomimicry: Innovation Inspired by Nature*. New York: Perennial (HarperCollins), 1997.

Bloch, Eric. "Testimony to Congress." National Science Foundation, 1988. In James J. Duderstadt, "Future of Higher Education in the Knowledge-Driven, Global Economy of the 21st Century" [online]. *175th Anniversary Symposium, October 31, 2002*. [Cited August 1, 2005]. Toronto: University of Toronto, 2002. <http://milproj.ummu.umich.edu/publications/toronto/download/Toronto_103102.pdf>.

Bloch-Nevitte, Susan. "University Bolsters GTA Economy with $4.7 Billion Impact" [online]. [Cited August 16, 2005]. *University of Toronto News*. Toronto, December 9, 2003, updated January 12, 2004. <http://www.news.utoronto.ca/bin5/031219a.asp>.

Board of the Millennium Ecosystem Assessment. "Living Beyond Our Means: Natural Assets and Human Well-being, Statement from the Board," New York: United Nations, 2005.

Bok, Derek. *Universities in the Marketplace: The Commercialization of Higher Education*. Princeton, NJ: Princeton University Press, 2003.

Boulevard Transportation Group. "University of Victoria Transportation Demand Management Study." Victoria: University of Victoria, 2003.

Bourdieu, Pierre. *Homo Academicus*. Stanford: Stanford University Press, 1988.

Boverket, The National Board of Housing, Building and Planning. *Participatory Planning Processes: The National City Park* [online]. [Cited August 1, 2005]. <http://www.boverket.se/novo/filelib/arkiv10/progress/participatoryplanningprocess.pdf>; <http://www.boverket.se/index.htm>.

Bowers, Chet. *The Relevance of Eco-justice and the Revitalization of the Commons Issues to Thinking About Greening the University Curriculum* [online]. [Cited July 31, 2005]. Eugene, June 21, 2005. <http://www.c-a-bowers.com/>.

Bracken, Len. *Guy Debord, Revolutionary: A Critical Biography*. Los Angeles, CA: Feral House, 1997. Available at <http://www.neravt.com/left/may1968.htm>.

British Columbia Archives. "Original Treaty." ADD. MSS772. Victoria.

Brown, Jeffrey, Daniel Baldwin Hess and Donald Shoup. "Unlimited Access," *Transportation*. Vol. 28, 2001, p. 243.

Bryce, Cheryl. *Interview*. October 26, 2006.

Bunt & Associates Engineering Ltd. *UVic Traffic Audit 2004*. Victoria, 2004.

Burkholder, Rex. *Interview*. January 20 & February 24, 2004.

Calamai, Peter. "Sustaining Biosphere's Legacy: Facility in London to Feature Sealed Environments; Federal Money for This and Project in Vancouver." *Toronto Star*. March 13, 2004, F5.

Calthorpe, Peter. *The Next American Metropolis*. New York: Princeton Architectural Press, 1993.

Camassia Learning Centre for Sustainable Living Society. "Camassia Learning Centre for Sustainable Living: Request for the Use of the Mystic Vale Farmlands." Unpublished document. Victoria, 1997.

Campbell, Colin and Anders Sivertsson. "The 2003 Update of the ASPO Oil & Gas Depletion Model." Paper presented at the 2nd International Workshop on Oil Depletion, Paris, France, May 26–27, 2003.

Campbell, Kenneth D. *University Patents Support 246,000 Jobs, Contribute Billions to Economy* [online]. [Cited July 25, 2005]. Boston: MIT News Office, 1999. <http://web.mit.edu/newsoffice/1999/patents-0113.html>.

Campbell, Robert. *Universities Are the New City Planners* [online]. [Cited September 1, 2005]. *Boston Globe*. Boston, March 20, 2005. <http://www.boston.com/ae/theater_arts/articles/2005/03/20/universities_are_the_new_city_planners/>.

Campus Consortium for Environmental Excellence. "Construction: Using Green Certified Wood, Middlebury." *Best Management Practices for Colleges and Universities*. New England, MA: United States Environmental Protection Agency, April 2003, p. 1. <www.epa.gov/ne/assistance/univ/pdfs/bmps/MiddleburyCertifiedWood.pdf>.

Capital Regional District Environmental Services. *Bowker Creek Watershed Management Plan* [online]. [Cited November 3, 2005]. Victoria: Bowker Creek Urban Watershed Renewal Initiative, January 2003. <http://www.crd.bc.ca/es/environmental_programs/stormwater/bowker_creek.htm>.

Capital Regional Planning Board of B.C. "University Study Area: A Report on Land Use and Major Roads in the Vicinity of Gordon Head University Campus." Victoria, June 1962.

Castle, Geoffrey, ed. *Saanich: An Illustrated History*. Victoria: The Corporation of the District of Saanich, 1989.

Castree, Noel and Matthew Sparke. "Introduction: Professional Geography and the Corporatization of the University: Experiences, Evaluations and Engagements." *Antipode*. Vol. 32, no. 3, 2000, pp. 222–29.

Centre for Interactive Research on Sustainability. *Accelerating Sustainability* [online]. [Cited August 19, 2005]. Burnaby: Simon Fraser University, 2005. <http://www.sfu.ca/~clayman/CIRSPPT.pdf>.

CEOs for Cities and the Initiative for a Competitive Inner City. *Leveraging Colleges and Universities for Urban Economic Revitalization: An Urban Action Agenda* [online]. [Cited August 2, 2005]. Chicago, 2002. <http://ceosforcities.org/research/2002/leveraging_colleges/colleges_1.pdf>.

Chan, Timothy. "The Social and Regulatory Relations of Metropolitan Victoria's Commercial Greenhouse Industry: 1900 to 1996."Thesis, University of Victoria, 1997.

City of Victoria. "Employment" [online]. [Cited October 14, 2005]. Victoria: City of Victoria, 2004. <http://www.city.victoria.bc.ca/common/pdfs/profiles_city_emplym.pdf>.

Collard, Rosemary. "Annual Savings by University Environmental Sustainability Programs." Adapted from Garrett W. Meiggs, *Campus Sustainability in Higher Education*. Ithaca: Cornell University, 2005.

Collins, Ron. "Wind-generated Electricity to Power Calgary's C Train" [online]. [Cited October 18, 2005]. Washington: American Public Transport Association, 2005. <http://www.apta.com/services/intnatl/intfocus/windelec.cfm>.

Community Food Security Coalition. "Farm-to-College Program." From *Information about Individual Programs*. Venice, CA: Community Food Security Coalition. <http://www.farmtocollege.org/list.php>.

Condon, Patrick. *Interview*. February 20, 2004.

Conca, Ken. "Beyond the Statist Frame: Environmental Politics in a Global Economy." In *Nature, Production, Power: Towards an Ecological Political Economy*, edited by Fred P. Gale and Michael M'Gonigle. Northampton: Edward Elgar, 2000.

Cornell Chronicle. *CU Designated by Government as a 'Best Workplace for Commuters'* [online]. [Cited October 27, 2005]. Ithaca: Cornell University, August 26, 2004. <http://www.news.cornell.edu/Chronicle/04/8.26.04/commuter_workplace.html>.

Creighton, Sarah Hammond. *Greening the Ivory Tower: Improving the Track Record of Universities, Colleges, and Other Institutions*. Cambridge: MIT Press, 1998.

Curry, Michael R. "The Fragmented Individual and the Academic Realms." In *Textures of Place: Exploring Humanist Geographies*, edited by P. Adams, et al. Minneapolis: University of Minnesota Press, 2001.

Curtis, Malcolm. "Radical Dockside Plan Wins Plaudits." *Times Colonist*. December 8, 2004, A1.

Daft, Richard L. *Organization Theory and Design*, 7th ed. Mason: South-Western Educational Publishing, 2001.

Daly, Herman E. *Steady-State Economics*, 2nd ed. Washington: Island Press, 1991.

Dautremont-Smith, Julian. "Students Flock to Organic Campus Farms." *Education for Sustainability Western Network Announcements* [online]. [Cited October 26, 2005]. Portland, July 20, 2005. <http://www.efswest.org/contact/contact.html>.

Department of Labor. *Employment in New York State* [online]. [Cited August 30, 2005]. March 2003. <http://www.labor.state.ny.us/workforceindustrydata/PDFs/enys0303.pdf>.

Derrida, Jacques. "White Mythology." In *Margins of Philosophy*, translated by Alan Bass. Chicago: University of Chicago Press, 1982.

DeVries, Jan. *The Economy of Europe in an Age of Crisis, 1600–1750*. Cambridge: Cambridge University Press, 1976.

Diamond, Jared. *Collapse: How Societies Choose to Fail or Succeed*. New York: Viking Books, 2005.

Dibert, Corinne. "The Parking Issue: Does UVic Need More Parking Lots?" Research paper, in possession of authors. Victoria: University of Victoria, 2003.

Dietrich, William. "A Tale of Three Cities." *Seattle Times*, February 2, 2003, 1.

Dorf, Michael C. and Charles F. Sabel. "A Constitution of Democratic Experimentalism." *Columbia Law Review*. Vol. 98, no. 2, 1998, pp. 267–473.

Dryzek, John S. *Rational Ecology: Environment and Political Economy*. New York: Blackwell, 1987.

Duderstadt, James J. *Future of Higher Education in the Knowledge-Driven, Global Economy of the 21st Century* [online]. [Cited August 1, 2005]. 175th Anniversary Symposium, October 31, 2002. Toronto, 2002 <http://milproj.ummu.umich.edu/publications/toronto/download/Toronto_103102.pdf>.

Duderstadt, James J. "Governance and Leadership." In *A University for the 21st Century*. Ann Arbor: University of Michigan Press, 2000.

Duff, Wilson. "The Fort Victoria Treaties." *BC Studies*. No. 3, Fall 1969, pp. 3–57.

Duke University. *Duke Green Power Challenge* [online]. [Cited August 19, 2005]. Durham: Duke University, August 5, 2005. <http://www.duke.edu/sustainability/green_power_challenge.html>.

Duke University Wetland Restoration Project. *Wetland Restoration* [online]. [Cited August 19, 2005]. Durham: Duke University, August 5, 2005. <http://www.duke.edu/sustainability/wetland_restoration.html>.

Dynes, Robert C., President. *University of California Policy on Green Building Design and Clean Energy Standards*. Oakland: University of California, Office of the President. June 16, 2004.

Eagan, David, J. and Julian Keniry. "Green Investment, Green Return: How Practical Conservation Projects Save Millions on America's Campuses." National Wildlife Federation: Campus Ecology Program, 1998.

Earth Negotiations Bulletin. December 12, 2005, vol. 12, no. 291. International Institute for
Sustainable Development. <www.iisd.ca/climate/cop11/>.

"The Ecologist." *Whose Common Future? Reclaiming the Commons*. Gabriola Island: New Society
Publishers, 1993.

Ehrenberg, Ronald G., ed. *Governing Academia: Who Is in Charge at the Modern University?* Ithaca:
Cornell University Press, 2004.

Eilperin, Juliet. "Colleges Compete to Shrink Their Mark on the Environment." *Washington Post*,
June 26, 2005, A01.

Elliott, Dave Sr. *Saltwater People*, edited by Janet Poth. Victoria: Saanich School District 63, 1983.

Enns, Cherie. "Complete Communities: Achieving a New Way of Living in the Lower Mainland."
Paper presented at the "Complete Communities Forum," New Westminster, BC, November
9–10, 1994.

Environmental Center. "Growing Without Increasing Traffic." In *Blueprint for a Sustainable Campus*.
[Cited August 31, 2005]. Boulder: University of Colorado, 2000.
<http://ecenter.colorado.edu/greening_cu/2002/page3.html>.

Environmental Compliance Office. "Stormwater Management Wetland Demonstration Project"
[online]. [Cited October 27, 2005]. Ithaca: Cornell University, Sustainable Campus, 2005.
<http://www.sustainablecampus.cornell.edu/natural-areas-freds.htm>.

Environmental Protection Agency. *Transportation Management: If You Build It They Will Come*
[online]. [Cited August 31, 2005]. New England: Environmental Protection Agency, April 2003.
<http://www.epa.gov/ne/assistance/univ/pdfs/bmps/CornellTransportation.pdf>.

Ewert, Henry. *Victoria's Streetcar Era*. Victoria: Sono Nis Press, 1992.

Facilities Management. *Annual Sustainability Report 2003* [online]. [Cited August 31, 2005]. Victoria:
University of Victoria, 2003.
<http://web.uvic.ca/fmgt/assets/pdfs/FACI%20Sustain%20report.pdf>.

Facilities Management. *Sustainability* [online]. [Cited July 27, 2005]. Victoria: University of Victoria,
June 29, 2005. <http://web.uvic.ca/fmgt/sustain.html>.

Facilities Management. *TDM: History and Travel Statistics* [online]. [Cited July 27, 2005]. Victoria:
University of Victoria, updated June 29, 2005 (by Al Butler).
<http://web.uvic.ca/fmgt/TDM-history.html>.

Fallis, George. "The Mission of the University." In Government of Ontario, *Postsecondary Review:
Higher Expectations for Higher Education*. Toronto: York University, October 2004.
<http://www.cou.on.ca/content/objects/The%20Mission%20V3.pdf>.

Filho, Walter Leal. "European Reference Point for Technology Transfer for Sustainable Development:
Mission and Projects." In *Proceedings: Committing Universities to Sustainable Development*. Graz,
Austria: Graz University, 2005.

Financial Report to the Board of Overseers of Harvard College, Cambridge: Harvard University, 2004. <http://vpf-web.harvard.edu/annualfinancial/pdfs/2003discussion.pdf>.

Fogler, James and Bruce Estes. *The Ithaca Journal* [online]. [Cited August 30, 2005]. Ithaca: Gannett, 2005. <http://www.gannett.com/map/ataglance/ithaca.htm>.

Ford, Marcus. *Beyond the Modern University: Towards a Constructive Post-Modern University*. Westport: Praeger, 2002.

Ford, Marcus. *Interview*. June 17, 2005.

Fortune Magazine. "The Fortune Global 500." New York, May 3, 1982.

Fortune Magazine. "The 2005 Global 500." New York, July 25, 2005.

Foucault, Michel. *Power/Knowledge: Selected Interviews and Other Writings 1972–1977*, edited by Colin Gordon. New York: Pantheon Books, 1980.

Foucault, Michel. *Society Must Be Defended: Lectures at the Collège de France, 1975–76*, edited by Mauro Bertani and Alessandro Fontana; translated by David Macey. New York: Picador, 2003.

Found, Jason and Michael M'Gonigle. *UnCommon Ground: Creating Complete Community at the University of Victoria*. Victoria: POLIS Project on Ecological Governance, March 2005.

Franklin, Carol, Teresa Durkin and Sara Pevaroff Schuh. "The Role of the Landscape in Creating a Sustainable Campus." *Planning for Higher Education*. March–May 2003, pp. 142–49.

Fung, Archon and Erik Olin Wright, (eds). *Deepening Democracy: Institutional Innovations in Empowered Participatory Governance*. London: Verso, 2003.

Gale, Fred P. and R. Michael M'Gonigle, eds. *Nature, Production, Power: Towards an Ecological Political Economy*. Northampton: Edward Elgar, 2000.

Gayton, D.V. "Ground Work: Basic Concepts of Ecological Restoration in British Columbia." Kamloops, BC: Southern Interior Forest Extension and Research Partnership, 2001.

Gehl, Jan and Lars Gemzøe. *New City Spaces*. Copenhagen: Danish Architectural Press, 2000.

Geller, Michael. *Interview*. February 16, 2004.

Gerbilsky, Lew. "Education for Sustainable Development: A Look from the Ukraine." In *Proceedings: Committing Universities to Sustainable Development*, Graz, Austria: Graz University, 2005.

Gerth, H.H. and C. Wright Mills, eds. *From Max Weber: Essays in Sociology*. London: Routledge & Kegan Paul, 1948.

Gertler, Meric S. *Manufacturing Culture: The Institutional Geography of Industrial Practice*. Oxford: Oxford University Press, 2004.

Gilbert, Daniel. "The Corporate University and the Public Intellectual." 2005.

Gilderbloom, John I. and R.L. Mullins. *Promise and Betrayal: Universities and the Battle for Sustainable Urban Neighborhoods*. Albany: State University of New York Press, 2005.

Gill, Aman Paul. "Staying the Course: Resisting Change in a Planned Middle Class Neighborhood." Master's thesis, University of Victoria, 2005.

Gillespie, Robert. *Interview*. January 10, 2005.

Gréard, Octave. "The Sorbonne in the Seventeenth Century." In *Nos adieux à la vieille Sorbonne.* Paris: Hachette, 1983, p. 94.

Green Buildings Design and Clean Energy Standards Steering Committee. *University of California Policy on Green Building Design and Clean Energy Standards.* Oakland: University of California, June 16, 2004.

Greenwood, Royston and C.R. Hinnings. "Understanding Radical Organizational Change." In *Organization and Governance in Higher Education, ASHE Reader Series,* edited by M. Christopher Brown II. Boston: Pearson Custom Publishing, 2000.

Gruenewald, David A. "The Best of Both Worlds: A Critical Pedagogy of Place." *Educational Researcher.* Vol. 32, no. 4, 2003, pp. 3–12.

Gruenewald, David A. "Foundations of Place: A Multidisciplinary Framework for Place-Conscious Education." *American Educational Research Journal.* Vol. 40, no. 3, 2003, pp. 619–54.

Habermas, J. *The Theory of Communicative Action I: Reason and the Rationalization of Society.* Boston: Beacon, 1984.

Hall, Shawn. "UVic Saves Vale." *The Martlet.* Victoria: University of Victoria Students' Society, 1993, 4.

Halwell, Brian. *Home Grown: The Case for Local Food in a Global Market, Worldwatch Paper 163,* edited by Thomas Prugh. Danvers: Worldwatch Institute, 2002.

Hanen, Marsha. *Interview.* July 8, 2005.

Harding, James. "The New Left in BC." In *The New Left in Canada,* edited by Dimitrios J. Roussopoulos. Montréal: Black Rose Books, 1970.

Harkavy, Ira and Harmon Zuckerman. *Eds and Meds: Cities' Hidden Assets* [online]. [Cited August 29, 2005]. Survey Series. Washington: The Brookings Institution, Center on Urban & Metropolitan Policy, 1999. <http://www.brookings.edu/es/urban/eds&meds.pdf>.

Harris, Cole. *Making Native Space: Colonialism, Resistance, and Reserves in British Columbia.* Vancouver: UBC Press, 2002.

Harvard Green Campus Initiative. "New Green Building Loan Fund Announced by President Summers." *Harvard Green Campus Initiative Newsletter.* Vol. 7, Spring 2005. <http://www.greencampus.harvard.edu/newsletter/>.

Harvey, David. *The Condition of Postmodernity.* Oxford: Basil Blackwell, 1989.

Harvey, David. "From Space to Place and Back Again: Reflections on the Condition of Postmodernity." In *Mapping the Futures,* edited by Jon Bird, Barry Curtis, Tim Putnam, George Robertson and Lisa Tickner. London: Routledge, 1993.

Hattori, Ruth Anne and Joyce Wycoff. *Innovation DNA* [online]. [Cited August 30, 2005]. Louiseville: Innovation Network. January 2002. <http://www.thinksmart.com/articles/new_world.pdf>.

Hawken, Paul, Amory Lovins and L. Hunter Lovins. *Natural Capitalism.* Boston: Little, Brown, 1999.

Heinberg, Richard. *The Party's Over: Oil, War and the Fate of Industrial Societies.* Gabriola Island: New Society Publishers, 2003.

Heller, Chaia. *The Ecology of Everyday Life: Rethinking the Desire for Nature*. Montréal: Black Rose Books, 1999.

Herman, Arthur. *How the Scots Invented the Modern World: The True Story of How Western Europe's Poorest Nation Created Our World and Everything in It*. New York: Crown Publishers, 2001.

Higgins, D.W. *The Mystic Spring and Other Tales of Western Life*. Toronto: William Briggs, 1904.

Hill, Richard. "Portland Trims Carbon Dioxide to 15-Year Low." *The Oregonian*, June 9 2005. <http://www.oregonlive.com/news/oregonian/index.ssf?/base/front_page/1118311291318380.xml&coll=7>.

Ho, Cheeying. *Interview*. February 20, 2004.

Hoskins, W.G. and L. Dudley Stamp. *The Common Lands of England and Wales*. London: Collins, 1963.

Hunt, Julian, ed. *London's Environment: Prospects for a Sustainable World City*. London: Imperial College Press. 2005.

Hunter, Iain. "Frozen Precut Sod Turned to Start Varsity Buildup." *Daily Times*, January 22, 1962, 11.

IFC Consulting. "California's Future: It Starts Here — UC's Contributions to Economic Growth, Health, and Culture." Prepared for the University of California, Oakland, 2003.

Ingbritson, Scott. *A Brief History of Transit in Victoria and the Lower Mainland* [online]. [Cited October 21, 2005]. Victoria: BC Transit. <http://www.transitworkers.novatone.net/PUBLIC/a_brief_history_of_transit.htm>.

Institute of Advanced Studies. *International Sustainable Development Governance: The Question of Reform — Key Issues and Proposals* [online]. [Cited September 1, 2005]. Tokyo: United Nations University, 2002. <http://www.ias.unu.edu/binaries/ISDGFinalReport.pdf>.

International Energy Agency. *World Energy Outlook 2005: Middle East and North Africa Insights, Executive Summary* [online]. [Cited November 29, 2005]. Paris: International Energy Agency, 2005. <www.worldenergyoutlook.org/>.

Irvine, Martin. *Emerging e-Education Landscape* [online]. [Cited July 10, 2005]. CIO Series: A Blackboard Strategic Whitepaper. 2002. <http://www.blackboard.com/docs/wp/CIOSeriesWhitePaper.pdf>.

Isitt, Ben. *Interview*. July 28, 2004.

Jackson, P. and N. Thrift. "Geographies of Consumption". In *Acknowledging Consumption: A Review of New Studies*, edited by D. Miller. London and New York: Routledge, 1995.

Jackson, Peter M. and Robert W. Esser. "Worldwide Liquids Capacity Outlook to 2010: Tight Supply or Excess of Riches." Cambridge: Cambridge Energy Research Associates, 2005.

Jacobs, Jane. *Dark Age Ahead*. New York: Random House, 2004.

Jacobs, Jane. *The Death and Life of Great American Cities*. New York: Vintage Books, 1961.

Jenks-Jay, Nan and Anthony Cortese. In *Conference Proceedings Summary* "Institutions, Climate Change and Civil Society: Acting Now to Protect Our Future," Medford, April 24, 1999.

Johnson, Geoff. *Interview*. March 2, 2004.

Johnston, Hugh. *Radical Campus: Making Simon Fraser University*. Vancouver: Douglas and McIntyre, 2005.

The John T. Lyle Center for Regenerative Studies. *About the Lyle Center* and *Masters of Science in Regenerative Studies* [online]. [Cited June 14, 2005]. Pomona, CA: The John T. Lyle Center for Regenerative Studies, September 15, 2004. <http://www.csupomona.edu/~crs/aboutcenter/index.html>.

Jones, Andy. *Eating Oil: Food Supply in a Changing Climate* [online]. [Cited April 09, 2005]. London: Sustain and Elm Farm Research Centre, 2001. <http://www.sustainweb.org/chain_fm_eat.asp>.

Jupp, Ursula. *Cadboro: A Ship, a Bay, a Sea Monster 1842–1958*. Victoria: Ursula Jupp, 1988.

Jupp, Ursula. *From Cordwood to Campus in Gordon Head 1852–1959*. Victoria: Ursula Jupp, 1975.

Jupp, Ursula. "Gordon Head: Since 1959." *The Islander*, November 16, 1980, 8.

Kane, Frank. "British to Help China Build 'Eco-cities.'" *The Observer*. London: Guardian Newspapers, November 6, 2005. <http://www.guardian.co.uk/china/story/0,1635246,00.html>.

Keddie, Grant. *Notes: Archaeological Sites in the Cadboro Bay Area, a Very Brief Overview*. Document in possession of the authors. Victoria: Royal BC Museum, 1990.

Keddie, Grant. *Songhees Pictorial: A History of the Songhees People as Seen by Outsiders, 1790–1912*. Victoria: Royal BC Museum, 2003.

Kerr, Clark. *The Uses of the University*, 5th ed. Cambridge: Harvard University Press, 2001.

Kezar, Adrianna. "What Is More Important to Effective Governance: Relationships, Trust, and Leadership, or Structures and Formal Processes?" *New Directions For Higher Education*. No. 127, 2004, pp. 35–46.

Kezar, Adrianna and Peter D. Eckel. "The Effect of Institutional Culture on Change Strategies in Higher Education: Universal Principles of Culturally Responsive Concepts?" *Journal of Higher Education*. Vol. 73, no. 4, 2002, pp. 435–60.

Kotkin, Joel. *The New Suburbanism: A Realist's Guide to the American Future* [online]. [Cited November 20, 2005]. Costa Mesa: The Planning Center, November 2005. <www.planningcenter.com/resources/index.html>.

Kreis, Steven. "1968: The Year of the Barricades." *The History Guide: Lectures on Twentieth Century Europe*. 2000.

Kunstler, James Howard. *Geography of Nowhere: The Rise and Decline of America's Man-made Landscape*. New York: Simon & Schuster, 1993.

Kushner, James A. *The Post-automobile City: Legal Mechanisms to Establish the Pedestrian-friendly City*. Durham: Carolina Academic Press, 2004.

Land in Farms. Adapted from USDA National Agricultural Statistics Service, Quick Stats U.S. & All States Data, Land in Farms. <http://151.121.3.33:8080/QuickStats/PullData_US>.

Latour, Bruno. *We Have Never Been Modern*. Cambridge: Harvard University Press, 1993.

Lee, Ingmar. *Interview*. July 22, 2004.

Leff, Enrique. *Green Production: Toward an Environmental Rationality*. Margaret Villanueva, trans. New York: Guilford Publications, 1995.

Lehman, Jeffrey. President. "Presidential Inauguration Speech." Ithaca: Cornell University, 2003.

Lehman, Jeffrey. President. "State of the University Address." [Cited October 26, 2005]. Ithaca: Cornell University, October 2004. <http://www.sustainablecampus.cornell.edu/org-policy-Lehman10-29-04-4thOrder.htm>.

Licamele, Greg. "Gauging GW's Impact on the Local Economy" [online]. [Cited August 2, 2005]. *By George!*. Washington: George Washington University, 2002. <http://www.gwu.edu/~bygeorge/juneByG!/impact.html>.

Lipsitz, George. "Consumer Spending as State Project." In *Getting and Spending: European and American Consumer Societies in the Twentieth Century*, edited by Charles McGovern, Matthias Judt and Susan Strasser. Cambridge: Cambridge University Press, 1999.

Litman, Todd. *Interview*. January 8, 2004.

Litman, Todd. *Parking Management Best Practices: Draft*. Victoria: Planners Press, 2004.

Lovelock, James. *The Revenge of Gaia: Why the Earth Is Fighting Back — and How We Can Still Save Humanity*. London: Allen Lane, 2006.

Lowy, Michael. "A 'Red' Government in the South of Brazil." In *Monthly Review*. Vol. 52, no 6, November 2000.

Lucas, Tim. *Construction Begins on DUWC Wetland Restoration Project* [online]. [Cited August 31, 2005]. Durham: Duke University Wetland Center News, 2004. <http://www.env.duke.edu/wetland/newsitems804.htm>.

Luke, Timothy W. "Global Cities vs. 'global cities': Rethinking Contemporary Urbanism as Political Ecology." *Studies in Political Economy*. No. 70, 2003, pp. 11–34.

Lyman, Francesca. "What Makes a Great Place? The New City Beautiful." In *Yes! Magazine*. Summer 2005. <http://www.yesmagazine.org/default.asp?ID=149>.

Mackie, Al. *Personal communication* with Jessie Cowperthwaite. October 21, 2005.

MacKinnon, James. "Unique UVic Habitat Disappearing." *The Martlet*. Victoria: University of Victoria Students' Society, October 29, 1992.

MacNair, Emily. "A Baseline Assessment of Food Security in British Columbia's Capital Region." Victoria: Capital Region Food and Agriculture Initiatives Round Table, 2004.

MacNair, Emily and Shannon McDonald. *A Path Less Taken: Planning for Smart Growth at the University of Victoria*. Victoria: POLIS Project on Ecological Governance, 2001.

Makovsky, Paul. "Pedestrian Cities: Copenhagen's 10-Step Program." *MetropolisMag.com*. August/September, 2002. <http://www.metropolismag.com/html/content_0802/ped/index.html>.

Mankoff, Al. "Revisiting the American Streetcar Scandal." *In Transition Magazine*, Newark, Summer 1999, vol. 4. Quoted in Jane Jacobs, *Dark Age Ahead*. New York: Random House, 2004.

Marcuse, Peter and Cuz Potter. "Columbia University's Heights." In *The University as Urban Developer*, edited by David C. Perry and Wim Weiwel. Armont: M.E. Sharpe, 2005.

Martin, Fernand and Marc Trudeau. "The Economic Impact of University Research." *Research File.* Vol. 2, no. 3, March 1998.

The Martlet. "Taylor Refuses Last Student Plea." Victoria: University of Victoria Students' Society, April 7, 1967.

Marullo, Sam and Bob Edwards. "From Charity to Justice: The Potential of University–Community Collaboration for Social Change." *American Behavioral Scientist.* Vol. 43, no. 5, 2000, pp. 895–912.

Massey, Doreen. "Geographies of Responsibility." *Geografisa Annaler.* Vol. 86B, 2004, p. 11.

Massey, Doreen. "The Political Place of Locality Studies." *Environment and Planning A.* Vol. 23, 1991, pp. 267–81.

Massey, Doreen. "Questions of Locality." *Geography: Journal of the Geographical Association.* Vol. 78, no. 1, 1993, pp. 142–49.

Matthaei Botanical Gardens and Nichols Arboretum. *Home* [online]. [Cited July 31, 2005]. Ann Arbor: University of Michigan, 2005. <http://sitemaker.umich.edu/mbgna>.

McCulloch, Sandra. "Pierre Berton Dies at 84." *Times Colonist*, December 1, 2004, A1.

Merrick, Paul. *Interview.* November 5, 2004.

Merrifield, A. "Place and Space: A Lefebvrian Reconciliation." *Transactions of the British Institute of Geographers.* Vol. 18, 1993, pp. 516–31.

M'Gonigle, Michael. "Between Globalism and Territoriality: The Emergence of an International Constitution and the Challenge of Ecological Legitimacy" *The Canadian Journal of Law and Jurisprudence.* Vol. XV, no. 2, July 2002, pp. 159–174.

M'Gonigle, Michael and Justine Starke. "Minding Place: Towards a Political Ecology of the Sustainable UniverCity." *Journal of Environment and Planning D: Society and Space.* Vol. 24, no. 3, 2006 (forthcoming).

M'Gonigle, R. Michael. "A Dialectic of Centre and Territory: The Political Economy of Ecological Flows and Spatial Relations." In *Nature, Production, Power: Towards an Ecological Political Economy*, edited by Fred P. Gale and R. Michael M'Gonigle. Northampton: Edward Elgar, 2000.

M'Gonigle, R. Michael. "A New Naturalism: Is There a (Radical) 'Truth' Beyond the (Postmodern) Abyss?" *Ecotheology.* Vol. 8, January 2000, pp.8–39.

Middlebury College Trustees. *Designing the Future: Guiding Principles of Middlebury College* [online]. [Cited August 1, 2005]. Middlebury College, 1999. <http://community.middlebury.edu/~enviroc/gbprinciples.html>.

Minaker, Dennis. *The Gorge of Summers Gone: A History of Victoria's Inland Waterway*. Victoria: Dennis Minaker, 1998.

Mintzberg, Henry. *Structure in Fives: Designing Effective Organizations*. Englewood Cliffs: Prentice Hall, 1993.

Mjolsness, Adam. *Bowker Creek History: A Mini-Ethnography*. A special research report, in the possession of the authors. Victoria: University of Victoria, April 2003.

Monbiot, George. "With Eyes Wide Shut: Climate Change Threatens the Future of Humanity, But We Refuse to Respond Rationally." *The Guardian*, August 12, 2003. London: Guardian Newspapers. <http://www.guardian.co.uk/>.

Morand, Michael. *Interview*. July 15, 2005.

Morrison, Brad. *The Life, Family and Accomplishments of Richard Biggerstaff Wilson 1904–1991*. Private manuscript in possession of the authors, Victoria, 1996.

Mouffe, Chantal. *The Democratic Paradox*. New York: Verso, 2000.

Municipality of Saanich Archives. "Collection of Statistics on Estimated Population and Area in Saanich." Victoria: Municipality of Saanich, n.d.

Murdoch, G. "A History of the Municipality of Oak Bay." Unpublished document, Victoria, 1968.

National Association of State Universities and Land Grant Colleges. *Value Added: The Economic Impact of Public Universities* [online]. [Cited July 25, 2005]. Washington: Office of Public Affairs, 1997. <http://www.nasulgc.org/publications/Value_Added.pdf>.

National Center for Education Statistics. *Chapter 3: Postsecondary Education: Faculty, Staff and Salaries* [online]. [Cited August 1, 2005]. Digest of Education Statistics. Washington, 2003. <http://nces.ed.gov/programs/digest/d03/ch_3.asp#2>.

National Center for Education Statistics. *Expenditures of Title IV Degree Granting Institutions: United States, Fiscal Year 2001* [online]. [Cited July 25, 2005]. Washington, 2001. <http://nces.ed.gov/>.

National Center for Education Statistics. *NCES Fast Facts: Postsecondary Enrollment 2001* [online]. [Cited July 25, 2005]. Washington, 2005. <http://nces.ed.gov/fastfacts>.

Nechyba, Thomas J. and Randall P. Walsh. *Urban Sprawl* [online]. [Cited July 26, 2005]. Working paper. Cambridge, 2004. <http://www.lincolninst.edu/pubs/dl/924_Nechyba_PDF.pdf>.

Newman, Julie. *Interview*. June 20, 2005.

Newman, Julie. "The Onset of Creating a Model Sustainable Institution: A Case Study Analysis of Yale University." In *Proceedings: Committing Universities to Sustainable Development*. Graz, Austria: Graz University, 2005.

New Urbanism. *Pedestrian Cities* [online]. [Cited August 10, 2005]. 2005. <http://www.newurbanism.org/pages/519562/>.

New York State Supreme Court, Appellate Division, Third Judicial Department. Case number 96595. March 17, 2005.

Nicholson, Bill. *Interview*. April 1, 2004.

Normile, Dennis. "Conservation Takes a Front Seat as University Builds New Campus." *Science*. Vol. 305, no. 5682, 2004, pp. 329–31.

Northeast Energy Services Company Inc. (NORESCO). "Columbia University" [online]. [Cited August 2, 2005]. *Higher Education*. Westborough, 2000. <http://www.noresco.com/site/content/CaseStudy_174.asp>.

Office of New Haven and State Affairs. *Strong Neighborhoods: Homeownership* [online]. [Cited August 30, 2005]. New Haven, 2004. <http://www.yale.edu/onhsa/homeowner.htm>.

Office of New Haven and State Affairs. *Yale and New Haven* [online]. [Cited August 1, 2005]. New Haven, 2005. <http://www.yale.edu/onhsa/facts.htm>.

Orr, David. *Ecological Literacy: Education and the Transition to a Postmodern World*. Albany: State University of New York Press, 1992.

Orr, David. *Interview*. February 27, 2005.

Oxfam America. *Buy Local Food and Farm Tool Kit: A Guide for Student Organizers and the Community Food Security Coalition* [online]. [Cited August 17, 2005]. 2002. <http://www.farmtocollege.org/index.htm>.

Pagani, Freda. "UBC: Canada's Unexpected Leader in Campus Sustainability." Paper presented at the North American Conference on Sustainability and Higher Education, October 21–23, 2004. Portland, Oregon: Education for Sustainability Western, 2004.

Paris '68. "The Struggle Site" [online]. [Cited July 25, 2005]. 2005. <http://struggle.ws/pdfs/paris68.pdf>.

Parker, Martin. *Against Management: Organization in the Age of Managerialism*. Cambridge: Polity Press, 2002.

Pataki, George E. and Linda Angello. *Employment in New York State* [online]. [Cited August 30, 2005]. Albany: State of New York Department of Labour, Division of Research and Statistics, March 2003. <http://www.labor.state.ny.us/workforceindustrydata/PDFs/enys0303.pdf>.

Penn, Briony. *Interview*. April 18, 2004.

Perry, David C. and Wim Weiwel. *The University as Urban Developer: Case Studies and Analysis* Armont: M.E. Sharpe and Lincoln Institute of Land Policy, 2005.

Petersen, John. Comment on college website. Oberlin: Oberlin College, 2003–04. <http://www.oberlin.edu/ajlc/design_4.html>.

PFC Energy. *PFC Energy's Global Crude Oil and Natural Gas Liquids Supply Forecast* [online]. [Cited August 2, 2005]. 2005. <http://www.csis.org/energy/040908_presentation.pdf>.

Pierce, Neal. *Wake-up Call for Academia* [online]. [Cited August 2, 2005]. Washington Post Writers Group, May 29, 2002. <http://www.ceosforcities.org/press/>.

Planning Department of Saanich. "A Plan for the University Area." Victoria: District of Saanich, 1965.

Pocklington, Tom and Allan Tupper. *No Place to Learn: Why Universities Aren't Working.* Vancouver: UBC Press, 2002.

Polanyi, Karl. *The Great Transformation: The Political and Economic Origins of Our Time.* Boston: Beacon, 1944.

POLIS Project on Ecological Governance. *Planning for a Change: Innovation and Sustainability for the 21ˢᵗ Century at the University of Victoria.* Victoria: University of Victoria, October 2003.

Ponting, Clive. *A Green History of the World.* New York: Penguin, 1991.

"Population Distribution." Adapted from *Suburbs and Suburban Sprawl.* Michigan State University: Land Use and Cover Change. <http://www.landuse.msu.edu/related/sprawl_report.pdf>.

Potter, Sheila. "Camas Comeback." *Saanich News.* July 1, 2005, C1.

Potter, Sheila. "Gillespie's Trail." *Saanich News.* December 15, 2004, B1.

Powell, Loraine. "Shedding a Tier: Flattening Organisational Structures and Employee Empowerment." *International Journal of Educational Management.* Vol. 16, no. 1, 2002, pp. 54–59.

Prato, Maurita. *Interview.* January 25, 2005.

Quinn, Daniel. In Richard Heinberg, *The Party's Over: Oil, War and the Fate of Industrial Societies.* Gabriola Island: New Society Publishers, 2003.

Ray, Arthur. *I Have Lived Here Since the World Began: An Illustrated History of Canada's Native People.* Toronto: Key Porter, 2005.

Raygor, Jill. "Paving Paradise." *Ithaca Times.* June 16, 2004 [online]. [Cited December 12, 2005]. <www.ithacatimes.com>; <http://www.zwire.com/site/news.cfm?newsid= 11976664&BRD=1395&PAG=461&dept_id=216620&rfi=8>.

Redbud Woods Faculty Working Group. *Redbud Woods: Home Page* [online]. [Cited August 2, 2005]. Ithaca: www.redbudwoods.org, 2005. <http://www.redbudwoods.org/>.

Redbud Woods Faculty Working Group. *Statement Read on Behalf of the Redbud Woods Faculty Working Group* [online]. [Cited August 2, 2005]. Ithaca: www.redbudwoods.org, July 18, 2005. <http://www.redbudwoods.org/Faculty-Statement.html>.

Rees, William. "Impeding Sustainability? The Ecological Footprint of Higher Education." *Planning for Higher Education.* Vol. 31, no. 3, March–May, 2003, pp. 88–98.

The Ring. "Board Approves Campus Planning Report." Victoria: University of Victoria, March 4, 2004.

The Ring. "Campus Traffic Patterns Changing, Audit Shows." Victoria: University of Victoria, January 2005, vol. 31, no. 1, 1.

Roberts, Susan M. "Realizing Critical Geographies of the University." *Antipode.* Vol. 32, no. 3, 2000, pp. 230–44.

Robson, G.A. University of Victoria Facilities Management. "Re: CJVI Property Proposal for Use as the Camassia Learning Centre for Sustainable Living." Letter to Sol Kinnis, Camassia Learning Centre for Sustainable Living Society, November 13, 1997.

Rojas, Alejandro. *Interview.* August 23, 2004.

Rosan, Richard M. *The Key Role of Universities in Our Nation's Economic Growth and Urban Revitalization* [online]. [Cited July 28 2005]. Cambridge: Lincoln Institute of Land Policy, 2002. <http://www.uli.org/AM/Template.cfm?Section=Search&template=/CM/HTMLDisplay.cfm&ContentID=5524>.

Rouche, Ken. "Streetcars and Fairfield." *Fairfield Observer*, Victoria: Fairfield Community Association Newsletter, March 2001, pp. 1–2.

Ruppert, Michael C. *Peak Oil and the Big Picture* [online]. [Cited July 28, 2005]. Speech, August 31, 2004. YubaNet, <http://www.yubanet.com/cgi-bin/artman/exec/view.cgi/13/15732>.

Sandercock, Leonie. *Towards Cosmopolis: Planning for Multicultural Cities.* London: John Wiley and Sons, 1998.

Sanders, Elizabeth. *Email* to Michael M'Gonigle and Justine Starke. August 1, 2005.

Sanders, Elizabeth. *Interview.* July 12, 2005.

San Francisco Municipal Railway. *On the Move Over 90 Years: 1919–2002.* San Francisco: State of Muni, 2002.

Saul, John Ralston. *Voltaire's Bastards: The Dictatorship of Reason in the West.* Toronto: Penguin, 1992.

Scharner, Nathan. *The Medieval University.* New York: A.S. Barnes, 1962.

Schmidt-Bleek, Friedrich. "Chapter 1: Making Sustainability Accountable: Putting Resource Productivity into Praxis." In *A Report by the Factor 10 Club* [online]. [Cited October 19, 2005]. 1999. <http://www.factor10-institute.org/pdf/F10REPORT.pdf>.

Schwenk, Charles Ransom. *Identity, Learning and Decision Making in Changing Organizations.* Westport: Quorum Books, 2002.

Seattle.gov. December 13, 2005. <http://www.seattle.gov/News/detail.asp?ID=5725&Dept=40>.

Second Nature. *The University Modelling Sustainability as an Institution* [online]. [Cited September 23, 2005]. Boston, 2001. <http://www.secondnature.org/pdf/snwritings/factsheets/UnivModelSust.pdf>.

Senge, Peter M. *The Fifth Discipline: The Art and Practice of the Learning Organization*, 1ˢᵗ ed. New York: Doubleday/Currency, 1990.

Sharp, Leith. "Green Campuses: The Road from Little Victories to Systemic Transformation." *International Journal of Sustainability in Higher Education.* Vol. 3, no. 2, 2002, pp. 128–45.

Sharp, Leith. *Interview.* June 23, 2005.

Shepherd, William R. *Historical Atlas.* New York: Henry Holt, 1923, p. 100.

Sherry, Barbara. "Universities as Developers: An International Conversation." In *Land Lines Newsletter.* Cambridge: Lincoln Institute of Land Policy, 2005.

Shriberg, Michael P. "Sustainability in U.S. Higher Education: Organizational Factors Influencing Campus Environmental Performance and Leadership." Doctoral thesis, University of Michigan, Ann Arbour, 2002.

Silverman, Julia. *Students Flock to Campus Organic Farms* [online]. [Cited August 2, 2005].
SFGate.com. *San Francisco Chronicle* (Associated Press), July 22, 2005.
<http://www.sfgate.com/cgi-bin/article.cgi?file=/news/archive/2005/07/21/national/
a121337D32.DTL>.

Singer, Andy. *CARtoons*. Prague: CARBusters, 2001.

Skelsey, Geoffrey. *The ALRV and CLRV Turn at the Canadian National Exhibition Terminus, in the
Shadow of the Gardener Expressway, September 2000* [online]. [Cited October 20, 2005]. Tramway
Resources, 2000. <http://www.tramwayresources.com/trams/ttc10.html>.

Slaughter, R.A. "Universities as Institutions of Foresight." *Journal of Future Studies*. Vol. 1, no. 3,
November, 1998, pp. 51–71.

Smith, Alisa. "UVic Ignores Claim to Mystic Vale." *The Martlet*. Victoria: University of Victoria
Students' Society, 1993, 1.

Smith, Anthony and Frank Webster, eds. *The Postmodern University? Contested Visions of Higher
Education in Society*. Bristol, PA: Taylor and Francis, 1997.

Smith, Peter L. *A Multitude of the Wise: UVic Remembered*. Victoria: The Alumni Association of the
University of Victoria, 1993.

Snyder, Thomas D. *120 Years of American Education: A Statistical Portrait* [online]. [Cited August 31,
2005]. U.S. Department of Education: National Center for Education Statistics, 1993.
<http://nces.ed.gov/pubs93/93442.pdf>.

Soley, Lawrence C. *Leasing the Ivory Tower: The Corporate Takeover of Academia*. Boston: South End
Press, 1995.

Starik, M., T.N. Schaeffer, P. Berman and A. Hazelwood. "Initial Environmental Project
Characterizations of Four US Universities." *International Journal for Sustainability in Higher
Education*. Vol. 3, no. 4, 2002, pp. 335–45.

Statistics Canada. "The Loss of Dependable Agriculture Land in Canada." *Statistics Canada Rural and
Small Town Canada Analysis Bulletin*. Vol. 6, no. 1, January 2005. Ottawa: Statistics Canada.

Statistics Canada. *Post-secondary Graduates, Proportion of Population Aged 25 to 54, Canada, 1996, Table
109-0005* [online]. [Cited July 25, 2005]. Ottawa: Statistics Canada, 1996.
<http://estat.statcan.ca>.

St. Clair, Matthew. *Interview*. June 27, 2005.

St. Clair, Matthew. "The University of California Goes Solar: How Students Convinced One of the
Largest University Systems in the United States to Adopt an Ambitious Sustainability Policy."
Paper presented at the *Sustainable Development Education: Holistic and Integrative Educational
Management Approaches for Ensuring Sustainable Societies" (A Global Conference for Educators and
Educational Policy Makers)*, ed. Campus Monterrey Tecnológico de Monterrey. Monterrey,
Mexico: Environmental Management for Sustainable Universities, June 2004.

Strayhorn, Carol K. *The Impact of the State Higher Education System on the Texas Economy* [online]. [Cited July 28, 2005]. Austin, Window on State Government, Texas Comptroller of Public Accounts, 2005. <http://www.window.state.tx.us/specialrpt/highered05/>.

Tennant, Paul. *Aboriginal Peoples and Politics: The Indian Land Question in British Columbia, 1849–1989.* Vancouver: UBC Press, 1990.

Tierney, William G. "The Autonomy of Knowledge and the Decline of the Subject: Postmodernism and the Reformulation of the University." *Higher Education.* Vol. 41, 2001, pp. 353–72.

Tierney, William G. and James T. Minor. "A Cultural Perspective on Communication and Governance." *New Directions For Higher Education.* No. 127, 2004, pp. 85–94.

Toor, William. "Sustainable Transportation for Campus Communities." Paper presented at the EFS West's "North American Conference on Sustainability and Higher Education," October 21–23, Portland, 2004.

Toor, William and Spense Havlick. *Transportation and Sustainable Campus Communities: Issues, Examples, and Solutions.* Portland: Island Press, 2004.

Tornatzky, Louis G., Paul G. Waugaman and Denis O. Gray. *Innovation U: New University Roles in a Knowledge Economy* [online]. [Cited July 25, 2005]. Southern Growth Policies Board, 2002. <http://ip.research.sc.edu/PDF/InnovationUniversityBook.pdf>.

Toronto Transit Commission. *Operating Statistics: Key Facts* [online]. [Cited October 5, 2005]. Toronto, 2004. <http://www.toronto.ca/ttc/pdf/operatingstatistics2004.pdf>.

Turner, Jane and Don Lovell. *The Changing Face of University of Victoria Campus Lands.* Victoria: University of Victoria Archives, 1999.

2020 Long Range Development Plan (LRDP) Litigation Settlement Agreement. Between the University of California, Berkeley, the Regents of the University of California and the City of Berkeley, May 25, 2005.

UBC Public Affairs. *Fact and Figures: 2004/2005* [online]. [Cited August 28, 2005]. Vancouver, May 30, 2005. <http://www.publicaffairs.ubc.ca/ubcfacts/index.html >.

University of California at Berkeley. *UC Berkeley's Economic Impact: Generating Jobs on Campus and Beyond* [online]. [Cited August 2, 2005]. Berkeley: University of California, 2005. <http://www.berkeley.edu/econimpact/jobs.html>.

University of Victoria. *Campus Plan 2003* [online]. [Cited August 29, 2005]. Victoria: University of Victoria, Vice-President Finance and Operations, 2003. <http://web.uvic.ca/vpfin/campusplan/>.

University of Victoria. *Facts and Figures* [online]. [Cited July 27, 2005]. Victoria: Vice-President Finance and Operations, July 18, 2005. <http://www.uvic.ca/about/factsfigures/>.

University of Victoria Archives. University Secretary's Fonds. Accession No. 94-088, Box 1, File 31. "Mortgage Agreement 1964." Victoria: University of Victoria, 1964.

University of Victoria Board of Governors. *Open Session Minutes*. Victoria: University of Victoria, Office of the Secretary, May 12, 2003.

University of Wisconsin Arboretum. *About the Arboretum* [online]. [Cited July 31, 2005]. Madison, 2005. <http://uwarboretum.org/about/>.

Urban Systems. *U-Pass Review: Final Report* [online]. [Cited August 20, 2005]. Vancouver, May 4, 2005. <http://www.trek.ubc.ca/research/pdf/U-Pass%20Review%20Final%20Report.pdf>.

U.S. Department of Education. *Postsecondary Educational Institutions and Programs Accredited by Accrediting Agencies and State Approval Agencies Recognized by the U.S. Secretary of Education* [online]. [Cited July 25, 2005]. 2005. <http://ope.ed.gov/accreditation/>.

Van Belleghem, Joe. *Speech*. Victoria, December 7, 2004.

van Dam-Mieras, M.C.E. "RCE-Europe: Regional Centres of Expertise in the Context of the UN Decade Education for Sustainable Development." In *Proceedings: Committing Universities to Sustainable Development*, Graz, Austria: Graz University, 2005.

Volkswagen AutoUni, Wolfsburg, Germany. [Cited October 27, 2005]. <http://www.autouni.de/autouni_publish/master/en/communications/contact.html>.

Walljasper, Jay. "Enlightened Cities Around the World: 7 Urban Wonders." *UTNE Reader*, November–December 2001, pp. 80–83.

Wals, Arjen E.J. and Bob Jickling. "'Sustainability' in Higher Education: From Doublethink and Newspeak to Critical Thinking and Meaningful Learning." *International Journal of Sustainability in Higher Education*. Vol. 3, no. 3, 2002, pp. 221–32.

Ward, Doug. "Mountaintop Fourth Avenue: There Will Be Nothing of the Suburban Mall Look to SFU's New UniverCity Community" [online]. [Cited August 29, 2005]. *Vancouver Sun*, April 27, 2004. <http://www.univercity.ca/bmcp/vancouversunapril27-04.html>.

Watt-Gremm, Graham. "Towards Ecological Stewardship and Planning at the University of Victoria, British Columbia." Unpublished document, 2003.

Webb, Sarah. *Interview*. May 13, 2004 and July 11, 2005.

Webb, Walter Prescott. *The Great Frontier*. Austin: University of Texas Press, 1951.

Weber, Max. *On Charisma and Institution Building*. Chicago and London: University of Chicago Press, 1968.

Wikipedia. *History of Higher Education in the United States* [online]. [Cited August 2, 2005]. 2005. <http://en.wikipedia.org/wiki/Education_in_the_United_States#Higher_Education>.

Winterhoff, Thomas. "Hobbs Creek Is at Risk." *Saanich News*, February 7, 2001, 10.

Wisenthal, M. *Table W 1-9, Total Full-time Enrollment 1950–1974* [online]. [Cited July 26, 2005]. Historical Statistics of Canada, Section W (Education), F.H. Leacy, ed. Ottawa: Statistics Canada, n.d. <http://www.statcan.ca/english/freepub/11-516-XIE/sectionw/sectionw.htm>.

Wisenthal, M. *Table W 41-46: Total Expenditures on Education 1950–1974* [online]. [Cited July 26, 2005]. Historical Statistics of Canada, Section W (Education), F.H. Leacy, ed. Ottawa:

Statistics Canada, n.d.
<http://www.statcan.ca/english/freepub/11-516-XIE/sectionw/sectionw.htm>.

Wolfe, D.A., and C.H. Davis, M. Lucas. "Global Networks and Local Linkages: An Introduction" in Wolfe, D.A. and M. Lucas, eds., *Global Networks and Local Linkages: The Paradox of Clusters in an Open Economy.* Montreal and Kingston: McGill-Queens University Press. 2005.

Wolfenden, Richard (Government Printer). "Che-Ko-Nein Tribe: Point Gonzales to Cedar Hill," *Papers connected with the Indian Land Question 1850–1875, 1877.* Victoria: Government Printing Office, 1987 (orig. ed. 1875).

Worldwatch Institute. *Curbing Sprawl to Fight Climate Change* [online]. [Cited July 26, 2005]. Washington: Worldwatch Institute, 2002. <http://www.worldwatch.org/press/news/2002/06/28/>.

Worldwatch Institute. *Vital Signs 2005.* New York: W.W. Norton, 2005.

York, Michelle. "Protests Slow Cornell's Effort to Build a Parking Lot." *New York Times*, June 7, 2005, B5.

Young, Dwight. *Alternatives to Sprawl* [online]. [Cited July 26, 2005]. Cambridge: Lincoln Institute of Land Policy, 1995. <http://www.lincolninst.edu/pubs/dl/864_Alt%20to%20Sprawl.pdf>.

Young, Iris. *Inclusion and Democracy.* New York: Oxford University Press, 2002.

Young, Stephen C., ed. *The Emergence of Ecological Modernization: Integrating the Environment and the Economy?* London: Routledge, 2000.

Zanetto, Gabriele. "Ca'Foscari University of Venice from Local to International Cooperation." In *Proceedings: Committing Universities to Sustainable Development.* Graz, Austria: Graz University, 2005.

Zimmermann, Friedrich M. "The Role of Management in Sustainable Universities." In *Proceedings: Committing Universities to Sustainable Development.*Graz, Austria: Graz University, 2005.

INDEX

About the Illustrations

The Symbolic Representations of the Tarot Cards

WHEN ASKED TO COME UP WITH AN ARTISTIC INTERPRETATION of this book's different themes, I was very drawn to the classic archetypal battle of the tree-sit in Cunningham Woods. Here we had young principled students defending trees, symbolic of knowledge and inhabited by Owls, a traditional bird of wisdom in many cultures, from the excesses of the Ivory Tower — an institution isolated from society and governed by an outdated system. Because the university holds such a powerful symbolic position within society, this struggle to determine the university's ultimate purpose had even more significance to the wider public. I knew this well because I was working as a television news reporter at the time, and the news producers, the great arbiters of the public taste, were curious about this struggle and assigned me to follow the issue through to its bitter end.

Because these symbols and archetypes are represented in popular forms like Tarot cards, I used them as my source of inspiration. Tarot cards also share the same early European origins and evolving traditions as the institution of the university. Both traditions have been resilient, a parallel that intrigued me. The other source of inspiration was the plants and animals that occupied Cunningham Woods before they were cut down. The Lekwungen people who lived in this region drew inspiration from local species such as the Owl, Raven, Arbutus and Frog for qualities of wisdom, truth, conservation and communication respectively. These were the very qualities that the students challenged the University not to preach but to practice. The rich cultural crossover between the local stories and some of the universal meanings of these species took this story from a regional context to a global one. The story of Cunningham Woods repeats itself on campuses around the world, which in turn are mirrors of society. In each case, the same elements, tensions, symbols and context unfold. Can we live well in, and respect the genius of, local places within a global society?

The first four sections of the book seemed to fall naturally into the four suits of the Tarot, (which evolved into the suits of our modern-day playing cards). The final chapter of the Visionary is the Joker or Fool card.

Swords (Spades) — The Rebel

The tree-sit (student rebellion) represents Swords (Spades) and documents the tension between the use of a sword to clear for opportunity (cutting down the Woods to make way for buildings of learning) and the need to defend equally important places of learning (forests) and cut away delusions and deceptions. The Rebel is fashioned around the archetype of Justice, commonly a figure holding a sword facing downwards. On his chest is Sisiyutl, a West Coast double-headed serpent that made warriors powerful. In the background, is the archetype of the Tower (the Ivory Tower), which is a transformational card. The burning of the Tower indicates change, renovation and restoration. It dismantles what is false and artificial. The figure falling out of the tower represents unauthentic ways of expressing oneself. Raven is the transformer character in all the Coastal cultures. Sometimes he can appear as a bumbling fool and other times as a wise, inspired genius.

Cunningham Woods provided habitat for four species: 1) The Owl is an ancient symbol of knowledge in Greek, Celtic and West Coast cultures. The threat to the Owl by cutting down its habitat is a metaphorical threat to knowledge. Feathers were also used in Egyptian times to measure the truth of one's heart and occur in the Justice archetype; 2) Garter snakes are also a symbol of shedding a skin and expressing a desire for change; 3) Arbutus, an evergreen deciduous tree unique to this region, were cut down in Cunningham Woods. In Coast Salish culture, the roots of the Arbutus are responsible for holding the world together and consequently are viewed as sacred; and 4) The Oak is the most revered of all Celtic trees. It bestows vision and wisdom and engenders high standards of morality and the determination to tell the truth. Several ancient Garry Oak, another unique and at-risk species, had been cut down adjacent to the Cunningham Woods to make way for a Centre for Innovative Learning a few years earlier. Students, not missing the irony, had protested then but with no success. The defense of this tree again symbolizes defense of wisdom and truth.

Pentacles (Diamonds) — The Teacher

The history of the University is represented by Pentacles (Diamonds) and the tension between the material foundation of our learning and teaching and the spiritual foundations. Pentacles express opportunity and abundance. The tension is portrayed through the two archetypes of learning. In Egyptian traditions, Osiris, God of Reason (Tarot used a papal figure or Hierophant), married Isis (High Priestess, Copper Woman in West Coast cultures), Goddess of Intuition. Traditional cultures recognize the importance of marrying intuition to reason in teaching and learning. In this card, the Hierophant is sharing power with the High Priestess, shown by the transfer of the staff with the planetary symbol of Jupiter on it. This hints at the potential shift from old opportunities through credentialism and corporatism to those of ecological and societal justice.

The four other symbols are guides to learning and teaching: 1) Beaver (Taurus), to remind one to take action on ideas; 2) Raven (Aquarius), on originality and pioneering; 3) Wolf (Scorpio), loyalty to something that has meaning and commitment to our hearts; and 4) Frog, the symbol in many cultures of communication to all people. Each of these icons has disappeared historically on campus through incremental development of the University, but are being restored symbolically through the restoration of their habitat. The ruined Tower appears again in the background, ready for restoration with the regrowth of the forest as an equally important place of learning.

Wands (Clubs) — The Innovator

Innovations are symbolized in Wands (Clubs) by budding sticks thrust into the earth. Here the tension is between the need to allow creativity to blossom, especially in solving problems, and the need to harness creativity so that it is not harmful to the whole. The Sun in all cultures is the life force that is exuberant, creative and with unlimited energy. Too much Sun energy and it becomes destructive. The Sun is generally portrayed as masculine in nature. The yang of the Sun is typically married to the yin of the Moon. Using resources carefully is a creative task and is symbolized by harnessing the Moon's energy and feminine nature.

The Chariot is a symbol of change through innovation. The use of innovative forms of energy is symbolized by the innovator harnessing the Sun and the Moon, both important forms of alternative energy. The rays are reins and one is held tightly to symbolize the discipline of applying ideas and the practice of restraint and energy conservation. The other rein is held loosely to allow full creativity.

There is also innovation in the way we adapt ideas to the local context and environment. This is symbolized in the substitution of the Martlet (mythical flying bird and symbol of UVic) for a native Winter Wren. In European heraldry, the Martlet celebrated virtue and merit over inheritance. The Wren is a real bird that lived in Cunningham Woods amongst the Sword Ferns. It is a West Coast symbol of greatness through humility. Similarly, the Fern is a symbol of healing in many cultures. There is innovation in healing and restoring the land.

Cups (Hearts) — The Governor

Governance is symbolized by Cups (Hearts), our emotional balance. Overfilled they represent emotional indulgence; underfilled they symbolize lack of emotional development. In the governance of universities, there is a move toward the filling of cups and emotional stability and rigour. The tension lies between the governance of the institution through mind, logic and efficiency, in order to meet the material needs of the institution, and governance through heart, intuition and democracy, in order to meet the spiritual needs of the institution.

There are two archetypes dealing with governance: The Emperor (Eagle in West Coast cultures) is the yang of leadership through power: the builder, the doer, etc. He has the ability to make things stable, solid and secure for himself and others. The Empress (Raven) is the yin of leadership through love, wisdom and humour. The Empress is the only symbol in all the deck that shows the heart and the mind in equal balance and proportion. It is the trusting, balanced heart, not the protective, controlling one. Emperor/Empress (Eagle/Raven) formed the yang/yin, the two halves of the great whole. The Empress is situated under the crescent Moon, which symbolizes the magnetic pull of the feminine nature of love with wisdom. Historically, governance has been unbalanced towards the Emperor. The Empress and the Moon rising to meet the Emperor on an equitable basis shows the potential for a more heart/mind, democratic style of governance.

The talking feather symbolizes communication, allowing no one to interrupt while the speaker holds the feather. Frog is a great communicator and "the voice of the people" in both Celtic and West Coast cultures. Restoration of wetlands (the springs of the university) and banning the use of pesticides that kill amphibians are a metaphorical call to communication and accessibility for all.

The Joker — The Visionary

The final chapter projects a vision for the future. In Tarot, the Visionary is the archetype of the Fool (Raven). The Fool (androgynous being) represents the vision that one has been close to death (stepping off the cliff) — truth stripped of all delusions with immense courage and risk taking. It is the Joker in the pack, the Trickster; it trumps all suits. It is the rebel upside down — the rebel with a sense of humour, humility, joy and no attachment to outcome. The Raven is also upside down in playful flight. Visionaries attain this state to be truly open to situations and solutions. The river is flowing up the mountain with swimming Salmon, a symbol of regeneration, restoration and perseverance. One day, Salmon might swim again up Bowker and Mystic Vale Creeks. Wolf stands by, showing loyalty to something that has meaning, next to Wren, the symbol of humility. The visionary is holding a Camas flower as a gesture for the restoration of land and understanding with First Nation cultures.

Great horned Owl

A natural symbol of wisdom, the owl has long been associated with careful study and thoughtfulness, as well as with clarity and power. For these reasons, we chose an icon of the great horned owl to lead the reader into each chapter. These owls do a lot of tree-sitting (Chapter 1). They used to reside commonly on the campus, but their numbers have dwindled over the years due to loss of forest, and clearing of wildlife trees. They nest (Ch. 2) in old-growth trees, commonly on branches or the cavities of snapped trunks and limbs, and they especially like Douglas-fir. With suburbanization, they have become common casualties from electrical lines, road kills and poisoning (Ch.3). Great horned owls are magnificent flyers (Ch.4), and without the aid of fossil fuels! The design of their feathers is so aerodynamically clever that they make no noise when they fly. In the city (Ch.5), great horned owls have adapted well to parks and open areas where they hunt rodents, such as introduced rats. In the urban commons (Ch.6), they are able to locate their prey

About the Illustrator

Briony Penn is an environmental educator who has worked in a variety of fields from writing and lecturing to television and museum design.

She holds a doctorate in geography from the University of Edinburgh.

with incredible precision, because their vision is 10 times better than humans in daylight, and 100 times better at night. Their talons have evolved to grab onto prey like a vice grip so that they can rip it apart. They are truly structured power (Ch.7). Great horned owls are protective of their place and their young. Through a process of mantling (Ch.8), they spread their wings over what they intend to protect. Although they are solitary creatures, they stick together when they are young (Ch. 9). For these young, the return of the mother with a night's hunting in her beak is a time of great celebration. As one generation sustains the next (Ch.10), it is a time of re-enchantment.